Diversity and Inclusion Research

Series Editor
Thomas Köllen, Institute of Organization and HRM
University of Bern, Bern, Switzerland

The book series ‘Diversity and Inclusion Research’ examines the facets of diversity in a variety of contexts, as well as approaches to and perspectives on diversity and inclusion. It presents organizational research on workforce diversity, and covers diversity and inclusion-related issues within communities, cities, regions, nations, and societies.

The series welcomes functional and intersectional perspectives on diversity, as well as constructivist perspectives on processes of “doing” or “performing” diversity. In terms of inclusion, it welcomes research on broader initiatives (such as generalized diversity management approaches), as well as on practices of inclusion that focus on specific dimensions of diversity; these can include age, appearance, ethnicity, disability, gender, gender identity, nationality, race, religion, sexual orientation, sex, or any other characteristic or demographic in which persons can differ from each other, or, conversely, which they share.

The series publishes research from the broad range of academic disciplines within the social sciences (e.g. economics and business administration, linguistics, political science, history, law, psychology, sociology, geography, and education) and humanities (e.g. philosophy and religion). It strongly encourages interdisciplinary and transdisciplinary research, as well as critical perspectives on diversity and inclusion-related issues. By welcoming research from a variety of sectoral, national, and cultural contexts, the series will make an essential contribution to shaping the academic discourse on diversity and inclusion.

Taijrani Rampersaud-Skorka

Community Radio in South Asia

Mapping the Alternative Mediascape in Nepal, India, and Bangladesh

Springer

Taijrani Rampersaud-Skorka
University of Guyana
Georgetown, Guyana

ISSN 2662-5997 ISSN 2662-6004 (electronic)
Diversity and Inclusion Research
ISBN 978-3-031-85200-8 ISBN 978-3-031-85201-5 (eBook)
https://doi.org/10.1007/978-3-031-85201-5

This Springer imprint is published by the registered company Springer Nature Switzerland AG
The registered company address is: Gewerbestrasse 11, 6330 Cham, Switzerland

Self-actualisation

I took a peep past the physical façade,
attempting to see the depths within.
What monsters lay beyond the veil?
It was a journey I was determined to begin…
With trembling hands and a skipping heart,
I slowly drew the fabrics apart.
Cautiously, I went forth in the unknown;
into the darkest abyss, I did bemoan…
But as I beheld the beauty inside
—swirling mixtures of darkness and light,
I remembered that I am a being of strength,
from a unique position I did fight.
Today, I am a free spirit, shackled by none,
my imagined bonds are now undone.
And even though this adventure is now complete,
I did realise that I am not obsolete.
(By: Taijrani Rampersaud, April 2019)

To all the strong, talented, guiding lights of the Community Radio Sector of South Asia—without your dedication to creating positive changes in your societies, so many voices would remain unheard, suppressed. You truly are examples worth following. The joy and dedication I observed in all of you will remain with me forever.

~ Follow the light and be guided by the Morning Star, always!

Foreword

With immense pleasure and pride, we introduce Taijrani Rampersaud-Skorka's important work, '*Community Radio in South Asia: Mapping the Alternative Mediascape in Nepal, India, and Bangladesh*'. This book, derived from her PhD research, meticulously maps the community radio (CR) sector in South Asia, emphasising the vital role of voice infrastructures in the Global South. Rampersaud-Skorka's in-depth research and thorough analysis of the policy and socio-cultural environments make this work a significant contribution to media studies and community development.

Rampersaud-Skorka's book provides comprehensive data on the alternative media sector within South Asia, with a particular focus on CR in Nepal, India, and Bangladesh. CR is the most pervasive and popular alternative media in these three countries. Although based on a global interpretation of the concept and practice of alternative media, the author analyses the CR scenario in these countries from the perspective of the South Asian media ecology and policy environment. This dual approach offers a nuanced understanding that is both globally informed and locally grounded.

The book is structured into ten chapters, beginning with an introduction that sets the stage for the detailed exploration that follows. This chapter also includes a synopsis of the methodology, which outlines the systematic approach adopted to map the CR sector across the three countries. By adopting a combination of thematic, reference, and conceptual mapping methodology, Rampersaud-Skorka examines both primary and secondary data on CR within each country. This methodological rigour ensures the reliability and validity of the findings, presenting a Community Media Database (CMD) for South Asia organised under suitable and search-friendly categories.

The second and third chapters delve into the CR sector in South Asia. Chapter 2 offers a historical overview of Nepal, India, and Bangladesh, focusing on their unique geographical and cultural developments. It then examines the general media landscape and traces the introduction and sustainability of community media in these countries. Chapter 3 presents thematic entry points for understanding community media, consolidating various perspectives from academics, authors, and thinkers into five key themes.

Rampersaud-Skorka presents the CMD as a crucial research output in the fifth chapter. This chapter charts the regional diversity of CR in Nepal, India, and

Bangladesh, providing extensive information about various CR initiatives. Detailed profiles of these initiatives include establishment data, geographical locations, community profiles, thematic programming areas, and production genres. This carefully collated database is a valuable resource for researchers, policymakers, and practitioners interested in community media.

Chapters 6–9 offer theme-specific analyses of CR practices, providing a wide-ranging overview of the CR sector in Nepal, India, and Bangladesh. The data that Rampersaud-Skorka gathered through her visits to different parts of India, Nepal, and Bangladesh in the form of in-depth interviews with stakeholders and case study analyses (note: profiles of each case are captured in Chap. 4) are fractured into four thematic areas: policy environment, ownership and management, community, and programming. These thematic categories are linked to the core principles CR stations adhere to in these countries, which could serve as the basis for starting CR stations in other countries of the region.

In Nepal, Rampersaud-Skorka explores the integration of CR practices with mainstream systems by tracing their historical development, policy environment, and the unique challenges CR initiatives face in the absence of clear policies. By focusing on the innovative approaches adopted by CR stations to engage and empower local communities, the research shows that CR has become a crucial part of the media sphere in Nepal.

Through analyses of the policy frameworks, ownership and management structures, and community participation strategies of CR stations in India, this book illustrates the potential of CR to serve as a platform for marginalised voices, promoting social inclusion, cultural diversity, and participatory democracy. The analysis of the Indian context reveals the dynamic nature of CR and its role in supporting democratic processes and cultural expression.

In Bangladesh, the focus is on nurturing youth voices for development through CR. Rampersaud-Skorka's analysis of the Bangladeshi CR sector unwraps the engagement of the youth in their endeavour to promote education, health, and social awareness among younger generations. Through a focus on the policy and regulatory environment, the importance of supportive frameworks for the sustainability of CR is emphasised. The CR stations in Bangladesh showcase youthful energy as an enabling factor to drive social change and development.

The concluding chapter synthesises insights from the theme-specific chapters and ties them together to present a coherent picture of the CR sector in South Asia. Rampersaud-Skorka identifies key principles guiding the operation of CR stations and discusses challenges and sustainability techniques relevant to the region. This chapter offers a reflective summary of the contributions of CR to community empowerment and development, making a compelling case for the continued support and expansion of CR initiatives.

The theoretical framework of this study is grounded in Participatory Communication and Development and the concepts of Community, the Public Sphere, and Civil Society. These frameworks highlight the role of Community Radio as an Alternative Media and Citizens' Media, featuring the broader implications of Rampersaud-Skorka's book for the practice of community media.

In conclusion, Rampersaud-Skorka's work stands out for its academic rigour and practical relevance. As an international scholar from outside the region, she demonstrates remarkable adaptability and cultural sensitivity to successfully navigating the diverse socio-political environments of South Asia. We consider this book to be a validation of her dedication and passion for community media and a noteworthy addition to the literature on community radio and media studies in Nepal, India, and Bangladesh. We are confident that this book will be a substantial resource for years to come for scholars, practitioners, policymakers, and anyone interested in the power of media to drive social change in the Global South.

At the UNESCO Chair on Community Media, the only one of its kind in the world, our research outputs, as well as the community resources we have generated over the last decade, have focused, among other things, on: the emergence of community radio in India within a development paradigm and a social change matrix; the evolution of CR in India as primarily NGO radio and the pitfalls that accompany it; the complexity of policymaking around the democratisation of airwaves in South Asia; the history and establishment of a dynamic community radio sector in the region, amounting to reclaiming of the airwaves in various ways; building the capacities of radio stations to undertake self-assessment through a methodology of peer-learning; and instilling gender sensitivity in the programming and policies of stations. This volume by Rampersaud-Skorka, who has been one of the important researchers at the Chair, is a significant addition to this collection of works on community radio in South Asia. It brings in a valuable mapping methodology to offer a set of analytical anchors within which to understand community radio in India, Bangladesh, and Nepal. If someone is looking for an overview of the community radio sector in the region, this book eminently serves the purpose.

Vinod Pavarala, Kanchan K. Malik, Vasuki Belavadi
UNESCO Chair on Community Media
University of Hyderabad,
Hyderabad, India

Acknowledgements

I began my doctoral degree journey with much uncertainty—a new step in academia, moving away from my home (again), and returning to a not so new world but still a very different one. That journey comprised phases of rest, of peace, and of harmony; likewise, there were phases of conflict, of uncertainty, and of a need to evolve to accommodate changes. These characteristics appear to have been transferred to the conversion of my doctoral thesis into this book. Alas! I see the horizon.

In my mind, this book is not a reflection of my abilities alone; it displays the personalities of everyone who helped from the beginning of my doctoral studies to the end of the journey. Saying *'thank you'* seems like a diminutive sentiment to express the depth of gratitude I feel; however, I do recognise the importance of their contributions.

First and foremost, Mom and Dad, Dhanwanti Rampersaud and Ramdat Rampersaud, you have always supported my dreams and aspirations; you encouraged me to keep aiming for the stars, even on the cloudiest of nights. Thank you for believing in me, always. To my husband and daughter, Julian Skorka and Viktoria Skorka, you provided the final motivation for me to complete this task! *Danke euch!*

Apart from my personal community, it is most important to acknowledge those who were directly involved with my doctoral project as their knowledge and experiences truly provided the best foundation for me to soar. To all the stakeholders who made the time to speak with me about this passion, I thank you sincerely. While I might not mention you by name here, you are all noted throughout this book, and I trust I have adequately shared your stories. Additionally, there are a few organisations I must mention for their help in introducing me to the experts and arranging my travels around the beautiful countries of Nepal, India, and Bangladesh: the UNESCO Chair on Community Media, the World Association of Community Radio Broadcasters (AMARC-Asia Pacific), and Bangladesh NGOs Network for Radio and Communication (BNNRC).

Finally but most important, the participants of community radio in Nepal, India, and Bangladesh— **you are all awesome!** Thank you for answering my numerous questions, giving me tours around the facilities, and sharing your cultures with me.

I enjoyed the chai, samosas, and all the other delicious snacks you shared as you told me your stories with such enthusiasm. It truly was an honour and a pleasure to meet all of you, to have these shared experiences, and to learn from you.

Thank you to all of you!

Competing Interests The author has no competing interests to declare that are relevant to the content of this manuscript.

Contents

Abbreviations

ACORAB	Association of Community Radio Broadcasters (Nepal)
AMARC	World Association of Community Radio Broadcasters (French: *Association Mondiale Des Radiodiffuseurs Communautaires*)
BCRA	Bangladesh Community Radio Association
BNNRC	Bangladesh NGOs Network for Radio and Communication
CMD	Community Media Database
CR	Community Radio
CRS	Community Radio Stations
FM	Frequency Modulation
ICT	Information and Communication Technology
INGO	International Non-governmental Organisation
LGBTQ	Lesbian, Gay, Bi-sexual, Transgender, Queer/Questioning
MoU	Memorandum of Understanding
NGO	Non-governmental Organisation
PSA	Public Service Announcement
PWD	Persons with Disabilities
RTI	Right to Information
SAARC	South Asian Association for Regional Cooperation
SANCOM	South Asia Network on Community Media
SMS	Short Message Service (ref. mobile phones)
UNESCO	United Nations Educational, Scientific and Cultural Organisation
W	Watts

Community Media in South Asia

1

> An alternative to commercial and state radio, community radio's most distinguished characteristic is its commitment to community participation at all levels. While listeners of commercial radio are able to participate in the programming in limited ways – via open line telephone shows or by requesting a favourite song, for example – community radio listeners are the producers, managers, directors, evaluators, and even the owners of the stations. (Girard, 2001, p. 2)

Around the world, community radio (CR) is characterised using a variety of perspectives depending on the reasons for the establishment of these initiatives, their objectives, and their products. Different conceptual points-of-view put forth by various key thinkers in the field provide a multitude of entry points into understanding this phenomenon. The typology of alternative and radical media highlighted by Atton (2001), the Rhizomatic Approach presented by Bosch (2010), and the four theoretical approaches presented by Carpentier et al. (2002) are some of the theoretical bases for CR. However, regardless of the approach taken to explain this phenomenon, there are some universally acceptable and foundational aspects associated with CR: (1) they ideally operate on a not-for-profit basis; (2) they feature content produced by local communities who are generally marginalised or ignored by mainstream media; (3) stations are used to address the needs of these communities; and (4) they are owned, operated, and managed by the members of these communities. In essence, community radio stations (CRS) are used by marginalised communities to share their own stories, firstly among themselves and secondly with the wider population, when necessary, especially since mainstream media[1] often ignore or pay minimum attention to these marginalised communities (AMARC Asia-Pacific, n.d.-b; Carpentier, 2016).

[1] Mainstream media encompass government-owned (public) and privately run (commercial) media outlets. They reflect dominant views held by society—particularly those views by people who control (through ownership or financial support) these entities (Herman & Chomsky, 1998).

T. Rampersaud-Skorka, *Community Radio in South Asia*, Diversity and Inclusion Research, https://doi.org/10.1007/978-3-031-85201-5_1

1.1 Reasons for the Establishment of CR

In the beginning, mass media were considered as instruments to foster a truly representative public sphere. However, as they became bigger and more commercially inclined, they were used to broadcast content from a powerful minority to the perceived powerless majority; their content enforced ways of thinking that empowered the elites and disempowered the poor. In addition, the subsequent quest for world domination resulting in the world wars and the ensuing mass poverty led to some "less developed" societies regressing as resources became scarce (Atton, 2001; Cleaver, 1999; Downing, 2008; Rodríguez, 2001).

To alleviate poverty, ideas of development, from an economic point of view, started to surface in the 1970s. This approach to development[2] supported the impression that economically and technologically advanced societies are better than those "lagging behind" or those showing a preference for age-old wisdom and oral traditions; thus, it diminished the importance of traditional knowledge from grassroots people. As this top-bottom approach to development was implemented, problems arising from excluding people in their own processes of development were discovered. Trying to correct this, these people were then included in the process, albeit, in minuscule foci at either the beginning of projects, in brief consultations during project implementation, or in a feedback capacity at the end. All the arising problems laid the foundation for a paradigm addressing a bottom-up approach, which ensured societies progress in a manner benefitting the majority, if not all. This paradigm did not focus on making the rich wealthier and the poor poorer but on positive social change for all—on sustainable development[3] (Chatterjee, 1998; Fraser, 1992; Kamat, 2002; Kidd, 1998; Rodríguez, 2001).

From the 1990s onwards, participatory communication entered the social change discussion as it directly addressed key challenges associated with the development era. Participatory communication focused on the people at the grassroots and employed techniques that laid the groundwork for community media—a phenomenon that has metamorphosised to suit contemporary times. For many, the use of community media (newspapers, radio, video, theatre, mobile, folklore, or some other form) filled a gap by providing fora where common people can address their interests and even provide solutions to problems they face among their social groups. As such, community media are "conceived, owned, run and sustained by a section of society and used to fight poverty and social injustice" (Malik, 2011,

---

[2] As Seers (1969, p. 2) puts it, "development is inevitably treated as a synonym for improvement" by copying the development paths perceived as desirable from first-world countries and imposing them onto third-world countries.

[3] "Sustainable development is a multi-dimensional concept aimed at achieving economic, environmental, social, cultural, and governance goals in an inter-temporal context; its focus is on meeting the needs of future and current generations" (Keser, 2023); should not compromise future generations to meet their own needs (Sustainable Development, n.d.).

p. 23); they provided a forum for the voiceless[4]—a public arena for them to express themselves.

1.2 Background to CR in South Asia

Since the introduction of *Miners' Radio* in 1949, this phenomenon has been in a continuous state of change. With beginnings traced to the isolated mountains of Bolivia, South America—several hours away from the nearest city—the very first CRS was used in mining towns and encampments (thus the name) as an important means of communication for almost 30 years (O'Conner, 1990, p. 102). Since then, it has transformed into a tool for social change. As a result of this dynamism, CR is referred to by a variety of different names including, but not limited to, *alternative radio, rebel radio, cooperative radio, educational radio, free radio, participatory radio*, and *rural radio.* Irrespective of the term used for this phenomenon, and regardless of the content being broadcast, location, audience reach, ownership structure, funding, or any other factor, if the initiative focuses on promoting participation of members from a community and endorses the processes of interaction and communication over the product, then this highlights what CR encompasses today. The world over, these initiatives provide an avenue for the voiceless to be heard and the marginalised to express themselves since these initiatives are ideally *in* the community, *for* the community, *about* the community, and *by* the community—whether those communities are identified by the geographical reach of the stations or by interests exhibited by the members of the communities (Pavarala & Malik, 2007; Tabing, 2002). In short, with such humble beginnings, CR today focuses on people's participation—to motivate them to become active change agents and enable them to share their stories as they fill existing information gaps present within mainstream media (Atton, 2001; Downing, 2008; Rodríguez, 2001; Servaes, 1999; White, 1994).

Regarding South Asia, according to Pavarala (2015, p. 1), "the two-decade old community radio movement in South Asia is something that seems to be perpetually 'under progress'" due to multiple challenges within Nepal, India, and Bangladesh (as well as other countries in the region). He continued by highlighting that even though CR has been a reality in the region for over two decades, with many individuals and organisations advocating for (enabling) policies and the official establishment of stations within their countries, this phenomenon is still in a state of development in the region.

With specific reference to the origins of CR in the region, Nepal is credited as the forerunner in the sector through the establishment of *Radio Sagarmatha* in 1997; today, the country boasts of over 300 CRS, even though there is no specific policy for the CR sector (ACORAB, n.d.-b). CR stations in Nepal are represented by the Association of Community Radio Broadcasters (ACORAB), which aims to

[4] People identified as being voiceless do not have an avenue to share their knowledge due to a lack of access or resources to access a public forum (Tacchi, 2008, p. 1).

promote, protect, and strengthen the medium as a tool for communication (ACORAB, n.d.-a). India had a longer time to wait before welcoming the first campus CRS—*Anna Community Radio,* in 2004 and the first rural CRS—*Sangham Radio*, in 2008; today, there are over 200 operational CRS across the country (List of Operational Community Radio Stations in India as on *31-05-2019,* 2019). Finally, Bangladesh has been involved in the struggle for CR since the 2000s, guided by the Bangladesh NGOs Network for Radio and Communication (BNNRC), which has resulted in the establishment of the first official CRS—*Radio Padma*, in 2011 (BNNRC, n.d.).

Even though CR has been present in the South Asia region since the 1990s, there was no formal attempt to address the larger geographic region until 2014 when the foundation for the South Asia Network on Community Media (SANCOM)[5] was laid. This network provides a forum for promoting freedom of expression and the strengthening of community media development within the region as it supports capacity and knowledge sharing, and advocates for community media to engage the SAARC countries in democratic problem solving and dialogue (SANCOM, n.d.).

1.3 Unifying Factors for CR in South Asia[6]

Overall, Nepal, India, and Bangladesh boast of large populations with most people residing in rural areas. Additionally, there are multi-cultural societies with diversity in spoken languages, religious practises, and everyday cultural practises. Through these similarities across Nepal, India, and Bangladesh, one can see that there are unifying factors for CR in South Asia. This is supported by Pavarala[7] (in-depth interview, July 11, 2018), who highlighted that there is a variety of unifying factors such as politics and culture; however, the prominent binding factor for the South Asian countries is the "development logic" that prevails—these countries are considered as being in a developmental state.[8] He expands on this by stating that late in the 1980s and the 1990s, there was a ferment that led to civil society exploring the possibilities of non-government organisations (NGOs) playing a role in development—as was the case around the world—with regard to a more participatory approach being created and implemented to address the challenges of the domi-

[5] SANCOM was launched at the World Radio Day event in New Delhi, India, on February 13, 2015. It was devised to spearhead the CR movement in the region and is an initiative of the UNESCO Chair on Community Media (SANCOM, n.d.).

[6] Please see *Chap. 2: (Media) History of Nepal, India, and Bangladesh* for a brief overview of the histories of the three countries and information about their media environment.

[7] Prof. Vinod Pavarala is a Professor and Chairholder, UNESCO Chair on Community Media, University of Hyderabad, India. He has over 20 years of teaching, research, and advocacy experience in the development communication and community media fields (Pavarala, in-depth interview, July 11, 2018).

[8] "The developmental state not only refers to the collective economic and human development, but also describes the state's essential role in harnessing national resources and directing incentives through a distinctive policy-making process" (Charlotte, 2008).

nant development paradigm. As a result, there was a move away from the more state-centric model of development. Pavarala continued by stating that the emerging development logic could have ideally been used by media to disseminate states' goals of national development as well as the values and principles of modernisation. However, due to the *broadcasting* method endorsed by mainstream media, CR emerged to accomplish this feat and to encourage people's participation. These points are supported by Basnet[9] (in-depth interview, April 23, 2018), who expressed that people wanted control over a communication channel that would allow them "unhindered expression of self" where they speak for themselves and not have others do it for them; this thinking was linked to the idea that by having control over a channel of communication, they would have some influence over politics and their lives.

In general, the South Asia countries, specifically the grassroots communities in Nepal, India, and Bangladesh, were unified in their fight to counter the negatives of globalisation since, being categorised as part of the Global South, they were affected by the economically and technologically advanced countries. Huesca (2002, p. 3) explains:

> Development programs and research projects falling out of this philosophical frame tended to focus on individual attitudes and effects while ignoring social, political, and economic structures that frequently stood in contradiction to development goals. [A situation] detrimental to the region's social context.

These challenges informed the decision that led to CR being identified as an ideal medium to foster participatory communication where everyone would have the opportunity to share in their own development. By supporting the ideas of freedom of expression and the right to information—foundational elements for societies to live with dignity—these initiatives perpetuate diversity, equity, and inclusion (DEI) by highlighting the multi-cultural beauty of communities, by promoting impartiality considering the disparities that exist in society, and by safeguarding against discrimination to ensure marginalised groups are given a forum to express themselves. Overall, CR enables people's inclusion in society "on their terms through self-determination [using their] voices [and participating] in decision-making processes that affect them" (AMARC Asia-Pacific, n.d.-a).

[9] Suman Basnet is the Regional Coordinator of AMARC Asia-Pacific—the World Association of Community Radio Broadcasters. For more than 15 yrs, he has been working in the community media field as an advocate and activist for CR with a focus on (1) disaster risk reduction and CR, (2) women's empowerment, and (3) empowerment of the marginalised societies (Basnet, in-depth interview, April 23, 2018).

1.4 Methodology

Even though these initiatives have been utilised to create social change for over three decades, there has not been any significant work detailing the field *in totality* in the South Asia region. While there is information about various projects and the more popular initiatives in the individual countries, there is currently no consolidated information which maps and analyses these initiatives across a larger geographical area transcending national borders. CR, for all its contributions towards the development of societies around the world, is still an anomaly to those researching this phenomenon. There is a variety of information available via various projects, articles, reports, etc.; however, many of those tend to focus on specific countries or select initiatives, or a combination of both sometimes. While such information, at the micro-level, is valuable, there is a paucity of data at a macro level that can be used to better understand the sector in its entirety across a region.

With the aim and objectives of the author's doctoral project (displayed in Box 1.1), a *mixed-methods mapping methodology* was created to bridge the information gap since it provided a foundation to conceptually address the sector. Through application of this methodology, the author was able to centralise information about the sectors within Nepal, India, and Bangladesh, as well as the individual CRS in each of the three countries.

Box 1.1 Aim and Objectives of Doctoral Project

The purpose of the study of this so-called alternative media sector, with a focus on Nepal, India, and Bangladesh, was to understand the structure, location, and significance vis-à-vis the larger mediascape within each of these nations. The mapping of this specific sector provided a consolidated volume of information surrounding community radio within this region.

1. Develop a technique and framework, based on an international understanding of alternative media, for adequately mapping the community media sector of South Asia.
2. Analyse the media ecology of South Asia and understand the techno-social policy environment surrounding the establishment and continuation of community radio endeavours in Nepal, India, and Bangladesh.
3. Systematically study the structure and political economy of the community radio sector in Bangladesh, India, and Nepal.
4. Analyse the notions of participation and empowerment adopted by stakeholders for community radio initiatives in Nepal, India, and Bangladesh.
5. Examine the endeavours by stakeholders to establish and/or be part of networks in order to strengthen the policy environment and promote good practices locally, nationally, regionally, and internationally.

Source: Rampersaud, T. (2020). *Mapping Community Radio in South Asia: A Systematic Analysis of the Alternative Mediascape in Nepal, India, and Bangladesh*. (Unpublished Doctoral Thesis).

The mapping methodology was selected as it was best suited for creating and presenting clear pictures—both literal and metaphorical—of the CR sector in South Asia. Apart from the traditional cartographic maps,[10] concept maps and mind maps were used as they "demonstrate how people visualize relationships between various concepts [and] might also include other sorts of visual or graphic representation of concepts and/or propositions that attempt to convey an understanding or relationships among different concepts within a map" (Wheldon & Faubert, 2009, p. 69). For these reasons, the mapping methodology was selected as it can lead to "patterns being better identified, recognized, and understood through more graphic representations of knowledge, experience, and perception" (Wheldon & Ahlberg, 2012, pp. 125). By combining multiple mapping approaches, a mapping methodology specific to CR was created which (1) recorded detailed data about the sector and (2) presented the information utilising both images and words in relation to physical locations and thematic areas.

Through the *mapping methodology*, the data collected were explored, analysed, and described by combining both qualitative and quantitative techniques. The key instruments used were desk review of existing data, in-depth interviews with stakeholders, and an interview schedule to document observations regarding the case studies during field visits.

While it would have been ideal to map the entire South Asia region with regard to all traditional community media initiatives—community newspapers, community television, participatory video, and community radio—the lack of resources forced some limitations on the project in relation to the type of medium and the countries chosen for data collection, as well as the individuals identified for in-depth interviews. Due to the nature of the project and the data available in the public forum, non-probability sampling techniques were employed at all stages, that is each stakeholder, country, and initiative was selected for specific reasons based on the findings from the desk review process. Specifically, purposive sampling was utilised since the main goal was to focus on characteristics identified during the desk review stage which were of interest (*Non-probability sampling*, n.d.).

1. *Countries*: The eight members of the South Asian Association for Regional Cooperation (SAARC)[11] comprised the population; these countries are Afghanistan, Bangladesh, Bhutan, India, The Maldives, Nepal, Pakistan, and Sri Lanka. Nepal, India, and Bangladesh were selected through purposive non-probability sampling because they have well-developed and operational CR sectors with about 10 years or more of history.

[10] According to Foote and Crum (1995), maps are a fundamental part of society for several reasons: recording and storing information, analysing location distribution, and presenting information and communicating findings.

[11] This organisation was established on December 08, 1985, to enable member countries to work together for their growth regionally, the promotion of their socio-cultural backgrounds, and collectively addressing issues such as technology, trade, climate change, and so forth, which affect the region (SAARC, n.d.).

2. *Initiative*: Following the desk review process, it was found that CR was the best-documented community medium in the target countries since CRS need to be licensed to operate. Thus, it was easy to use public records from government departments and key stakeholder organisations to identify the number of initiatives within each country. Also, CR appeared to be the medium of choice for grassroots people due to its advantages over other media. As a result, a profile based on secondary information was created for each operational CRS as of December 2017.
3. *Case Studies*: A combination of convenience and expert sampling were used to identify stations in Nepal, India, and Bangladesh. With regard to expert sampling, the first CRS to legally broadcast content in Nepal, India, and Bangladesh were selected: *Radio Sagarmatha* in Nepal, *Sangham Radio* in India, and *Radio Padma* in Bangladesh. Apart from this, the remainder were selected using convenience sampling: easily accessible, have environments conducive to interviews in English or with a translator present, and the stations should be in operation for at least 2–3 years in order to be able to provide data based on experience. The other CRS visited were *Radio Namobuddha* and *Radio Sindhu* in Nepal; *Radio Luit, Tilonia Radio*, and *Waqt ki Awaaz* in India; and *Radio Bikrampur*, *Borendro Radio*, and *Radio Sarabela* in Bangladesh.
4. *Stakeholders*: For these in-depth interviews, experts and/or individuals with large amounts of experience in the CR sector who can provide key insights about each country and the South Asia region in general were selected through expert sampling technique. These interviews were conducted in person and through video conferencing.

These multiple approaches, techniques, and tools within the mapping methodology made it possible to curate existing information and uncover new data regarding the CR sectors in Nepal, India, and Bangladesh.

1.5 Overview of the Book

This book has ten chapters, comprising both secondary and primary data gathered and organised by themes. This chapter*: Community Media in South Asia* introduces the topic and situates community media in the region as well as provides a brief overview of the methodology employed for data gathering and analysis. *Chapter 2: (Media) History of Nepal, India, and Bangladesh* introduces the larger media sector and then addresses the community media sectors of the three countries. *Chapter 3: Contextualising Community Radio* provides the thematic entry points for understanding the data gathered with a focus on five key areas: paradigmatic shifts in understanding communication; participatory communication and development; public sphere, counter public sphere, and civil society; community; and alternative media, community media, citizens' media. *Chapter 4: Profiles of Case Studies* comprises overviews of the 11 case studies in Nepal, India, and Bangladesh, where primary data via in-depth interviews and observations were gathered; this chapter informs the content in Chaps. 6–9. *Chapter 5: Descriptive Mapping of CR in SA* provides a quantitative analysis of the created Community Media Directory across all three countries and is based on data gathered during the desk review stage of the author's doctoral research. *Chapter 6: Media Policy Environment*, *Chap. 7: Ownership and Management Philosophies*, *Chap. 8: Community Radio Practitioners*, and *Chap. 9: Community Radio Programmes* are the thematic chapters that address key content expressed in their titles across Nepal, India, and Bangladesh. Finally, *Chap. 10: Conclusion: Tracing Regional Multiplicity of the Alternative Mediascape in South Asia* summaries the community radio sector in each country and presents the 21 guiding principles observed by the author—these principles could be utilised by initiatives in the region.

References

ACORAB. (n.d.-a). *About Us*. Retrieved June 30, 2019, from http://www.acorab.org.np/index.php?pagename=aboutus

ACORAB. (n.d.-b) *Members*. Retrieved November 30, 2017, from https://www.acorab.org.np/index.php?pagename=member&page=1

AMARC Asia-Pacific. (n.d.-a). *Homepage*. Retrieved May 31, 2018, from http://amarc-ap.org/

AMARC Asia-Pacific. (n.d.-b). *What is community radio?* Retrieved May 30, 2019, from http://www.amarc.org/?q=node/47

Atton, C. (2001). *Approaching alternative media: Theory and methodology*. Napier University.

BNNRC. (n.d.). *Community Radio in Bangladesh*. Retrieved January 30, 2017, from http://www.bnnrc.net/

Bosch, T. (2010). Chapter 3 - theorizing citizens' media: A Rhizomatic approach. In C. Rodríguez, D. Kidd, & L. Stein (Eds.), *Making our media: Global initiatives toward a democratic public sphere, volume 1—Creating new communication spaces* (pp. 71–87). Hampton Press.

Carpentier, N. (2016). Community media as rhizome: Expanding the research agenda. *Journal of Alternative and Community Media, 1*(1) Retrieved July 31, 2019, from https://www.researchgate.net/publication/312020956_Community_media_as_rhizome_Expanding_the_research_agenda

Carpentier, N., Lie, R., & Servaes, J. (2002). Is there a role and place for community media in the new remit?. *Broadcasting & Convergence: Articulating a New Remit, International Conference RIPE@2002, Helsinki-Tampere*, 2002.

Charlotte, N. G. (2008, June 15). *The 'Developmental State' and Economic Development. E-International Relations*. Retrieved November 30, 2019, from https://www.e-ir.info/2008/06/15/the-developmental-state-and-economic-development/

Chatterjee, P. (1998). Community in the East. *Economic and Political Weekly, 33*(6), 277–282.

Cleaver, F. (1999). Paradoxes of participation: Questioning participatory approaches to development. *Journal of International Development, 11*, 50–62.

Downing, J. (2008). Social movement theories and alternative media: An evaluation and critique. *Communication, Culture & Critique, 1*(1), 40–50.

Fraser, N. (1992). Rethinking the public sphere: A contribution to the critique of actually existing democracy. In C. Calhoun (Ed.), *Habermas and the public sphere* (pp. 56–80). MIT Press.

Girard, B. (Ed.). (2001). *A passion for radio: Radio waves and community* (2nd ed.). Comunica.

Herman, E., & Chomsky, N. (1998). *Manufacturing consent—The political economy and the mass media*. Pantheon Books.

Huesca, R. (2002). Chapter 8—Tracing the history of participatory communication approaches to development: A critical appraisal. In J. Servaes (Ed.), *Approaches to development communication*. UNESCO.

Kamat, S. (2002). *Development hegemony—NGOs and the state in India*. Oxford University Press.

Keser, I. (2023). Interdependence and complementarity of a multi-dimensional concept of sustainable development and the integrated approach to urban governance - case Study City of Zagreb. *Sustainability, 15*(12). https://doi.org/10.3390/su15129213

Kidd, D. (1998). *Ph.D. dissertation - chapter 3: The commons and enclosures*. Simon Fraser University.

List of Operational Community Radio Stations in India as on 31-05-2019. (2019, May 31). *Ministry of Information and Broadcasting, India*. Retrieved October 30, 2019, from https://mib.gov.in/sites/default/files/List%20of%20251%20Operational%20CRS%20in%20India%20as%20on%2031-05-2019%28new%29.pdf

Malik, K. K. (2011). Community radio: Guidelines on management and ownership. In *UNESCO. Ground realities, Community Radio in India*. UNESCO.

Non-probability sampling. (n.d.). *Laerd dissertation*. Retrieved April 30, 2016, from http://dissertation.laerd.com/non-probability-sampling.php#step3

O'Conner, A. (1990). The miners' radio stations in Bolivia: A culture of resistance. *Journal of Communication, 40*(1), 102–110.

Pavarala, V. (2015). Community radio 'under Progress'—Resuming a paused revolution. *Economic and Political Weekly, 50*(51), 14–17.

Pavarala, V., & Malik, K. K. (2007). *Other voices: The struggle for community radio in India*. Sage Publications India Pvt Ltd.

Rodríguez, C. (2001). *Fissures in the Mediascape: An international study of citizens' media*. Hampton Press.

SAARC. (n.d.). *About SAARC*. Retrieved July 31, 2015, from http://www.saarc-sec.org

SANCOM. (n.d.). *History*. Retrieved November 30, 2015, from https://sancomonline.net/history/

Seers, D. (1969). *The meaning of development. IDS communication 44*. Institute of Development Studies.

Servaes, J. (1999). *Communication for development: One world, multiple cultures*.

Sustainable Development. (n.d.). *International Institute for Sustainable Development (IISD)*. Retrieved September 30, 2024, from https://www.iisd.org/mission-and-goals/sustainable-development

Tabing, L. (2002). *How to do community radio: A primer for community radio operations*. UNESCO.

Tacchi, J. (2008). *Voice and poverty*. Media Development, 2008/1.

Wheldon, J., & Ahlberg, M. K. (2012). *Visualizing social science research: Maps, methods, and meaning*. Sage.

Wheldon, J., & Faubert, J. (2009). Framing experience: Concept maps, Mind maps, and data collection in qualitative research. *International Journal of Qualitative Methods, 8*(3), 68-83.

White, S. A. (1994). Introduction - the concept of participation: Transforming rhetoric to reality. In S. A. White, K. S. Nair, & J. Ascroft (Eds.), *Participatory communication: Working for change and development* (pp. 15–34). Sage Publications.

(Media) History of Nepal, India, and Bangladesh

2

2.1 Nepal

The Federal Democratic Republic of Nepal ("Nepal" for short) was declared a democratic republic in 2008 following a decade-long period of violence and turbulent negotiations because of a strong Maoist insurgency from 1995 to 2006. Prior to this insurgency, Nepal has a past comprising an isolated existence and turbulent political and monarchical rule. From 1846 to 1950, the country had hereditary prime ministers, known as *Ranas* (meaning: King or Prince), who reportedly dominated the monarchy and dictated the country's isolation. In 1950, there was a revolt that resulted in the restoration of the crown's authority in 1951 and a parliamentary system to govern the nation. However, this was overturned in 1960 by King Mahendra, who established a non-political party system—a *panchayat* (meaning: council) where he suspended parliament and the constitution, and ruled the country. Three decades later, in 1991, democracy returned to Nepal when the Nepali Congress Party won the very first democratic election in the country. In 2008, the monarchy was abolished in Nepal (Nepal country profile, n.d.; Zuberi et al., 2017).

Geographically, Nepal is bordered by India to the east, south, and west, and the Tibetan region of China to the north. Comprising an area of 147,181 kms^2, the country has a population of close to 31 million people with 82% living in rural areas and 18% in urban areas. Approximately three-quarters of the country is mountainous with the remainder comprising flat, fertile plains for agriculture, and marshy areas due to the many rivers. With an approximate 85% literacy rate, Nepal is also multicultural as can be seen in the language dynamics where the principal language is Nepali with other common languages including Hindi, Tibetan, and English, where the use of English is widely associated with communication and educational organisations. Further, there are a total of 122 languages of which 109 are indigenous and 13 are non-indigenous because of immigrant communities including Assamese, Chinese, Eastern Punjabi, and Sindhi. In addition, Hinduism, the major religion, is practised by 81.3% of the population, with other key religions being Buddhism,

T. Rampersaud-Skorka, *Community Radio in South Asia*, Diversity and Inclusion Research, https://doi.org/10.1007/978-3-031-85201-5_2

Islam, Kiratism,[1] and Christianity (Naskar, n.d.; Nepal - Basic Data, n.d.; Nepal country profile, n.d.; Zuberi et al., 2017).

Community radio (CR) was introduced in Nepal to provide an alternative to the so-called power elites, which comprised media owners, industrialists, traders, and the government, in addition to representatives from the political, economic, and academic sectors, according to Mainali.[2] These elites who owned and controlled mainstream media utilised said entities to share self-promoting, subjective content to the wider population; as a result, there was a need for media that can be "held" directly by the community people with the aim of fostering their development. As a result, CR was introduced to address this gap as well as for being used to create and support peace, social harmony, and skills development. Today, in Nepal, this alternative medium is used for information and knowledge sharing among communities, as well as for entertainment purposes such as the sharing of songs, stories, and drama about folk cultures (Mainali, in-depth interview, April 26, 2018).

In Nepal, private broadcasting has flourished as has public broadcasting with the government having its radio, television, and print outlets; CR has also been very prominent in the country but only since the late 1990s. Regarding the media sector, the foundation of media can be traced back to 1898 when the first newspaper, *Sudhasagar*, was published. Following this, *Radio Nepal*—the state-owned broadcaster—was established in 1950 and television followed in December 1985. Today, while the press has a limited reach, many Nepalis have access to information via radio—the medium of choice due to it being "strong, popular, and credible with a larger following of listeners" (Paudyal, 2013 cited in Acharya, n.d.). As suggested by Humagain (2011, p. 2), radio is "the most influential medium in the context of uneven geographical territory, lower literacy rate and [the] poor economic condition of people, [it] is the best means of communication which can effectively flow the information to the different sectors of society." With these ideas in mind, CR was seen as the solution to the existing challenges (Lamichhane,[3] in-depth interview, April 27, 2018) (Kasajoo, 2002; Nepal - Basic Data, n.d.; Nepal profile – Media, n.d.; Shakya, 2015).

Nepal has a remarkably diverse community media sector comprising community radio, community television, community newspapers, and participatory video projects (Mainali, in-depth interview, April 26, 2018). Regarding CR, according to the

[1] Kiratism is an ancient religion practised by four tribes of the Himalayan Mountain Range and comprises worship of ancestors, nature, heavenly bodies, the elements, and some other Gods (Naskar, n.d.).

[2] Raghu Mainali is a community media activist who has been an advocate for and a key stakeholder of the community media sector in Nepal and South Asia for approximately 26 years, since the early 1990s. He has been involved in the development communication field for approximately 31 years. Mainali was involved in the set-up of *Radio Sagarmatha* and, today, continues his activism with CRSC and NEFEJ (Mainali, in-depth interview, April 26, 2018).

[3] Dr. Ramchandra Lamichhane is the Executive Director, ACORAB, Nepal. He has been involved with development communication for approximately 24 years (since 1993) and CR for 5 years. Lamichhane is deeply motivated towards the continuity of CR since they are beneficial to communities (Lamichhane, in-depth interview, April 27, 2018).

Association of Community Radio Broadcasters Nepal (ACORAB),[4] there were approximately 340 operational stations in Nepal as of June 2019. The history can be traced to the early 1990s when the democratic movement following the Panchayat Regime in Nepal occurred; this was a historical, political event that created a climate for activists to learn about the use of radio (FM (frequency modulation) in particular) in relation to participatory communication techniques. This led to activists approaching UNESCO for assistance around 1991. One year later, the *National Communication Policy 1992* was introduced, which created a more enabling policy environment. Following this major development, it took approximately 5 years for the first community radio station (CRS) to be granted a licence to operate—*Radio Sagarmatha* was established in 1997. Once the first licence was granted, activists and other stakeholders were then able to promote the use of CR across Nepal as they established the Community Radio Support Centre (CRSC)[5] in 2002 and continued the advocacy for more CRS. Throughout the activism, from the 1990s onwards, the Nepal Forum of Environmental Journalists (NEFEJ)[6] has been a key organisation to advocate for CR in Nepal (Mainali in-depth interview, April 26, 2018).

However, the CR movement was not without challenges. In 2005, when the King took control of Nepal, he sent armies to the then 20 operational CRS and other media houses to ensure the ban on news was enforced. This was met with protests in the form of the Save Independent Radio Movement, where the ban on news was circumvented by creative programming such as the singing of the news (a form of entertainment) and narrations about fighting Ravana[7]—a juxtaposition to fighting an all-powerful person—through poetry (Ninan, 2005). In 2006, when democracy was re-established in Nepal, the facilitation for CRS became even stronger, and from 2006 to 2009 there was an "excessive growth" (Mainali, in-depth interview, April 26, 2018) of the sector. Mainali compared this growth to an increase in sales of a new product in demand—a metaphor highlighting that there was no need for more stations, but a requirement for more quality and focused programming via strategically located stations through the country. Today, CR serves mainly to protect local cultures from the dominant Nepali language media which are biased against marginalised groups which comprise 75% of the population and include Dalits, Madhesis, indigenous people, and Muslims (Pringle & Subba, 2007, p. 12; Kasajoo, 2002; Mainali, in-depth interview, April 26, 2018).

---

[4] "ACORAB [the umbrella organisation for CR in Nepal] was established in 2002 as an autonomous and politically non-partisan organisation to advance the cause of community radio, facilitate the sharing of knowledge and resources, and speak with one voice for the communities it represents" (About Us, n.d.).

[5] The CRSC is an arm of NEFEJ created to actively promote and support the "growth and strengthening of community radio with help desk, grant fund, technical and management funds, producers' capacity building, reference materials development, advocacy and lobbying, radio centre, etc." (NEFEJ, n.d.).

[6] NEFEJ is a private company established on June 01, 1986, and formally registered on August 23, 1990, as a forum for various stakeholders to "debate, report, and influence public policy for sustainable development" (NEFEJ, n.d.).

[7] Ravana is a great King of Lanka, in Hindu mythology, who wanted unlimited powers.

2.2 India

The Republic of India ("India" for short) was founded on August 15, 1947, when the country gained independence from Great Britain ("Britain" for short) after approximately 200 years of colonisation. Known as one of the world's oldest civilisations, India was dominated by the British influence since the 1500s. Towards the late 1800s, India began a long struggle for independence from Britain. Since then, the country has grown to become the world's largest democracy; however, there have been periods of unrest and instability in the country and much of the population is reportedly living in extreme poverty. Today, India is seen as a "rising economic powerhouse and nuclear-armed state and has emerged as an important regional power" (India country profile, n.d.) (Briney, 2019; India country profile, n.d.).

With an area of 3,287,590 kms^2, approximately 1.3 billion people reside in the country with roughly 70% in rural areas and 30% in urban areas. Comprising 29 states and 7 union territories, India accounts for a large section of the South Asia region. Afghanistan, Bangladesh, Bhutan, China, Myanmar, Nepal, and Pakistan are country borders with water borders including the Arabian Sea and Bay of Bengal to the east and west, respectively. Approximately 91% of the country comprises land (mountainous regions, desserts, and coastlands), while 9% comprise water bodies. There are debates about the official language of the country due to the diversity in culture; however, the most popular languages include Hindi, Bengali, Marathi, Telugu, Tamil, and English. Like the languages spoken, there are a variety of religions including Hinduism, Islam, Christianity, Sikhism, and Buddhism (India, n.d.; India country profile, n.d.).

The Bangalore Declaration on Radio, 1996, n.d. (p. 1) suggests that "information is a key element in socio-economic development. The capacity to communicate and have access to media greatly influences information use and its impact." These ideas are mirrored by Nagarajan[8] (in-depth interview, June 18 & 19, 2018), who posits that the community radio (CR) initiatives provide democratic access to media—especially those that are operated by marginalised groups in society and in turn empower them to contribute to public discourses. Likewise, Dutta[9] (in-depth interview, March 23, 2018) highlighted that mainstream media are *for* and *about* us; however, they are not *by* us since the general population does not contribute to these

[8] Mr. Ramakrishnan Nagarajan, Executive Director, Ideosync Media Combine, India, and member of the Community Radio Forum (India), has been working in the development communication field for approximately 24 years and specifically with CR for 19 years. He assists CRS in setting up and becoming operational, training activities for CRS, lobbying for CRS in India, and networking with other stakeholders for the betterment of CR in India and South Asia (Nagarajan, in-depth interview, June 18 & 19, 2018).

[9] Dr. Ankurran Dutta has been working in the development communication field for approximately 13 years. As a media teacher and various work experiences with organisations such as CEMCA (India), he is focused on promoting the use of community media in India since they allow the common people to be producers of their own stories (Dutta, in-depth interview, March 23, 2018).

initiatives; as a result, voice poverty [and representation] in the media environment is a major issue that CR addresses.

In India, media can be traced to the introduction of the first print publication, *the Doctrine of Christ*, which was published in 1557. Following this, the first radio programme was broadcasted in 1923, experimental television broadcast began in 1959, and internet explorations in 1987 (Shaju, 2014). Since then, the media environment has developed to reflect the country's cultural diversity by having "thousands of outlets operating in multiple languages" (India profile – Media, n.d.) including traditional and new media. However, due to the criticisms against government-run and privately owned media outlets, CR was established to provide an alternative to mainstream media—there was the need for a medium that would give voices to marginalised people and ensure content relating to their lives are broadcast (*India country profile*, n.d.; India profile – Media, n.d.).

In India, ideas relating to people's participation in media activities can be traced back to 1956 with the introduction of Radio for Rural Development (popularly referred to as Radio Farm Forum) by the Government of India—an initiative that encouraged rural dwellers to listen to broadcasts twice weekly via All India Radio (AIR), the state broadcaster, with subsequent group discussions about the content. However, this experiment was only implemented from February to April 1956. The next project, this time through video, was the Satellite Instructional Television Experiment (SITE), which lasted for 1 year from August 1975 to July 1976. This experiment fostered the broadcast of educational programmes to rural dwellers from approximately 2400 villages in Arunachal Pradesh, Bihar, Karnataka, Madhya Pradesh, Orissa, and Rajasthan. Due to the positive reception of SITE, INSAT (Indian National Satellite), launched in 1981, was used to provide educational and development programmes via 1000 low-powered television transmissions around the country. However, technical failures of the satellite while in orbit resulted in this initiative being abandoned in a few months. Even though these initiatives were not direct results of CR ideologies, they did highlight the importance of audience participation in the communication process and show the need for involvement of grassroots people in development (Agrawal, 2006).

On February 05, 1995, the Supreme Court declared that the "airwaves constitute public property and must be utilised for advancing public good"—an outcome of The Secretary, Ministry of Information and Broadcasting (MIB) vs. Cricket Association of Bengal case, which ended the monopoly on radio broadcast. Following this ruling, several events contributed to the advocacy activities for CR in India, such as the Bangalore Declaration of 1996 and the Pastapur Declaration of 2000 (Pavarala & Malik, 2007, p. 102). In 2002, the *Policy Guidelines for setting up Community Radio Stations in India* ("2002 Policy" for short) was introduced, which allowed educational institutions to set up community radio stations (CRS). As a result, Anna University launched the first station—*Anna Community Radio*—in February 2004. It is important to note that although the state monopoly on broadcasting ended in 1995, only private FM stations and campus radio stations were allowed to broadcast until 2006 when there was an amendment to the 2002 CR Policy. This resulted in the establishment of the first rural CRS, *Sangham Radio*, in

October 2008, which was licensed to a non-governmental organisation (NGO) (Nagarajan, in-depth interview, June 18 & 19, 2018).

By May 2019, the MIB's website had a list comprising 251 operational CRS in India (*List of Operational Community Radio Stations in India as on 31-05-2019,* 2019). In September 2019, it was announced that 118 new CRS are in the process of being set up in India—this was regarding the issuance of 118 Letters of Intent ("118 new community radio stations to be set up: Union Minister Prakash Javadekar, 2019). Additionally, it was announced that there will be two more dedicated frequencies for CRS as well as revisions with regard to the advertisement rates associated with CRS instead of the hike in rates for electronic advertisements in the market (DoT announces two additional frequencies for running community radio stations, 2019).

2.3 Bangladesh

The People's Republic of Bangladesh ("Bangladesh" for short) was founded on March 26, 1971, following an official declaration by Sheikh Mujibur Rahman. However, this declaration marked the commencement of the War of Liberation, which lasted until December 16, 1971, and resulted in the separation of then East Pakistan from West Pakistan—the former became present-day Bangladesh (New Internationalist Team, 2011; Szczepanski, 2019).

Today, Bangladesh is one of the most densely populated countries in the world, with approximately 162 million people inhabiting 143,995 kms^2. Spread across eight main districts, 28% of the population live in the urban areas while 72% reside in the rural and peri-urban areas. Approximately 98% of the population are ethnic Bengalis while the remaining 2% are classified as having heritage from Burma and Bihar. The major language is Bengali; however, English is commonly spoken in urban areas. Islam is the dominant religion with approximately 88% of the population practising this faith, while Hinduism is the largest minority religion followed by Christianity, Buddhism, and Animism.[10] Geography-wise, Bangladesh has rich, fertile soil due to the presence of the Brahmaputra, Ganges, and Meghna Rivers, which supply nutrients from the Himalayan Mountain Range. As a result of the vast coastal topography and sea-level existence of the country, Bangladesh is prone to flooding and cyclones. Overall, Bangladesh is a developing country with most of the population employed in the agriculture sector (New Internationalist Team, 2011; Bangladesh country profile, n.d.; Anwar, 2015; Szczepanski, 2019).

> In Bangladesh, community radio was established for the purposes of knowledge creation, knowledge preservation, knowledge dissemination, and knowledge utilization. These initiatives provide a forum for the voices of the rural people to be heard, for the marginalized to

[10] This is the "belief in innumerable spiritual beings concerned with human affairs and capable of helping or harming human interests" (Park, n.d.).

participate in their development, and for existing divides to be bridged keeping in mind these four purposes. (Rahman,[11] in-depth interview, December 04, 2017)

Combining the above ideas with information from other stakeholders about community radio (CR) in Bangladesh, the author deduced that activists in Bangladesh visualise this medium as a forum for true democracy—a place where every voice can be represented, and traditionally marginalised people can communicate with each other and share their knowledge for the betterment of their society.

In Bangladesh, CR was introduced in 2011 with the official launch of *Radio Padma*—the first of currently 17 stations in operation. However, the media history of the country can be traced back to 1860 when two of the earliest Bengali magazines were published in Dhaka. The next medium to be established was radio, almost eight decades after the first printed magazine, which began transmission on December 16, 1939, with the then Pakistani government controlling the medium. This resulted in the government radio station holding a monopoly on the airwaves until 2006 when privately owned FM stations began broadcasting. Almost three decades after the introduction of radio, television broadcast began with the introduction of the Pakistan Television Corporation network in 1964—which became Bangladesh Television (BTV) after independence. This was followed by the infrastructure for online media being introduced in 1996 when internet service providers began operating. However, even with such a diverse media environment, mainstream initiatives were still not able to address the challenges faced by the majority; thus, the activism for community media in Bangladesh began (New Internationalist Team, 2011; Bangladesh country profile, n.d.; Bangladesh profile – Media, n.d.).

The beginnings of CR in Bangladesh can be traced back to the 1990s when the reformed General Agreement on Tariffs and Trade (GATT) by the World Trade Organisation (WTO) highlighted that private and commercial avenues can be used for empowering communities with the idea of restructuring the world. This, coupled with the rising focus on technology in the globalised world, gave rise to the question: "*How can rural communities receive the positives of globalization?*" (Rahman, in-depth interview, December 04, 2017).

By 1998, with the knowledge that technology can be used for development purposes, the Participatory Research in Asia (PRIA) Workshop in Delhi, India, allowed AHM Bazlur Rahman, then an employee with ActionAid International, to network with regional practitioners and fully formulate an idea of how to use CR to address the challenges faced by rural communities. For the next 2 years, he advocated for CR along with like-minded activists, members of civil society, and non-governmental organisations (NGOs); he eventually established the Bangladesh NGOs Network for Radio and Communication (BNNRC) in 2000 to spearhead the movement. The

[11] AHM Bazlur Rahman is a community media activist and policy advocacy individual in Bangladesh with approximately 21 years of experience in this field. He is currently the CEO of BNNRC, an organisation he founded in 2000, which addresses community media development in the country (Rahman, personal interview, December 04, 2017).

next 8 years were used to mobilise stakeholders and popularise the idea of CR in Bangladesh (Rahman, in-depth interview, December 04, 2017; Ullah, 2010).

In 2008, when the Bangladesh Awami League political party came into power, they saw the necessity for CR to reach out to rural communities with context-specific broadcasting, since the state-owned media focused on macro-level social and national development messages and the commercial media catered to urban areas. Also, both government and commercial entities were criticised as being controlled by either the government or urban-based bureaucrats where people's participation was neglected in the media climate. This top-down, unidirectional flow of information was counterproductive and "with nearly three-quarters of Bangladeshi families earning their living in rural areas by farming, one of the main goals identified by the government was to bolster rural communities through the decentralization of broadcasting services along with the promotion of equitable and needs-based information and knowledge" (Reza, 2012 cited in Anwar, 2015) (Bangladesh country profile, n.d.; Ullah, 2010).

Consequently, CR emerged in 2010, 2 years after the approval of the Community Radio Installation, Broadcast and Operation Policy 2008, 2008 ("2008 Policy" for short). With a visible and dedicated organisation, the BNNRC, international donors and partners joined the advocacy programmes and were significant in providing the necessary financial and technical resources for the establishment of stations (Reza, 2012 cited in Anwar, 2015). Today, a total of 17 community radio stations (CRS) are operating at the local level across Bangladesh, providing a forum for grassroots people to be heard (BNNRC, n.d.).

It must be noted that there were several challenges leading up to the establishment of CR in Bangladesh. From 2000 to 2005, there was no funding available; therefore, stakeholders were self-motivated and campaigned at their expenses. Also, internet availability was limited, which delayed the collection of information from other initiatives and movements around the world. However, UNESCO was able to assist with networking from 2002 onwards via workshops organised in India and Sri Lanka that enable activists and practitioners from Nepal, India, Pakistan, and Bangladesh to interact. As of 2018, CR was the only form of community media present in Bangladesh; however, BNNRC is collaborating with other key stakeholders to implement community television initiatives (Rahman, in-depth interview, December 04, 2017).

References

118 new community radio stations to be set up: Union Minister Prakash Javadekar. (2019, September 14). *India Today*. https://www.indiatoday.in/india/story/new-community-radio-stations-prakash-javadekar-1598948-2019-09-14

Acharya, U. (n.d.). Nepal—Media Landscape. *European Journalism Centre*. Retrieved May 31, 2019, from https://medialandscapes.org/country/pdf/nepal

ACORAB. (n.d.). *About Us*. Retrieved June 30, 2019, from http://www.acorab.org.np/index.php?pagename=aboutus

Agrawal, B. C. (2006). Communication technology and rural development in India: Promises and performances. *Indian Media Studies Journal, 1*(1).

Anwar, M. (2015). *Women's Participation in Community Radio in Bangladesh* [Unpublished doctoral dissertation]. University of Guelph, Ontario, Canada.

Bangalore Declaration on Radio, 1996. (n.d.). Retrieved September 30, 2019, from http://www.cmarch.in/wp-content/uploads/2019/02/Bangalore-Declaration-on-Radio_1996.pdf

Bangladesh country profile. (n.d.). *BBC*. Retrieved May 30, 2019, from http://www.bbc.com/news/world-south-asia-12650940

Bangladesh profile – Media. (n.d.). *BBC*. Retrieved October 30, 2019, from https://www.bbc.com/news/world-south-asia-12650946

BNNRC. (n.d.). *Community Radio in Bangladesh*. Retrieved January 30, 2017, from http://www.bnnrc.net/

Briney, A. (2019, September 02). *Geography and History of India*. Retrieved November 30, 2019, from https://www.thoughtco.com/geography-and-history-of-india-1435046

Community Radio Installation, Broadcast and Operation Policy 2008. (2008). *Ministry of Information, People's Republic of Bangladesh*.

DoT announces two additional frequencies for running community radio stations. (2019, August 30). *The Economic Times*. Retrieved October 30, 2019 from https://telecom.economictimes.indiatimes.com/news/dot-announces-two-additional-frequencies-for-running-community-radio-stations/70904185

Humagain, D. (2011, April 20–21). *Commentary on the History of Radio Broadcasting Policy in Nepal, Nepal Study Day 2011*. Britain-Nepal Academic Council and Centre for Research in the Arts, Social Sciences and Humanities, Cambridge.

India. (n.d.). *Press Reference*. Retrieved September 30, 2019, from http://www.pressreference.com/Gu-Ku/India.html

India country profile. (n.d.). *BBC*. Retrieved October 30, 2019, from https://www.bbc.com/news/world-south-asia-12557384

India profile – Media. (n.d.). *BBC*. Retrieved October 30, 2019, from https://www.bbc.com/news/world-south-asia-12557390

Kasajoo, V. (2002). The Community Press in Nepal. In *Asia and the Pacific - the community press is alive*.

Naskar, S. (n.d.). *Religions in Nepal—The Repository of Ethnic Mosaic. holidify*. Retrieved October 30, 2019, from https://www.holidify.com/pages/religion-in-nepal-855.html

NEFEJ. (n.d.). *About*. Retrieved May 31, 2019, from https://nefej.org.np/history/

Nepal - Basic Data. (n.d.). *Press Reference*. Retrieved September 30, 2017, from http://www.pressreference.com/Ma-No/Nepal.html

Nepal country profile. (n.d.). *BBC*. Retrieved April 30, 2019, from https://www.bbc.com/news/world-south-asia-12511455

Nepal profile – Media. (n.d.). *BBC*. Retrieved September 30, 2017, from http://www.bbc.com/news/world-south-asia-12561481

New Internationalist Team. (2011, March 05). *Bangladesh—A Brief History*. Retrieved February 28, 2017, from https://newint.org/features/2001/03/05/history/

Ninan, S. (2005, July 31). Nepal's fading radio waves. *The Hindu*, Online Edition. Retrieved May 30, 2019, from https://www.thehindu.com/thehindu/mag/2005/07/31/stories/2005073100350300.htm

Park, G. K. (n.d.). Animism. *Britannica*. Retrieved October 30, 2017, from https://www.britannica.com/topic/animism/The-animistic-worldview

Pavarala, V. & Malik, K. K. (2007). *Other voices: The struggle for community radio in India*. Sage Publications India Pvt. Ltd

Pringle, I., & Subba, B. (2007). *Ten year on: The state of Community Radio in Nepal*. UNESCO.

Shaju, P. P. (2014). *Study material: History of mass media*. University of Calicut.

Shakya, R. M. (2015, January 11). History of Nepali Journalism. *Nepal Oregon News*. Retrieved September 30, 2017, from http://viewsonnepalmedia.blogspot.com/2015/01/history-of-nepali-journalism.html

Szczepanski, K. (2019). *Bangladesh - Facts and History*. ThoughtCo. Retrieved March 30, 2017, from https://www.thoughtco.com/bangladesh-facts-and-history-195175

Ullah, M. S. (2010). *Community radio movement in Bangladesh—Will they work as citizens' media?* University of Calcutta. Retrieved March 30, 2017, from http://www.caluniv.ac.in/global-mdia-journal/Article-june2010/m%20s%20ullah-%20banglades.pdf

Zuberi, M., Karan, P. P., Rose, L. E., & Proud, R. R. (2017). Nepal. *Britannic*. Retrieved September 30, 2017, from https://www.britannica.com/place/Nepal

Contextualising Community Radio 3

3.1 Paradigmatic Shifts in Understanding Communication

Since its official classification as a field of study, communication has been in a continuous state of evolution, moving from one paradigm[1] to another under two distinct eras. The diffusionist era encompasses the direct effects paradigm, indirect effects paradigm, and limited effects paradigm, while the participatory era encompasses the development paradigm and the participatory approach to development.

The direct effects paradigm of the 1930s was the first archetype about the field of communication and supported the idea that media had a powerful or direct effect on audience members, especially since communication was viewed as a one-way, linear process of information sharing. There was a shift from this paradigm to the indirect effects paradigm in the 1950s due to multiple criticisms from academics and thinkers. Through the indirect effects approach, communication was described as an interaction between the sender and receiver since the communication process featured a "feedback" element. Media, therefore, were described as having an indirect effect on people in this instance. However, this second paradigm maintained that communication was still linear as it occurred in one direction at a time—whether sending information or receiving feedback. This linearity resulted in a shift from the indirect effects paradigm to the limited effects paradigm in the 1960s. The new model posited that communication was a transactional process—individuals could send and receive messages simultaneously. However, it failed to consider that audiences were more than just active recipients of messages—that audiences were more involved in the process as creators and stakeholders within the entire communication process—that they not only received information being broadcast but were part of the meaning-making process as well (Rampersaud, 2019, pp. 26–29).

[1] A *paradigm* is "a set of assumptions, concepts, values and practices that constitutes a way of viewing reality for the community that shares them, especially in an intellectual discipline" (Paradigm, n.d.).

T. Rampersaud-Skorka, *Community Radio in South Asia*, Diversity and Inclusion Research, https://doi.org/10.1007/978-3-031-85201-5_3

This evolution in the perception of the audience ushered in a change from the diffusionist era to the participatory era. The development paradigm, implemented widely from the 1970s to the early 1990s, considered that people were involved in the processes of their own development. However, it had multiple challenges with regard to representation and inclusivity. As a result, the participatory approach to social change was devised to address said challenges. This new paradigm entered discourses surrounding communication and social change from the early 1990s onwards—a foundation on which community radio (CR) exists. This approach moved beyond a top-bottom method of sharing information since communication is dynamic and can occur using top-bottom, bottom-up, and horizontal tactics (Rampersaud, 2019, pp. 29–33).

With this background on how communication has changed since being identified as a discipline, the following four sections provide an understanding of the academic discourses that legitimise as well as critique CR as people's media with the potential to create democratic spaces for discussion and debates.

3.2 Participatory Communication and Development

Kidd (1998, p. 36) argued that the "commons regimes facing enclosure continue to be an everyday reality for the 'vast majority of humanity' in both the south and north"—the suppression of the perceived minority by the elites in society continues as the latter aimed to accumulate more wealth and power. This situation was not alleviated by the onset of the global village[2] but resulted in even more information flowing from the West to the East as the political rape, hegemony, and imperialism of the 1500s still had an impact on societies today (Appadurai, 1996, p. 30). Nevertheless, multiple groups operating outside the state[3] and market[4] attempted to correct these problems and ensured people have control over their own lives through notions of *development* (Appadurai, 1996; Dixon, 2009; Kidd, 1998).

Development, as envisioned on the world stage, proposed a perfect vision for all societies through a systematic, all-encompassing application (Kamat, 2002). However, some inequalities existed within and between societies that prevented development from occurring, and this resulted in other problems such as alienation of the East from the West, ecological destruction, and a re-colonisation of countries (Kamat, 2002). Kidd (1998) endorsed the perpetuation of inequalities and showed this through numerous examples of the rich versus the poor and men versus women. Also, the complete disregard for grassroots societies led to many problems as

[2] The global village is a phenomenon that sees the entire world as one community due to the use of technology to bridge geographical boundaries (McLuhan, 1964 as cited by Dixon, 2009).

[3] The state is the political community of a country—the government (State, n.d.).

[4] The market is the place where commercial business takes place, a location for economic-based activities (Market, n.d.).

people were dispossessed of their traditional knowledge[5] in the name of development which resulted in the loss of cultures and the imposition of new ways of life dictated by the West (Kamat, 2002; Kidd, 1998).

According to Kidd (1998), these problems of inequality can be traced to two distinct periods of enclosures—the first occurred between the mid-fourteenth century to the sixteenth century, and the second in the eighteenth and nineteenth centuries. The first redefined what class conflict was and set the tone for the beginnings of a capitalist society. In an attempt to address the inequalities of the rich and poor binary, as well as the gender inequalities being perpetuated, the radical press, most likely the first attempt at the idea of community media, was used to fill the gaps of representation through the creation of a public sphere. However, the lack of resources by the poor minimised the effects as the elites were able to overshadow them through the mass production of content via the commercial press (Kidd, 1998).

The inequality in wealth and power distribution which governed the mass media and, in turn, society, saw the media as tools to inculcate values of the elites—systematic propaganda which extends up to the present day. Herman and Chomsky (1998), through their five filters,[6] highlighted how the capitalist approach to development influenced mass media content due to their profit-making agenda and, by extension, the suppression of the masses. Thus, there was the need for a more inclusive kind of media that provided a forum for the voiceless. This call for alternative media was supported by Cleaver (1999), who depicted the stifling nature of the mainstream mediascape post-World War II, and Kamat (2002), who alluded to the fact that the development discourse tended to favour universality and hegemony as it sprung from the economic approach to achieving social change (Cleaver, 1999; Herman & Chomsky, 1998; Kamat, 2002; Kidd, 1998).

Regarding the paradigm shifts, Manyozo (2012) reaffirmed that the diffusionist era did not take into consideration the fact that communication is more than broadcasting information from senders to receivers. Communication is not just a process that starts at a specific point and ends at a specific point—it is continuously in motion since audience members are both receivers and creators of content. This position was shared by Pool (1983), who had prophesised that with the advent of new media, control would be in the hands of the consumers—they would become the producers of content. However, the use of communication for development was fraught with problems resulting from: (1) lack of understanding of what development really meant and (2) whose development was being targeted. Furthermore, the development paradigm took an economic approach to social change and saw an imposition of ideas from the West to the East[7] without thought to either the resources

[5] Knowledge that is specific, unique to certain cultures or societies; sometimes referred to as traditional knowledge (Traditional Knowledge, 2021).

[6] The five filters presented by Herman and Chomsky (1998) with regard to news: (1) size, ownership, and profit orientation of the mass media; (2) the advertising licence to do business; (3) sourcing mass media news; (4) flak and the enforcers; and (5) anti-communism as a control mechanism.

[7] *West* is used to refer to the "developed" countries or the first-world countries while *East* refers to the "underdeveloped" countries or the third-world countries, also referred to as the North and

societies had access to or the traditional knowledge that had guided them for generations (Manyozo, 2012; Pool, 1983; Seers, 1969).

As a result, participatory communication was seen as the answer to these challenges since this phenomenon emphasised people's participation in their own development. The people at the grassroots are important in those social change projects and activities that affected them; thus, their voices needed to be heard. What is key to note is that the emphasis was shifted to *social change* in the participatory era as opposed to the previous emphasis on *development*, which was an ineffective top-down method of problem-solving (Basnet, in-depth interview, April 23, 2018[8]; Pavarala, in-depth interview, July 11, 2018[9]).

Within the new participatory approach, CR was conceptualised to help address the gaps in the communication process within communities. It was envisioned as a tool that would ensure the voices of the people at the grassroots were heard. However, though effective to some degree, even the participatory approach had some criticisms. The way participation was conceptualised and implemented did not necessarily mean the involvement of all people. In most instances, the facilitators of development projects had simple consultations at the beginning and/or end to tick the box that people were consulted; the people of the communities were not truly involved from planning to implementation and feedback (George, 2015).

As a result, Dutta (interviewed by George, 2015) suggested a novel approach referred to as the "culture-centred approach," where the capacity of theorising was placed in the hands of subaltern communities. Here, the main gap identified in the participatory approach was addressed as there was proper consultation of the grassroots people at all stages; there was true knowledge sharing among all involved. Furthermore, this new approach addressed how the target audience in the past were transformed into the producers of the content being shared—there was awareness about knowledge generation in all areas of society and not just in the elite arena. Therefore, projects were not about fixing problems within society anymore but about involving the target audience in the processes and the people with privileges were seen as the possible new targets as they represented the largest obstacle in bringing about positive social change within society (George, 2015).

Regarding participatory communication and development, one must remember that social change is more than transposing ways of life from the West to the East as the differences in cultures and resources would mean that the results would not be the same. All societies are different and have access to diverse resources that need

---

South, respectively (Seers, 1969).

[8] Suman Basnet is the Regional Coordinator of AMARC Asia-Pacific—the World Association of Community Radio Broadcasters. For more than 15 yrs, he has been working in the community media field as an advocate and activist for CR with a focus on (1) disaster risk reduction and CR, (2) women's empowerment, and (3) empowerment of the marginalised societies (Basnet, in-depth interview, April 23, 2018).

[9] Prof. Vinod Pavarala is a Professor and Chairholder, UNESCO Chair on Community Media, University of Hyderabad, India. He has over 20 years of teaching, research, and advocacy experience in the development communication and community media fields (Pavarala, in-depth interview, July 11, 2018).

to be taken into consideration. Furthermore, traditional knowledge gained through experiences and oral cultures passed down through generations need to be considered as they provide solid foundations on which societies were built. Ignoring them in the past has led to resistance time and again as development had occurred and reoccurred; the *illiterate* and *poor* need to be able to voice their opinions as they possess important knowledge also. These traditionally marginalised groups have a lot to share and, therefore, need to be able to access platforms to share their stories—CR provides this access by creating a counter public sphere (Manyozo, 2012; Kamat, 2002; Kidd, 1998).

3.3 Public Sphere, Counter Public Sphere, Civil Society

According to Habermas (1989 referenced by Fraser, 1992), an ideal public sphere is a space where access is guaranteed to all citizens based on unrestricted inclusion and freedom of expression. However, this initial idea was problematic in that it focused on the elites, was male-dominated, and generalised participants as rational beings with formal education. As Fraser (1992) pointed out, in an attempt to correct this elitist approach to a public sphere, there was a need for a subaltern counter public sphere—a position supported by Mansell (2012) who highlighted the need for an alternative space for producing and sharing knowledge. The alternative public sphere would cater to the voiceless and be a space where all could communicate without the inherent discriminations of the original public sphere (Fraser, 1992; Mansell, 2012).

However, instead of traditional broadcast media, many saw new media[10] as the channel to foster participation. Since the original public sphere, premised on mass media, did not cater to everyone, the idea was that a global knowledge society[11] could be produced through the dispensation of information and communication technologies (ICTs). As Mansell (2012, p. 4) stated, there was caution about overemphasising technology in place of people as the focus of development should be about creating "an enabling environment for people to enjoy long, healthy and creative lives" and not just about increasing material resources. Hence, Mansell highlighted potential problems with technology-based development as they could marginalise alternative knowledge through practices, policymaking, and, most importantly, access. Thus, it is important to remember not to overemphasise the technology or the products but focus on the democratic processes of production (Mansell, 2012). Therefore, CR was cemented as the medium to reach the people.

When CR plays a role in ensuring that there is freedom, genuine participation, and equitable access to technologies, they become tools to enhance the effectiveness of civil society—the entity which keeps those with power (the elites) in check. As a

[10] These are technologies based on computing devices and the internet as opposed to traditional media such as newspapers, radio, and television (Socha & Eber-Schmid, n.d.).

[11] The global knowledge society is an ideal where everyone around the world is connected and shares a superior knowledge that boasts of cohesion and not differences (Mansell, 2012).

result, members of civil society are responsible for keeping the public arena free from discrimination (Kaviraj, 2001).

As Kaviraj (2001) put it, we can learn from Western social theory and use it as a tool for our societies, but *we must also be willing to discard the tool when it is no longer useful*. We have moved from a time where we held fast to our natural rights and the idea of survival of the fittest to one where we support civil rights due to the security and certainty they perpetuate. With the advent of the state, even though it brought with it an awareness of rights and responsibilities to keep public figures in check, there is a need for civil society to ensure these rights and responsibilities are adhered to—a group to keep the state in check. However, civil society cannot play its role if the state or its ally—the corporate sector—controls all information in the public sphere. They need diverse information sources that bring in perspectives from the non-elites and the non-powerful also (Kaviraj, 2001).

This is where alternative media, also referred to as community media and citizens' media (as well as a plethora of other names), enter the picture. They are the non-mainstream media that cater to the majority, those disenfranchised members of communities. Community media are the counter public sphere that civil society needs to keep the state in check and to ensure balance in society. However, before addressing the broader concepts of alternative or community media, there is the need to understand "community" and what it means in the context of community media.

3.4 Community

What is a community? How does one define a community? Conceptual questions like these have been the cause of disagreement among academics and thinkers for decades as they propose and oppose a variety of definitions. However, even though there is no universally accepted definition, there is a common understanding. As Anderson (2006) posited, like the concept *nation* and its various forms such as *nationalism* and *nationality*, a community comprises a feeling of oneness with others; there is some emotional legitimacy attached to the term that appeals to a large variety of individuals with a multitude of common interests. Also, even though one might not meet all the other members of the community—a state Anderson (2006) describes as being *imagined*—they have that feeling of belonging. Bailur (2012) and Browne (2012) also explored the concept of community, albeit, from different perspectives as the former refers to the community as a *who* while the latter sees community as a *what*.

Bailur (2012), after exploring multiple avenues addressing ownership and control and other concepts such as empowerment, conscientisation, and fragmentation of power, finally found some satisfaction with the definition of community adopted by Pavarala and Malik (2007, p. 17), which stated that it is "a territorially bound group with some commonality of interest." She accepted that the concept has fluid boundaries that allude to communities not being discrete but are more dynamic and cognitive in nature. In other words, the relationships within communities do not simply link two individuals with a straight line but resemble a spider web with many intersecting points. Thus, communities are dynamic in nature as members of various groups construct and reconstruct their identities through different relationships. Regarding the idea of cognition, Bailur (2012) posited that communities can think and make choices based on the social contexts in which they exist. Thus, community is seen as an entity, a living being, which could change depending on relationships and how they are portrayed.

Browne (2012), on the other hand, accepted that a community comprises (1) a local, geographical community or (2) a community of interest where people are members of a particular group—either explanation sees community as being a thing of which people are a part of. He referenced a variety of factors to consider when exploring the concept such as language, ethnicity, gender, generation, sexual orientation, and their interests as all these characteristics can include or exclude individuals from a group. Like Bailur (2012) and Browne (2012) accepted that the boundaries for defining this concept are fluid and finally use three ideals to apply for a better understanding: (1) community as participant, (2) community as audience, and (3) community comprising staff and volunteers. It is important to note he also stated that even though people might belong by association to one of these areas, they could opt out of being an active part of the community altogether.

Overall, regardless of how the idea of *community* is explained, community media's mandate is to represent the oppressed and the marginalised—the disenfranchised, to provide a public forum via alternative media for people to express themselves—whether bound by geography and/or by interest. However, questions surrounding the legitimacy regarding the ownership of community media initiatives, as well as issues about solidarity and alienation, need to be taken into consideration as it is important to remember that a community is defined by those it includes as well as those it excludes (Anderson, 2006; Bailur, 2012; Browne, 2012).

Based on these various perspectives, the final consensus drawn by the author is that community is a fluid concept that is best understood through application rather than an imposition of a universal definition, which, if applied, would be subscribing to a reductionist approach that would diminish its importance. In keeping with the many ideas that surround community and to ensure there is no miscommunication, there are various concepts used for community media initiatives including alternative media and citizens' media, which are less problematic when talking about grassroots media used by a community.

3.5 Alternative Media, Community Media, Citizens' Media

Traditional and new media have been criticised repeatedly for not being truly representative of the general population. They have been accused of not granting equal access to all, and the dynamics of power and control over them have been the cause for great concern, especially in the last few decades with the increased awareness of development-related issues. As Atton (2001) highlighted, the mass media are owned and controlled by a few powerful and influential elites; thus, they (the elites) are always shown in a positive manner while other groups are marginalised and disempowered. As a result, alternative media are the harbinger of positive social change—a truly representative counter public sphere. In essence, they are different, and not necessarily *against* the mainstream media (Atton, 2001; Rodríguez, 2001).

Rodríguez (2001) gave some detailed insight into the background for alternative media. She stated that the MacBride Report by UNESCO in 1980 detailed the turning point of the shift from mainstream to alternative media, which started to occur in the 1970s—a period of turmoil for international communication because the flow of information from the West to the East was ten times more than East to West. It went on to highlight that there was no South-to-South communication occurring and a few Western transnational communication corporations controlled most of the global media. To counter the problems of misrepresentation and underrepresentation, attempts were made to establish third-world press agencies. However, these failed as they could not compete with the larger corporations and the domination over content by the first world continued. The result was an erosion in local cultures, an undermining of national identities, and a limitation in the advancement of national communication industries. In addition, consideration about the internal flow of communication within countries, national communication policies, South-to-South communication, and a code of ethics for the mass media was not addressed. Further to the points from the MacBride Report, there were problems regarding the deregulation and privatisation of media which occurred in the late 1980s and early 1990s in the West—a period referred to as the Reagan/Thatcher Era, which resulted in the creation of new communication cartels. The pressures from the West to modernise communication through privatisation or the joining with transnational communication corporations and moving away from national policies in order to be a part of the "information society" in this era also added to the existing problems in the East. Finally, in 1990, the MacBride Roundtable addressed these problems and recognised the importance of alternative media and pointed out that information and communication-related issues were "in the arena of grassroots movements, representing ordinary men, women, and children who are directly affected by our current cultural and communication environments" (Rodríguez, 2001, p. 15).

Overall, the consensus following this back and forth about the mediascape resulted in alternative media being part of a movement that should question the status quo and what is happening in societies. They were seen as presenting a possible new battleground for a new communication order—a means to relocate the debate on the democratisation of communication in the present and have new debates focus on new conceptual frameworks that were truly representative of community participation (Rodríguez, 2001).

What, then, are alternative media? Like many other phenomena in the communication discipline, alternative media have a problematic conceptual framework. As Atton (2001) argued, alternative media are not necessarily limited to a political watchdog role and resistance movements. They encompass the sharing of newer cultural forms and focus on process and relation; these initiatives encompass the transformative potential of media in social change. He is supported by Rodríguez (2001) who also alluded to alternative media having a transformative ability as she discussed them changing the self-image individuals and societies might have of themselves when they see themselves from a new perspective. This can be empowering as the new way of looking at themselves can result in them challenging beliefs, the existing status quo, and stereotypes that disenfranchise them.

Rodríguez (2001) also mentioned that alternative media are perceived as a balance for the unequal distribution of communication resources from large media corporations that perpetuate binary conceptions of domination and subordination. Other communication thinkers such as Bailey et al. (2008) add to this understanding by stating that alternative media do not exist in a vacuum. The participatory model of democracy that alternative media support can result in a widening of the political sphere to encompass current issues such as gender, racism, women's rights, and empowerment as alternative media refute the authoritarian way of life (Bailey et al., 2008; Rodríguez, 2001).

All in all, these thinkers seem to approach alternative media from a point of view that the changing nature of the political arena, that is the changes in power relations taking place, affects how issues are represented, and alternative media provide a platform for voices from the grassroots to be heard.

Even though there is an understanding of what alternative media represent, there is still disagreement surrounding a formal definition. If one took the path of defining one of the synonymous forms, such as community media, there are still issues when we problematise the term as the notion of community media is not easy to define as both *community* and *media* are problematic in their own ways. However, there are few definitions that, when combined, aptly address this phenomenon. According to the Community Media Association (n.d.), "community media is community-owned and controlled, giving access to voices in the community and encourage diversity, creativity, and participation." The second definition[12] by the International Programme for the Development of Communication (IPDC) is in tandem with the first but takes it a step further by highlighting the need for transparency and a true representation of the community. According to SANCOM, community media are "technologically mediated forms of communication that are established by civil society organisations and educational institutions" (SANCOM, n.d.), which embrace true community participation in the production process[13] as well as in ownership and management of said media (Developing Community Media, n.d.).

With this understanding, the next logical question is, "What are alternative media *alternative* to?" Some individuals posit that they are complementary to mainstream media and not alternative. Others have problems with the actual word "alternative" as it seems to mean that the information will be different from those provided in the

[12] "Community-based media ensure media pluralism, diversity of content, and the representation of a society's different groups and interests. They encourage open dialogue and transparency of administration at the local level and offer a voice to the voiceless. They are established on the concepts of public access, sharing experiences and information" (Developing Community Media, n.d.).

[13] The production process includes three main stages: (1) pre-production where all the planning is done, (2) production where the plan is implemented, and (3) post-production where the information is reviewed, packaged, and distributed (Belavadi, 2013).

mainstream media yet messages from the grassroots are not always different. Even more see alternative media as being radical and oppositional to mainstream media. As Downing (2008) suggested, media and media-related phenomena are fluid and are, thus, hard to theorise. Due to the very nature of alternative media, it is difficult to have one definition, but there is a need for media that will be more specific to fulfilling the needs of the greater population, which are ignored in the power and profit battles in which mainstream media are engaged (Atton, 2001; Downing, 2008; Rodríguez, 2001).

To find some common ground, Atton (2001) postulated that radical media are not synonymous with alternative media as the latter also encompasses the former—radical media are one type of alternative media. Atton (2001) goes on to reference Fiske (1992), who stated that alternative media are the home for stories that are repressed and, thus, do not appear in the mainstream media. Furthermore, radical media are avant-garde and artistic in nature and tend to focus on opposing information from mainstream media; they are "counter informational." In short, alternative media coexist in the present hegemony and radical media are the specific avenue for social movements. Downing (2008) referred to the latter as "radical alternative media" to establish that radical media fall under the broad umbrella of alternative media.

On the other hand, by using the term "citizens' media," Rodríguez (2001) attempted to bring in the active participants who are empowered through the use of these media and refocus on the process involved and not the technology or technique. She made mention that this term is specifically favourable as it alludes to active citizenship intervening and transforming the established mediascape. Through the use of citizens' media, communities are empowered to deconstruct their subordinate identities and rebuild meanings through the eyes of the marginalised. Regardless of which term is used—community, alternative, radical, radical alternative, or citizen—as Rodríguez (2001, pp. 5–6) poetically put it, trying to define this phenomenon is like "trying to capture the beauty of a dancer's movements with one photograph."

3.6 Summary

Overall, alternative media play roles in advocacy and are the media of the grassroots—they are the best means of alternative news values, engagement, and direct participation. They are a counter for mainstream media content and for the absence of channels within marginalised communities; they have the ability to produce materials that are more relevant, useful, and appropriate for communities. We need to remember that the media can be immensely powerful; however, they are not all-powerful and those who participate in the processes of content creation and dissemination have a lot of control. Alternative media comprise a communicative phenomenon and the complexities that they represent can hardly be contained by the binary of power and powerless. Thus, alternative media need to be accessible, foster horizontal participation, and represent a collective democratic process that involves the communities they serve (Rodríguez, 2001).

References

Anderson, B. (2006). *Imagined communities: Reflections on the origin and spread of nationalism* (Revised ed.). Verso.

Appadurai, A. (1996). *Modernity at large—Cultural dimensions of globalization, public worlds, volume 1*. University of Minneapolis Press.

Atton, C. (2001). *Approaching alternative media: Theory and methodology*. Napier University.

Bailey, O., Cammaert, B., & Carpentier, N. (2008). *Understanding alternative media*. Open University.

Bailur, S. (2012). Who is the community in community radio? *Economic and Political Weekly, 47*(17), 92–99.

Belavadi, V. (2013). *Video production*, 2 Ed. Oxford University Press.

Browne, D. R. (2012). What is "community" in community radio? A consideration of the meaning, nature and importance of a concept. In J. Gordon (Ed.), *Community Radio in the Twenty-First Century* (pp. 153–171). Peter Lang.

Cleaver, F. (1999). Paradoxes of participation: Questioning participatory approaches to development. *Journal of International Development, 11*, 50–62.

Community Media Association. (n.d.). *Homepage*. Retrieved July 31, 2015, from https://www.communitymedia.uk/

Couldry, N. (2010). *Why voice matters: Culture and politics after neoliberalism*. SAGE Publications Ltd.

Developing Community Media. (n.d.). *UNESCO*. Retrieved November 30, 2015, from http://www.unesco.org/new/en/communication-and-information/intergovernmentalprogrammes/ipdc/priorities/developing-community-media/

Dixon, V. K. (2009). Understanding the implications of a Global Village. *Student Pulse, 1*(11) Retrieved October 30, 2019, from http://www.studentpulse.com/articles/61/understanding-the-implications-of-a-global-village

Downing, J. (2008). Social movement theories and alternative media: An evaluation and critique. *Communication, Culture & Critique, 1*(1), 40–50.

Fraser, N. (1992). Rethinking the public sphere: A contribution to the critique of actually existing democracy. In C. Calhoun (Ed.), *Habermas and the public sphere* (pp. 56–80). MIT Press.

George, C. (2015). Development and participation: Turning the tables, interview with Mohan J. Dutta. *Media Asia, 41*(4).

Herman, E., & Chomsky, N. (1998). *Manufacturing consent—The political economy and the mass media*. Pantheon Books.

Kamat, S. (2002). *Development hegemony—NGOs and the state in India*. Oxford University Press.

Kaviraj, S. (2001). Chapter 15 - in search of civil society. In S. Kaviraj & S. Khilnani (Eds.), *Civil society: History and possibilities* (pp. 287–323). Cambridge University Press.

Kidd, D. (1998). *Ph.D. dissertation - chapter 3: The commons and enclosures*. Simon Fraser University.

Lang, S. (2013). *NGOs, civil society, and the public sphere*. Cambridge University Press.

Mansell, R. (2012). *ICTs, discourse and knowledge societies: implications for policy and practice*. LSE Research Online. Retrieved May 30, 2019 from https://eprints.lse.ac.uk/39245/1/ICTs%2C_discourse_and_knowledge_societies%28lsero%29.pdf

Manyozo, L. (2012). *Media, communication and development—Three approaches*. Sage Publications.

Market. (n.d.). *Merriam Webster Dictionary*. Retrieved November 30, 2015, from https://www.merriam-webster.com/dictionary/market

Paradigm. (n.d.). *The American Heritage Dictionary*. Retrieved November 30, 2015, from ahdictionary.com/word/search.html?q=paradigm

Pavarala, V., & Malik, K. K. (2007). *Other voices: The struggle for community radio in India*. Sage Publications India Pvt. Ltd.

Pool, I. S. (1983). What Ferment?. In *Ferment in the Field: Journal of Communication (Special Issue)*.

Rampersaud, T. (2019). Paradigmatic shifts in understanding communication—From the 'Diffusionist' perspective to the 'participatory' perspective of communication. Labyrinthe, 10(4). (pp. 19–37). Authors Press.

Rodríguez, C. (2001). *Fissures in the Mediascape: An international study of citizens' media*. Hampton Press.

SANCOM. (n.d.). *History*. Retrieved November 30, 2015, from https://sancomonline.net/history/

Seers, D. (1969). The Meaning of Development. *IDS Communication 44*. Institute of Development Studies.

Servaes, J. (1999). *Communication for development: One world, multiple cultures*. Hampton Press.

Socha, B., & Eber-Schmid, B. (n.d.). *What is new media?*. Retrieved November 30, 2015, from http://www.newmedia.org/whatis-new-media.html

State. (n.d.). Merriam Webster Dictionary. Retrieved November 30, 2015, from https://www.merriam-webster.com/dictionary/state

Tacchi, J. (2008). Voice and Poverty. *Media Development, 2008/1*.

Traditional Knowledge. (2021, October 19). Convention on Biological Diversity. Retrieved on October 23, 2024, from https://www.cbd.int/traditional/intro.shtml

Profiles of Case Studies

4

4.1 Profiles of Case Studies from Nepal

The three case studies for Nepal were Radio Sagarmatha, Radio Namobuddha, and Radio Sindhu—all three from the Bagmati Administrative Zone.[1] Image 4.1 *Map of Nepal with case studies* highlights where the national border of the country occurs (on the outside), and the locations of the case studies visited.

4.1.1 Radio Sagarmatha 102.4 MHz

Radio Sagarmatha was established on May 19, 1997, by the Nepal Forum of Environmental Journalists (NEFEJ). Located in the city of Kathmandu, Bagmati, Nepal—an urban area—this station operates with approximately 22 staff and 12 volunteers (a total of 34 persons) on a daily basis comprising 16-h radio broadcast from 6 am to 10 pm, and 24-h online streaming via their website. The 1000 W transmitter allows coverage of the entire Kathmandu Valley, which comprises approximately 4.5 million people who listen to the station (Shrestha,[2] in-depth interview, April 26, 2018).

This station was selected as a case study because it was the first community radio station (CRS) to be established in Nepal and, by default, the first initiative in the South Asian region. Furthermore, the station is in an urban environment and has approximately 20 years of operational data to share. In addition, the station has also seen significant upgrades over the last two decades—the latest has been to ensure that the building and infrastructure are earthquake resilient following the devastating

[1] Due to financial constraints, the author was unable to travel more extensively in Nepal to visit stations in different zones. However, she did gather a variety of data from these three stations.

[2] Sahah Man Srerestha is the Station Manager for Radio Sagarmatha.

T. Rampersaud-Skorka, *Community Radio in South Asia*, Diversity and Inclusion Research, https://doi.org/10.1007/978-3-031-85201-5_4

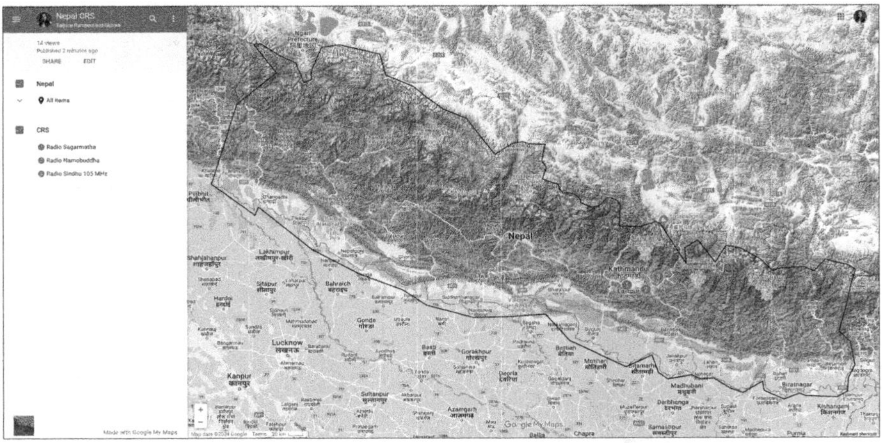

Image 4.1 Map of Nepal with locations of the three case studies (*Source*: Google Maps, n.d.-c)

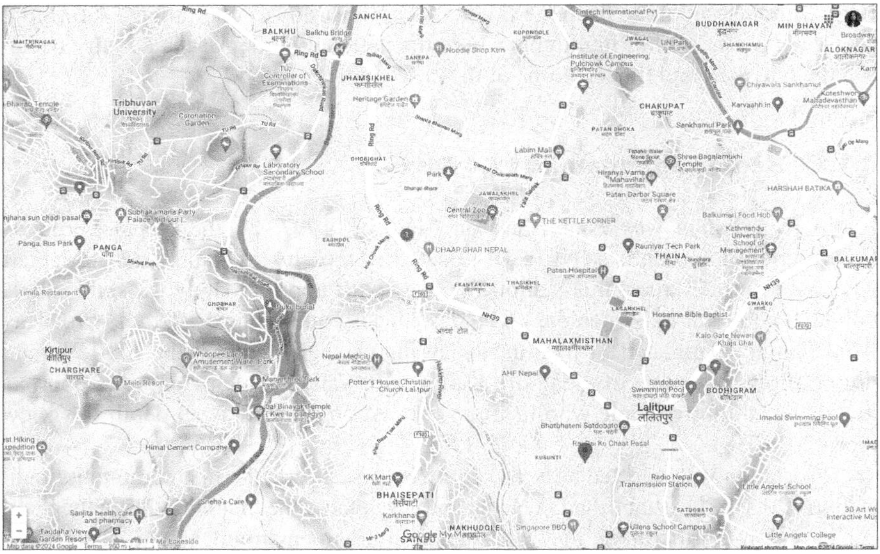

Image 4.2 Radio Sagarmatha and its surrounding urban environment (*Source*: Google Maps, n.d.-c)

occurrences of the 2015 earthquake when many CRS around Nepal were damaged (Basnet,[3] in-depth interview, April 23, 2018; Images 4.2, 4.3, and 4.4).

[3] Suman Basnet is the Regional Coordinator of AMARC Asia-Pacific—the World Association of Community Radio Broadcasters. For more than 15 yrs, he has been working in the community media field as an advocate and activist for CR with a focus on (1) disaster risk reduction and CR, (2) women's empowerment, and (3) empowerment of the marginalised societies (Basnet, in-depth interview, April 23, 2018).

Image 4.3 Picture of a community volunteer at Radio Sagarmatha (*Source*: Author's own picture)

Image 4.4 Picture of Radio Sagarmatha's antenna (*Source*: Author's own picture)

4.1.2 Radio Namobuddha FM 106.7 MHz

Radio Namobuddha was established on June 21, 2007, by Jugal Association Nepal—a local NGO. Located in the peri-urban environment in Kavre, Bagmati, Nepal, this station operates with approximately 18 staff (7 full-time and 11 part-time) on a daily basis comprising 12 h 30 min of radio broadcast from 5 am to 12 pm and 4:30 pm to 10:00 pm. The 100 W transmitter allows coverage of the communities in a 17 km radius which comprises approximately half a million people who listen to the station (Syangtan,[4] in-depth interview, April 25, 2018).

This station was selected as a case study because of its unique location in a peri-urban environment (adjacent to the Kathmandu Valley) and for it being the first station in that area. Furthermore, the CRS has been operational for over a decade with significant information and amount of experience to share. In addition, the secondary information gathered about the station by the author highlighted the station's commitment to marginalised communities—specifically those that do not speak Nepali. However, this station was finally selected due to its proximity to the author's base of operation, which was in Kathmandu, Nepal (Basnet, in-depth interview, April 23, 2018 Images 4.5, 4.6, and 4.7).

Image 4.5 Radio Namobuddha and surrounding environment (*Source*: Google Maps, n.d.-c)

[4] Bhakta Syangtan is the Station Manager for Radio Namobuddha.

Image 4.6 Picture of a community volunteer at Radio Namobuddha (*Source*: Author's own picture)

Image 4.7 Picture of rehearsal room at Radio Namobuddha (*Source*: Author's own picture)

4.1.3 Radio Sindhu FM 105 MHz

Radio Sindhu was established on November 27, 2007, by the Centre for Social Transformation and Human Development—a local NGO. Located in the rural environment in Kavre, Bagmati, Nepal, this station operates with approximately 30 people (24 staff and 6 volunteers) on a daily basis comprising 18 h of radio broadcast from 5 am to 11 pm. The 100 W transmitter allows for coverage of the communities for 57 km of mountainous terrain which comprises approximately one million people who listen to the station (Shrestha,[5] in-depth interview, April 25, 2018).

This station was selected as a case study because of its unique location in a rural environment located in the Himalayan Mountain Range, and it was the first station in that area. Furthermore, the current building and supporting infrastructure were new constructions since the old ones were severely damaged in the 2015 earthquake. As a result, the station has a strong focus on addressing disasters in that area such as floods, soil erosion, and earthquakes in addition to highlighting social issues relating to empowerment, gender, and child trafficking. However, this station was finalised due to its proximity to the author's base of operation located in Kathmandu, Nepal (Basnet, in-depth interview, April 23, 2018; Images 4.8, 4.9, and 4.10).

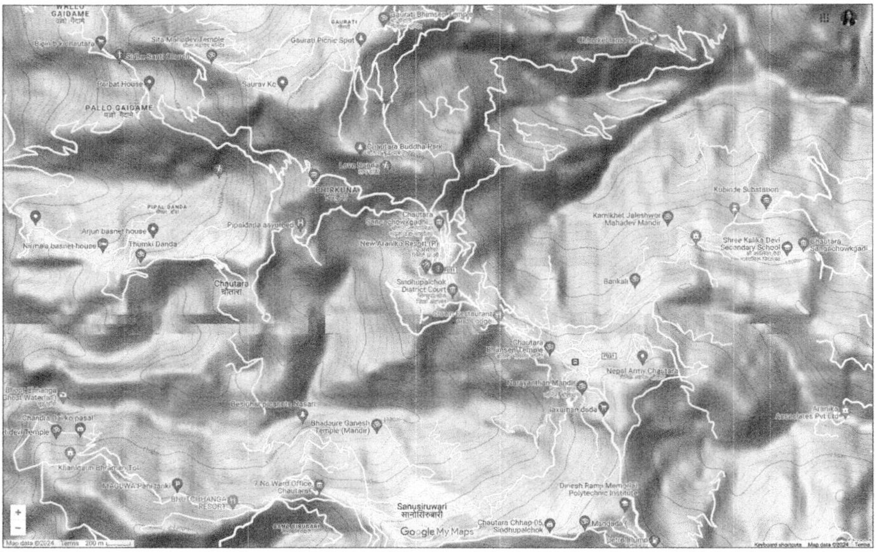

Image 4.8 Radio Sindhu and surrounding environment (*Source*: Google Maps, n.d.-c)

[5] Ratna Prasad Shrestha is the Station Manager for Radio Sindhu.

Image 4.9 Picture of community volunteers recording a programme at Radio Sindhu (*Source*: Author's own picture)

Image 4.10 Picture of Radio Sindhu's antenna and studio (*Source*: Author's own picture)

4.2 Profiles of Case Studies from India

The four case studies for India were Sangham Radio, Tilonia Radio, Radio Luit, and Waqt ki Awaaz—all four were in different areas of the country. *Image 4.17 Map of India with case studies* highlights where the national border of the country occurs (on the outside), and the locations of the case studies visited (Image 4.11).

4.2.1 Sangham Radio 90.4 FM

Sangham Radio 90.4 was established on October 15, 2008, by the Deccan Development Society (DDS), an NGO. Located in Medak, Telangana, India—a rural area—this CRS operates with two staff everyday comprising 2 h of radio broadcast from 7 pm to 9 pm to approximately 150 villages (General Narsamma,[6] in-depth interview, April 06, 2018).

This station was selected as a case study because it was the first rural CRS to be established in India and has approximately 10 years of operational information to share. Also, the station's focus on empowering disenfranchised groups, especially women and children, and the work done towards the preservation of local cultures were taken into consideration (*Community Radio for Good Governance*, 2015; General Narsamma, in-depth interview, April 06, 2018; Images 4.12, 4.13, and 4.14).

4.2.2 Tilonia Radio 90.4 FM

Tilonia Radio was established on November 02, 2009, by Barefoot College, a local NGO. Located in Tilonia, Rajasthan, India—a rural area—this station operates with two staff daily comprising 7 h of radio broadcast from 7 am to 9 am, 12 pm to 2 pm, and 6 pm to 9 pm. The 50 W transmitter allows coverage of approximately 30 villages comprising approximately 60,000 people (Aarti Devi,[7] in-depth interview, March 07, 2018).

This station was selected as a case study because of its remote location in Rajasthan in addition to having approximately 9 years of operational experience at the time of data gathering to share. Furthermore, the focus on preservation and sharing of folk cultures among the community and the use of the station to share policy information to grassroots people were key for its selection (*Community Radio for*

[6] General Narsamma is the Station Manager for Sangham Radio and a key figure in the CR movement in India.

[7] Aarti Devi is the Station Manager for Tilonia Radio.

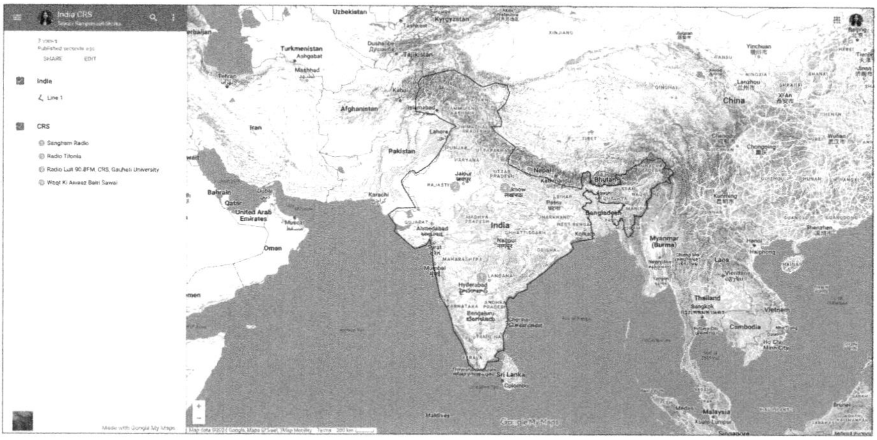

Image 4.11 Map of India with locations of case studies (*Source*: Google Maps, n.d.-b)

Image 4.12 Sangham Radio and surrounding environment (*Source*: Google Maps, n.d.-b)

Image 4.13 Picture of Sangham Radio's studio and antenna (*Source*: Author's own picture)

Image 4.14 Picture of a recording room at Sangham Radio (*Source*: Author's own picture)

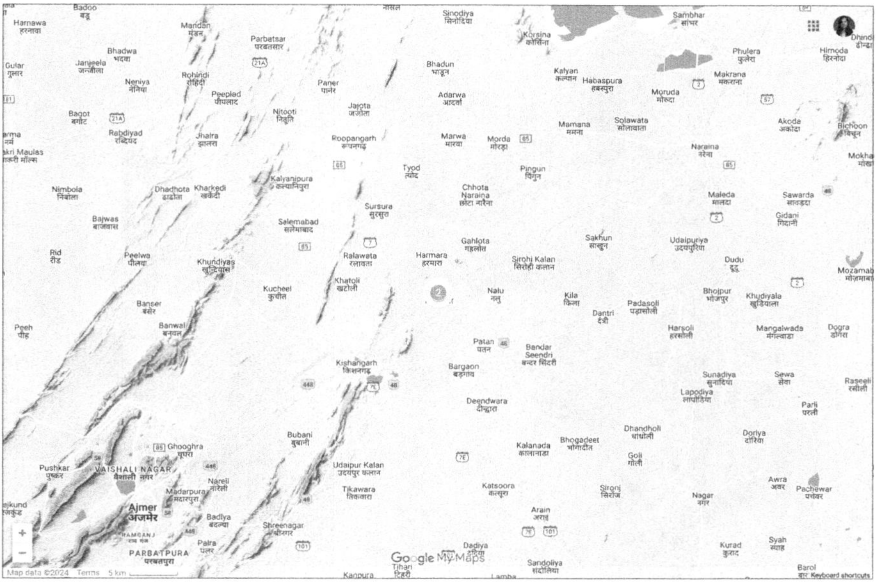

Image 4.15 Tilonia Radio and surrounding environment (*Source*: Google Maps, n.d.-b)

Good Governance, 2015; Aarti Devi, in-depth interview, March 07, 2018; Images 4.15, 4.16, and 4.17).

4.2.3 Radio Luit 90.8 FM

Radio Luit 90.8 was established on March 01, 2011, by Gauhati University, an educational institution. Located in Assam, India—an urban area—this station operates with 3 staff and approximately 25 volunteers on a daily basis for 12 h of radio broadcast from 8 am to 8 pm. The 100 W transmitter allows coverage of 10 km to 12 km comprising over 5000 people (Acharjya,[8] in-depth interview, February 05, 2018).

This station was selected as a case study because it was established by a university and is located in the North-East region of India and has been in operation for over 5 years. Also, the active volunteer population comprising media and communication students provided diversity with regard to the case studies selected (*Community Radio for Good Governance,* 2015; Acharjya, in-depth interview, February 05, 2018; Images 4.18, 4.19, and 4.20).

[8] Bhaskar Jyoti Acharjya is the programme executive of Radio Luit.

Image 4.16 Picture of volunteer editing audio content at Tilonia Radio (*Source*: Author's own picture)

Image 4.17 Picture of a recording in progress at Tilonia Radio (*Source*: Author's own picture)

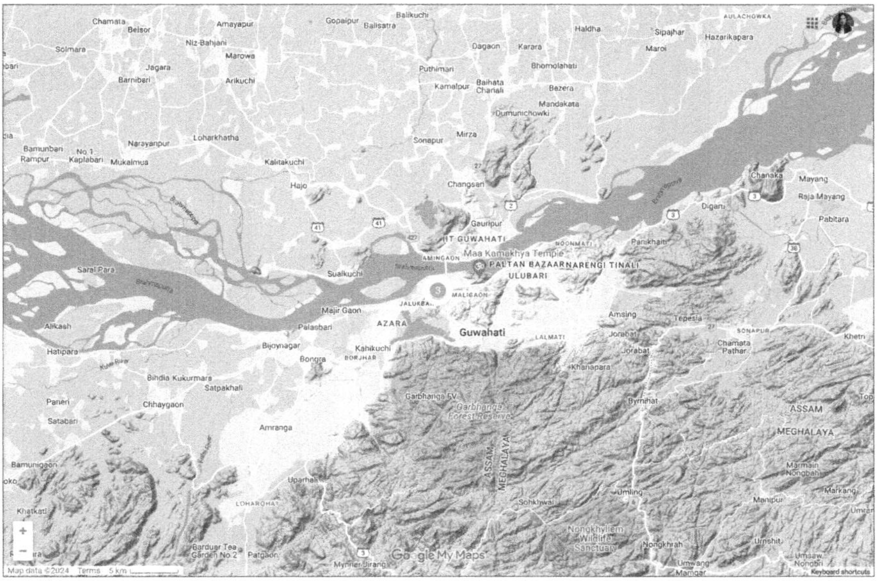

Image 4.18 Radio Luit and surrounding environment (*Source*: Google Maps, n.d.-b)

4.2.4 Waqt ki Awaaz

Waqt ki Awaaz was established on September 23, 2013, by Shramik Bharati, an NGO. Located in Kanpur, Uttar Pradesh, India—a rural area—this station operates with six staff on a daily basis for 9 h of radio broadcast from 6 am to 9 pm, 12 pm to 2 pm, and 6 pm to 10 pm. The station's transmitter reaches approximately 300,000 people from 303 villages (Shukla,[9] in-depth interview, March 08, 2018).

This station was selected as a case study because of its location and prominence due to the multiple awards won for work done. Furthermore, it has been in operation for over 5 years and has been actively used as a platform for the community to ask questions and seek answers for problems faced (*Community Radio for Good Governance,* 2015; Shukla, in-depth interview, March 08, 2018; Images 4.21, 4.22, and 4.23).

4.3 Profiles of Case Studies from Bangladesh

The four case studies for Bangladesh were Radio Padma, Borendro Radio, Radio Bikrampur, and Radio Sarabela—all four were in different areas of the country. *Image 4.35 Map of Bangladesh with case studies* highlights where the national

[9] Radha Shukla is the coordinator (instead of the title station manager) for Waqt ki Awaaz.

Image 4.19 Picture of student volunteers at Radio Luit (*Source*: Author's own picture)

Image 4.20 Picture of Radio Luit's antenna (*Source*: Author's own picture)

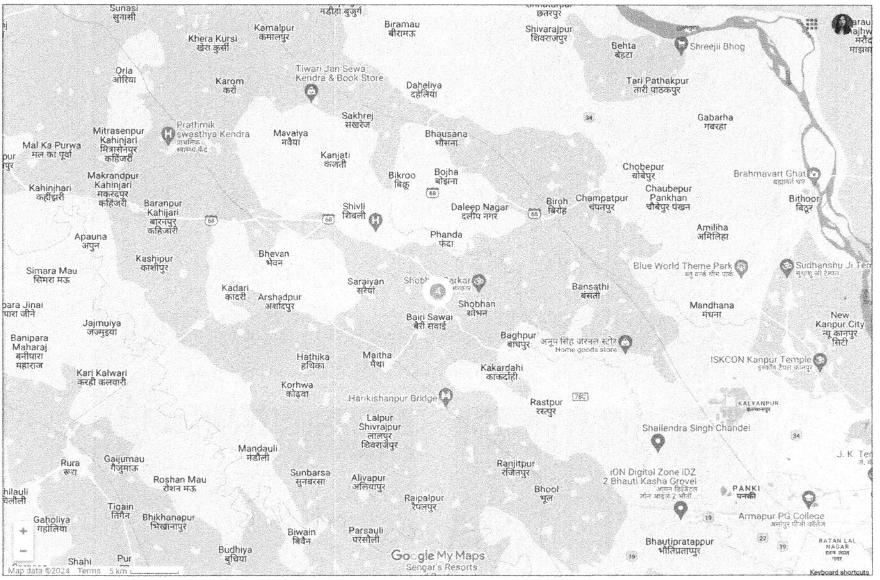

Image 4.21 Waqt ki Awaaz and surrounding environment (*Source*: Google Maps, n.d.-b)

border of the country occurs (on the outside), and the locations of the case studies visited (Image 4.24).

4.3.1 Radio Padma 99.2 FM

Radio Padma was established on October 07, 2011, by the Centre for Communication and Development, an NGO. Located in Rajshahi City, Rajshahi, Bangladesh—an urban area—this station operates with 10 staff and 70 volunteers on a daily basis comprising 14-h daily radio broadcast from 10 am to 2 am with the 250 W transmitter covering a radius of 32–34 kms and reaching approximately 600,000 people (Parveen,[10] in-depth interview, December 10, 2017).

This CRS was selected as a case study because it is the first official station to be established in Bangladesh and is located in a university town. Also, the station's aim of addressing the youth community and providing a platform for community participation—not only by students but also by various marginalised groups—were the final deciding factors. The fact that this CRS has been used to share emergency information—such as missing children alerts—and to connect people across various social groups within the community was extra justifications to make it a case study

[10] Shahana Parveen is the Station Manager for Radio Padma.

Image 4.22 Picture of the entrance to Waqt ki Awaaz (*Source*: Author's own picture)

Image 4.23 Picture of a recording in progress at Waqt ki Awaaz (*Source*: Author's own picture)

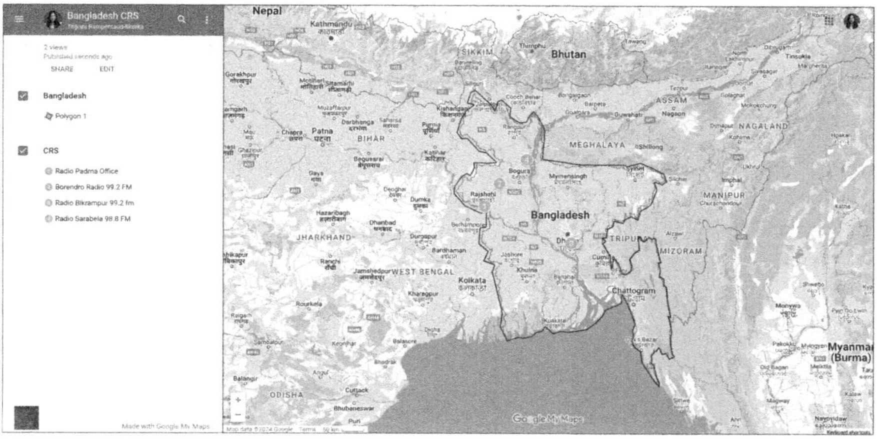

Image 4.24 Map of Bangladesh with locations of case studies (*Source*: Google Maps, n.d.-a)

(Parveen, in-depth interview, December 10, 2017; Rahman,[11] in-depth interview, December 04, 2017; Images 4.25, 4.26, and 4.27).

4.3.2 Borendro Radio 99.2 FM

Radio Borendro was established on March 08, 2012, by the Naogoan Human Rights Development Association, an NGO. Located in Naogoan, Dhaka, Bangladesh—a peri-urban area—this station operates with 3 staff and 31 volunteers comprising 9-h daily radio broadcast from 3 pm to 12 am with a 250 W transmitter covering a radius of 32–34 kms and reaching approximately 600,000 people (Sarkar,[12] in-depth interview, December 09, 2017).

Radio Borendro was selected because of its aim to create a platform for the grassroots people to utilise to reach the policymakers in the area. Since Radio Borendro began broadcasting, it has expanded its original aim of providing a forum for the voiceless to promoting participation among all those affected by different decisions made by policymakers within the area, creating linkages between the policymakers and grassroots people, and empowering the marginalised groups of people to act on

[11] AHM Bazlur Rahman is a community media activist and policy advocacy individual in Bangladesh with approximately 21 years of experience in this field. He is currently the CEO of BNNRC, an organisation he founded in 2000, which addresses community media development in the country (Rahman, personal interview, December 04, 2017).

[12] Shubrata Sarkar is the Station Manager for Radio Borendro.

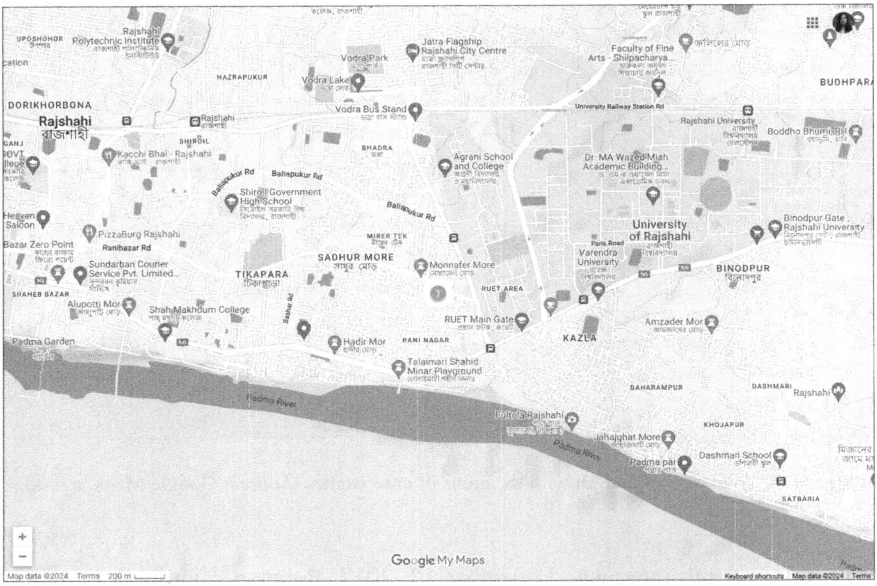

Image 4.25 Radio Padma and surrounding environment (*Source*: Google Maps, n.d.-a)

decisions affecting their livelihood (Rahman, in-depth interview, December 04, 2017; Sarkar, in-depth interview, December 09, 2017; Images 4.28, 4.29, and 4.30).

4.3.3 Radio Bikrampur 99.2 FM

Radio Bikrampur was established on May 01, 2012, by EC Bangladesh, an NGO that has since been rebranded as Ambala Foundation. Located in Munshigang, Dhaka, Bangladesh—an urban area—this station operates with 3 staff and 25 volunteers comprising 6-h daily radio broadcast from 4 pm to 10 pm with the 100 W transmitter covering a radius of approximately 17 kms and reaching approximately 700,000 people (Salahin & Pallobi,[13] in-depth interview, December 09, 2017).

This CRS was selected because of its proximity to Dhaka. Furthermore, its objectives of creating awareness about and addressing social issues affecting marginalised communities in the district by providing a platform for dialogue between the community members and policy level personnel were also key factors. Specifically, the interactions between the radio team and the community about child marriages and issues affecting Dalits were most interesting (Rahman, in-depth interview, December 04, 2017; Salahin & Pallobi, in-depth interview, December 09, 2017; Images 4.31, 4.32, and 4.33).

[13] M.D. Musfiqur Salahin, Senior Producer, and Israt Pallobi is a Producer at Radio Bikrampur.

Image 4.26 Picture of two volunteers at Radio Padma (*Source*: Author's own picture)

Image 4.27 Picture of a recording room at Radio Padma (*Source*: Author's own picture)

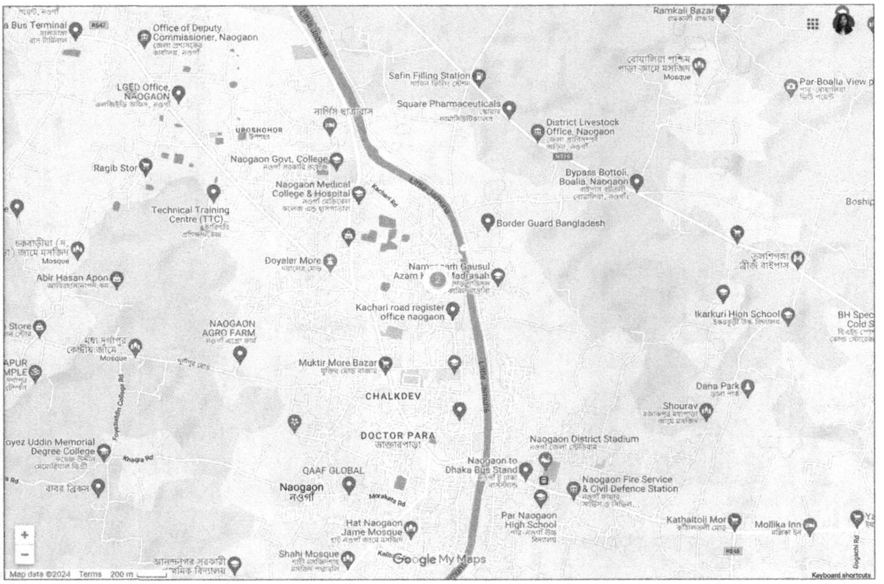

Image 4.28 Radio Borendro and surrounding environment (*Source*: Google Maps, n.d.-a)

4.3.4 Radio Sarabela 98.8 FM

Radio Sarabela was established on April 14, 2016, by SKS Foundation, an NGO. Located in Gaibandha, Rangpur, Bangladesh—a rural area—this station operates with 10 staff and 59 volunteers comprising 16-h daily radio broadcast from 7 am to 11 pm with the 100 W transmitter covering a radius of approximately 17 km and reaching approximately 200,000 people (Sutradar,[14] in-depth interview, December 09, 2017).

The key reason this station was chosen was that it was the latest to be established. Furthermore, the Gaibandha district is a *char* (meaning: island) community prone to flooding. As a result, the community actively voiced their need for a CRS for disaster information sharing, which resulted in the establishment of Radio Sarabela. Since establishment, the CRS has expanded its portfolio from disaster-related programming to development matters, connecting with policymakers, and creating a platform for the children, youth, and disenfranchised groups to express themselves (Rahman, in-depth interview, December 04, 2017; Sutradar, in-depth interview, December 09, 2017; Images 4.34, 4.35, and 4.36).

[14] Santa Rani Sutradar is the Station Manager of Radio Sarabela.

Image 4.29 Picture of two volunteers at Radio Borendro (*Source*: Author's own picture)

Image 4.30 Picture of the office space at Radio Borendro (*Source*: Author's own picture)

Image 4.31 Radio Bikrampur and surrounding environment (*Source*: Google Maps, n.d.-a)

Image 4.32 Picture of Radio Bikrampur's antenna (*Source*: Author's own picture)

Image 4.33 Picture of a recording room at Radio Bikrampur (*Source*: Author's own picture)

Image 4.34 Radio Sarabela and surrounding environment (*Source*: Google Maps, n.d.-a)

Image 4.35 Picture of volunteers recording a programme at Radio Sarabela (*Source*: Author's own picture)

Image 4.36 Picture of a volunteer editing a script at Radio Sarabela (*Source*: Author's own picture)

References

Google Maps. (n.d.-a). *Map showing the Bangladesh CRS used as case studies*. Retrieved November 29, 2024, from https://www.google.com/maps/d/u/0/embed?mid=1JucLdjwrQ98NId7UpSoLrn4LGEqoP40&ehbc=2E312F

Google Maps. (n.d.-b). *Map showing the India CRS used as case studies*. Retrieved November 29, 2024, from https://www.google.com/maps/d/u/0/embed?mid=1V-Taa5t6Qf4GHkwQ1oqlTwj7AjzgW0g&ehbc=2E312F

Google Maps. (n.d.-c). *Map showing the Nepal CRS used as case studies*. Retrieved November 29, 2024, from https://www.google.com/maps/d/u/0/embed?mid=1WMROlFFDnoS4WY0q-3xtr8MYKD3jyJA&ehbc=2E312F

5 Descriptive Mapping of CR in SA

The *South Asian Community Media Database (CMD) V.01*[1] is one of the outputs of the author's doctoral project. It signals the beginning of mapping active community media initiatives in South Asia as no other database like this currently exists. The first volume contains active community radio stations (CRS) in Nepal, India, and Bangladesh as of December 2017.[2]

Through foci on the policy environment, political economy, notions of participation and empowerment, and networking, the CMD specifically:

- Provides information about the media sectors of Nepal, India, and Bangladesh.
- Organises secondary data about CRS in Nepal, India, and Bangladesh in one location for easy access.[3]
- Provide opportunities to enhance possibilities of networking opportunities among CR participants which could result in capacity building and resource sharing.
- Identifies information gaps in secondary data with the aim of fostering research in this field so stakeholders could better understand and advocate for these initiatives.

Based on the data gathered, the CMD was created to contain data about three areas; they are illustrated in Fig. 5.1 with details about each section following.

---

[1]An excerpt of this database referred to as the *Community Media Directory*, which contains profiles of the active CRS in Nepal, India, and Bangladesh as of December 2017, was shared with the UNESCO Chair on Community Media team and is available via SANCOM's website: https://cmd.sancomonline.net/ (Rampersaud, 2019).

[2]See *Appendix 5.1 Lists of active CRS in Nepal, India, and Bangladesh as of December 2017.*

[3]The included data were found through a desk review of internet content from January 2017 to December 2017.

T. Rampersaud-Skorka, *Community Radio in South Asia*, Diversity and Inclusion Research, https://doi.org/10.1007/978-3-031-85201-5_5

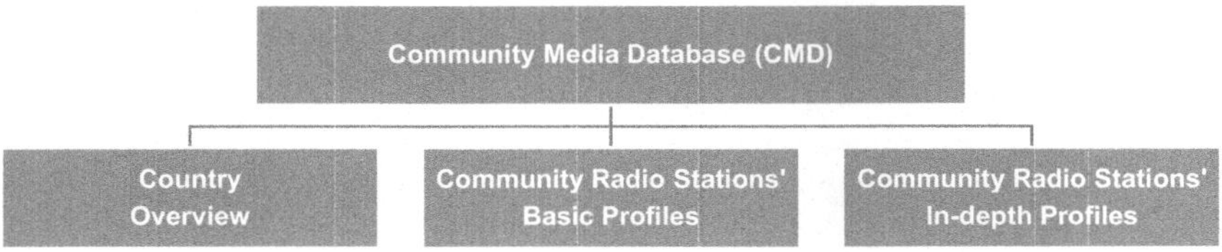

Fig. 5.1 Structure of the *South Asian Community Media Database (CMD) V.01* (*Source*: Author's own illustration)

The *Country Overview* and *Community Radio Stations' Basic Profiles*[4] parts of the database reflect the secondary data collected via desk review while the *Community Radio Stations' In-depth Profiles*[5] section reflects primary data gathered during the author's doctoral fieldwork. Regarding content, *Country Overview* and *Community Radio Stations' In-depth Profiles* organise information under eight identified categories: general information; management and networking; policies and guidelines; economic sustainability; participation; community; programming; and technology and infrastructure. The Community Radio Stations' Basic Profiles section is an overview of each active CRS in Nepal, India, and Bangladesh and contains information regarding name, type of community media, country, location, date established, description (which reflects the aim, objectives, and/or a simple explanation about the CRS), partners, contact information, audience profiles, programme themes and genres, and a miscellaneous section (for any additional information not captured under a given category). With regard to these identified categories, the author created them based on an international understanding of community media. Regarding the sources, information reflected in the CMD was gathered from CRS profiling done by the Association of Community Radio Broadcasters Nepal (ACORAB), Bangladesh NGOs Network for Radio and Communication (BNNRC), Ministry of Information and Broadcasting, India, the CR compendiums of India (Community Radio for Good Governance, 2015; Community Radio in India, Towards Diversity and Sustainability, 2016), initiative specific websites[6] in the public domain, and the *Community Radio Continuous Improvement Toolkit, Version 2.0* (Pavarala et al., 2014).

[4] See *Appendix 5.2: Screenshot of CRS Basic Profile Form in Microsoft Access.*

[5] See *Appendix 5.3 Screenshot of CRS In-Depth Profile Form in Microsoft Access.*

[6] See *Appendix 5.4 List of CRS websites accessed as of December 2017.*

5.1 Nepal

Analysis of different lists[7] revealed 309 operational CRS in Nepal as of December 2017 across the 14 administrative zones (FM radio frequencies licenced in Nepal, n.d.; List of Community and Commercial Radio Stations in Nepal, n.d.; Name List of All FM Radio Stations in Nepal, n.d.; Radio Stations in Nepal, n.d.).[8]

5.1.1 Nepal Country Mapping

General Information The general ideas shared via the initiatives' online platforms highlighted that stations were focused on sharing information for development purposes—especially from marginalised communities.

Management and Networking There was no significant information about networking possibilities in Nepal beyond the presence of the Association of Community Radio Broadcasters (ACORAB)—an organisation that facilitates networking among practitioners and stakeholders. Regarding management, the limited information available pointed to an internal hierarchy within stations as there was mention of station managers and various supervisory positions such as finance and human resource officers/heads.

Policies and Guidelines Nepal does not have a CR-specific policy; as a result, all CRS operate within the national media framework of the country. Some of the key media policies found included: *Rastriya Samachar Samiti Act 1962, Press and Publication Act 1965, Second Press and Publication Act 1975, National Communication Policy 1992, National Broadcast Act 1993*, and *Broadcast Regulations 1995*. It must be noted that many of these documents were in Nepali and/or in an image-related format (.jpeg or .pdf) which the author was unable to translate using the free Google platform. As a result, it was hard to ascertain if there were any other key policies that govern the operation of CRS in Nepal (Media of Nepal, n.d.).

Economic Sustainability CRS in Nepal appeared to have *for-profit* mechanisms since many of the initiatives' websites publicised advertising services via radio broadcasts or spots via online platforms.

---

[7] Lists consulted were available via the following websites: ACORAB, Asia Waves, I Am Nepal, Nepal Radio, and Tech Sansar.

[8] Nepal's administrative zones are Bagmati, Bheri, Dhawalagiri, Gandaki, Janakpur, Karnali, Kosi, Lumbini, Mahakali, Mechi, Narayani, Rapti, Sagarmatha, and Seti.

Community Apart from general descriptions such as "catering to the marginalised" and "for the development of society," specific information about the audiences for the various initiatives highlighted men, women, and youth communities.

Programming The content appeared to be diverse and ranged from general community-based information to entertainment and commercial genres. There were a variety of formats utilised such as news, talk-shows, and features. Popular thematic areas included culture, education, and environment while some stations mentioned unique focus areas such as religious programming and traffic updates.

Technology and Infrastructure The only information found related to the transmitters used for broadcasting which included varying powers: 50 W, 100 W, 200 W, 500 W, and 1000 W (Members, n.d.).

5.1.2 Nepal Initiatives' Mapping

5.1.2.1 Establishment Information

Figure 5.2 visually presents the data relating to the years of establishment for 235 CRS (76.1% of 309 operational CRS); no data was found for the other 74 CRS for this category. As can be seen, there was a slow start to the establishment of these initiatives with a sudden surge in the mid-2000s followed by a peak thereafter and a gradual decline towards 2017.

The first CRS that became operational was *Radio Sagarmatha* on May 19, 1997, in Bagmati. This was followed by the launch of two stations in the 2000–2002 period, five stations in the 2003–2005 period, 82 stations in the 2006–2008 period, 71 stations in the 2009–2011 period, 49 stations in the 2012–2014 period, and 25 stations in the 2015–2017 period.

With regard to the overall goal, mission, aim, and/or objectives, only 41 initiatives (13.3% of 309 CRS) had any information available. Figure 5.3 illustrates the

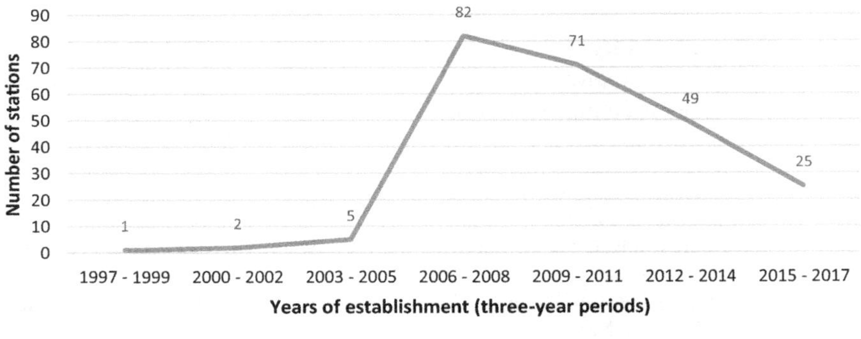

Fig. 5.2 Number of CRS established in Nepal over 3-year periods (*Source*: Author's own illustration)

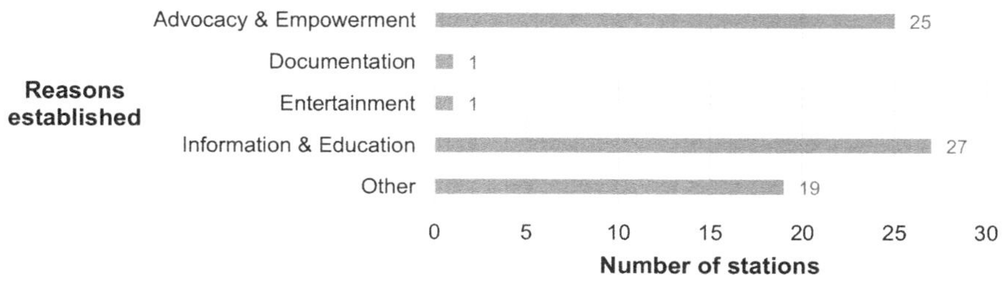

Fig. 5.3 Reasons for the establishment of CRS in Nepal (*Source*: Author's own illustration)

distinct reasons for the establishment under five categories.[9] It must be noted some CRS identified several reasons.

The main reason for the establishment of CRS was *information and education* with 27 of the 41 CRS identifying this reason while *advocacy and empowerment* was the second highest with 25 stations; and one station each highlighted *documentation* and *entertainment* purposes. Regarding the *other* categorisation identified by 19 stations, this was used when reference was made to reasons that did not fit under any of the four identified categories—these included: communication, persuasion, service to the community, journalism, access to media, development, and impacting life.

In relation to ownership (or licence holder), only five stations (1.6% of 309) had any information available. Of these five stations, three were licensed to non-governmental organisations (NGOs), and two were licensed to community-based organisations (CBOs).

Similarly, there was a paucity of information with regard to partnerships. Only eight of the 309 stations (2.6%) mentioned having any type of partner; data regarding these partners are illustrated in Fig. 5.4.

In total, there were 11 unique partners: four partner organisations were NGOs, three were international non-governmental organisations (INGOs), two were media entities, and one each was a community-based organisation (CBO) and a religious organisation. These partnerships were further classified based on their scale of operation; this is illustrated in Fig. 5.5.

Of the 11 different partners, 5 partners were operating at the local level, 1 partner operated at the national level, and the remaining 5 partners operated at the international level. While the local partners comprised three development-focused organisations and one religious organisation, the national-level partner was identified as ACORAB and the international partners were the British Broadcasting Corporation (BBC), the US Agency for International Development (USAID), and a China-Australia INGO.

[9] These categories were developed to reflect common reasons for establishment across the three countries and are in keeping with key CR ideals uncovered during the literature review.

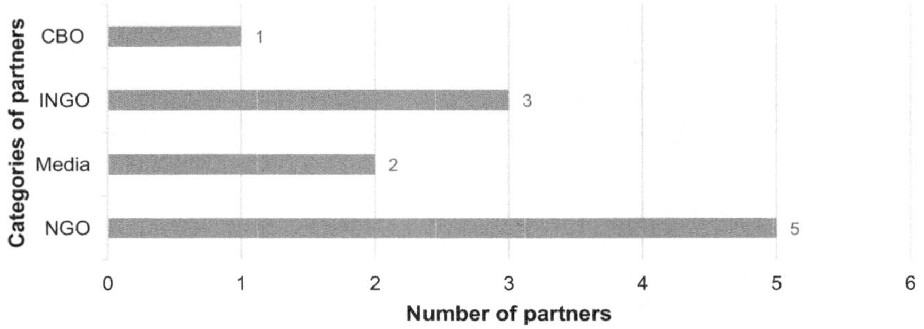

Fig. 5.4 Partners' classifications regarding CRS in Nepal (*Source*: Author's own illustration)

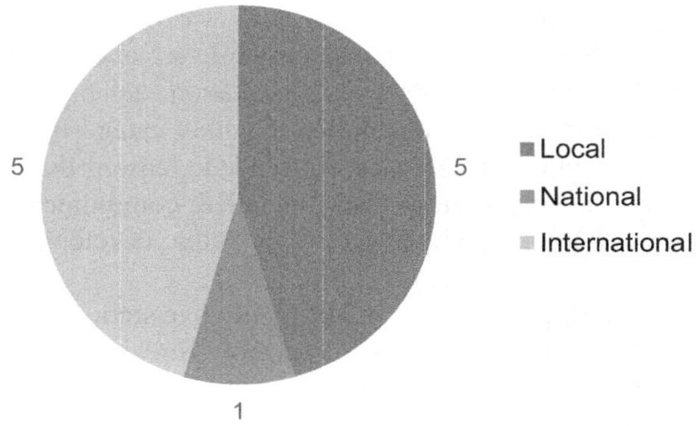

Fig. 5.5 Levels of operation regarding partners of CRS in Nepal (*Source*: Author's own illustration)

5.1.2.2 Location: Administrative Zones and Environmental Classification

Figure 5.6 visually presents the active CRS within each administrative zone. Of the 309 stations, information for 307 CRS (99.4%) was known while information for two CRS (0.6%) could not be deduced due to incomplete street addresses.

As can be seen, Bagmati and Rapti zones each had 33 initiatives in Nepal. The subsequent zones, from highest to lowest number of CRS were Janakpur with 30 initiatives, Gandaki with 28 initiatives, Narayani with 27 initiatives, Lumbini with 25 initiatives, Sagarmatha and Seti each with 21 initiatives, Bheri with 20 initiatives, Mahakali with 19 initiatives, Karnali with 17 initiatives, Kosi with 16 initiatives, Dhawalagiri with 9 initiatives, and Mechi with 8 initiatives.

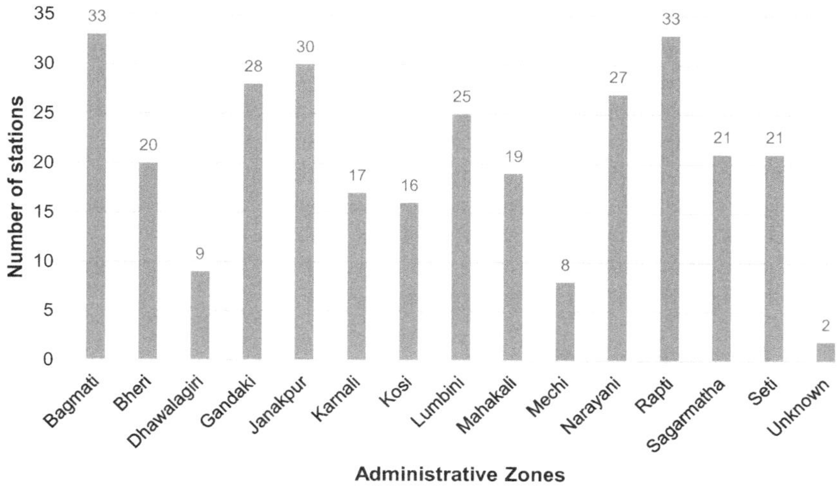

Fig. 5.6 Location of CRS in Nepal with regard to Administrative Zones (*Source*: Author's own illustration)

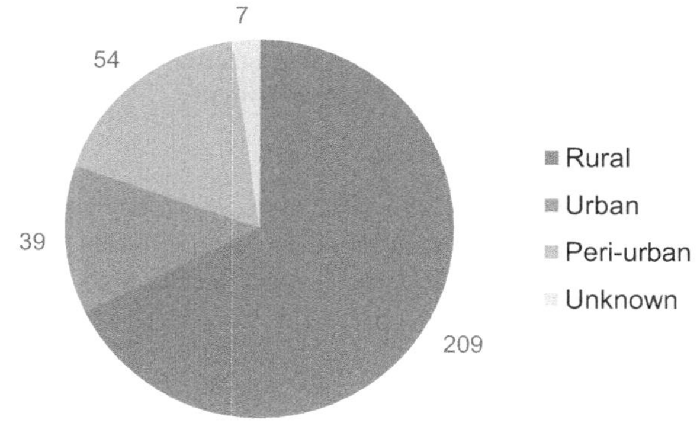

Fig. 5.7 Location of CRS in Nepal according to environmental classifications (*Source*: Author's own illustration)

Further to this, the locations of these CRS were also analysed based on the type of environment.[10] Figure 5.7 illustrates the environmental classification of these CRS.

[10] Rural areas were identified when primary activities such as farming and fishing were common; urban areas were identified when secondary activities such as processing and banking were common; and peri-urban areas were identified when there was a hybrid of rural and urban activities—elements for both were present.

As can be seen, the rural environment contained the majority with 209 stations (67.0% of 309 stations). These were mostly located in villages and small towns throughout the country—specifically in the Himalayan mountain range. The next most populated environment was peri-urban which accounted for 54 stations (17.5%). Finally, the urban environment, which includes major cities, accounted for 39 stations (12.6%). It was not possible to ascertain the environments for seven stations (3.0%) since their exact locations were not stated. Overall, Bagmati had the most stations located in the rural environment with 26 initiatives (8.5%), while Bheri had the most in the urban areas with 8 initiatives (2.6%), and Rapti had the most in the peri-urban areas with 13 initiatives (4.2%).

5.1.2.3 Contact Information

The contact information regarding CRS in Nepal was mostly traditional in nature with a few stations utilising new media (online) platforms. Figure 5.8 visually presents the types of contact information available for the 309 stations.

Regarding street addresses, only two stations (0.7% of 309 stations) had no specific information. Of the remaining 307 stations (99.3%), 226 stations had complete addresses while 81 stations only had information relating to the administrative zones and/or districts. While 254 stations had telephone numbers, 13 of these were inaccurate—they were incomplete or did not follow the format for landline or cell phone numbers in Nepal. There were 302 stations (97.3%) with e-mail addresses and 193 stations (62.5%) with websites. Of the 116 that had no website, 6 stations had Facebook pages to share their information virtually.

5.1.2.4 Community Profiles

Of the 309 stations, 148 stations (47.9%) had some information about the communities being catered to or involved in the initiatives. The different types of communities identified were children, youth, women, men, people with disabilities (PWD),

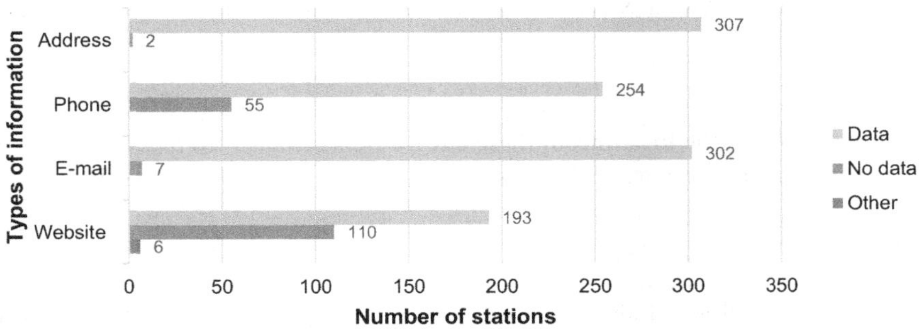

Fig. 5.8 Types of contact information available regarding CRS in Nepal (*Source*: Author's own illustration)

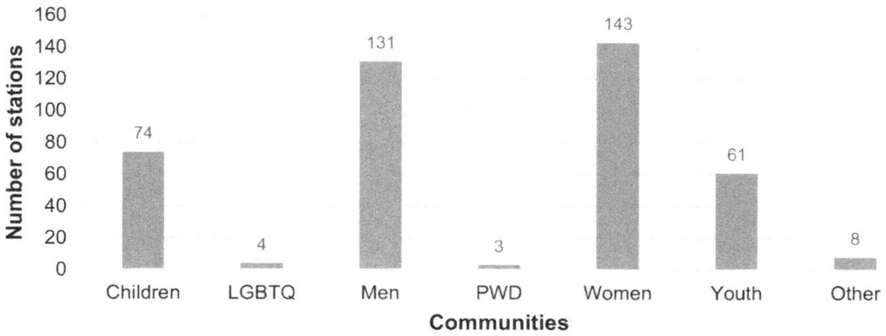

Fig. 5.9 Communities of CRS in Nepal (*Source*: Author's own illustration)

lesbian, gay, bisexual, transgender, and queers (LGBTQ),[11] and *other* (such as Dalits, farmers, and tribal). Figure 5.9 presents this information.

The most recurring community being catered to was *women* with 143 stations producing programmes for them. This group was followed by *men* which was highlighted by 131 stations, *children* were highlighted by 74 stations, *youth* were highlighted by 61 stations, *LGBTQ* were highlighted by 4 stations, *PWD* were highlighted by 3 stations, and *other* communities were highlighted by 8 stations.

Further analysis of these communities showed that only one of 148 stations (0.7%) catered to all seven categories. The information in Fig. 5.10 illustrates the number of communities being addressed by different CRS.

There were six stations that catered to five different communities—all six addressed *children* and *men*; five addressed *PWD* and *youth*; three addressed *women* and *other*; and two addressed *LGBTQ*. Within the 44 stations that catered to four different communities, all addressed *women* and *youth*; *children* and *men* were addressed by 42 stations; *other* were addressed by 3 stations; and one station addressed *LGBTQ*. Of the 23 stations that catered to three different communities, all addressed *women*; *men* were catered to by 22 stations; *children* by 18 stations; *youth* by 5 stations; and, *other* by 1 station. Within the 68 stations that catered to two communities, the *women* community was the strongest with 66 stations catering to them followed by *men* who were catered to by 60 stations, *children* by 7 stations, and *youth* by 3 stations. Finally, of the six stations that catered to just one type of community, three stations catered to *women* while three catered to *youth*.

[11] These were the general types of communities identified from the literature review and secondary data. It must be noted that the various categories are not mutually exclusive, for example, PWD can also be children, youth, men, women, and LGBTQ. As the project focuses on a macro level, these categories were used since communities of interest would be too diverse to classify.

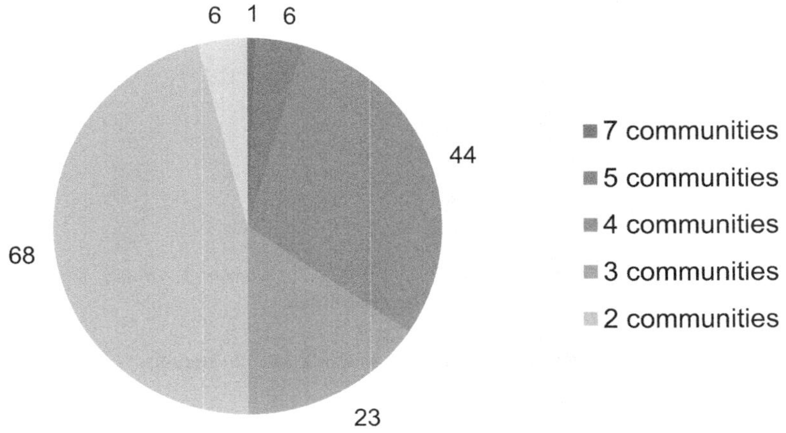

Fig. 5.10 Number of CRS catering to different amounts of communities in Nepal (*Source*: Author's own illustration)

5.1.2.5 Thematic Areas[12] for Programming

Only 100 of the 309 stations (32.4%) had any information about the thematic areas that guided programme production; Fig. 5.11 illustrates this.

The most popular thematic area was *culture* with 81 stations producing this type of content. This was followed by *education* in 59 stations, *health* in 49 stations, *agriculture* in 46 stations, and *entertainment* in 30 stations. The remaining thematic areas were environmental, gender, youth and children,[13] economics, disaster, human rights, weather, edutainment, tourism, and other. The *other* category was used when data highlighted programming in relation to general development and government-related content.

Programming was also classified based on the number of thematic areas addressed by each CRS; this is represented in Fig. 5.12.

Of the 100 stations that identified thematic areas, 25 stations highlighted five focus areas with the popular ones being *agriculture, culture, education,* and *health.* Following this, 20 stations highlighted four areas with the most recurring themes being *culture* and *education.* Nineteen stations highlighted three areas with an almost equal mix of themes among *agriculture, culture, education,* and *health.* Of the 12 stations that highlighted six areas, *agriculture, culture,* and *entertainment* were the most popular. There were nine stations each that highlighted seven and two

[12] To code the data for analysis, the author had to use broad categories to represent the data gathered. These categories were common across all three countries and informed by literature review, while the "other" classification catered to the differences.

[13] Even though differentiation was made between youth (13–30 years) and children (less than 13 years) in "communities," they are identified by one label under thematic area as most CRS did not differentiate between these two groups regarding data for this sub-section.

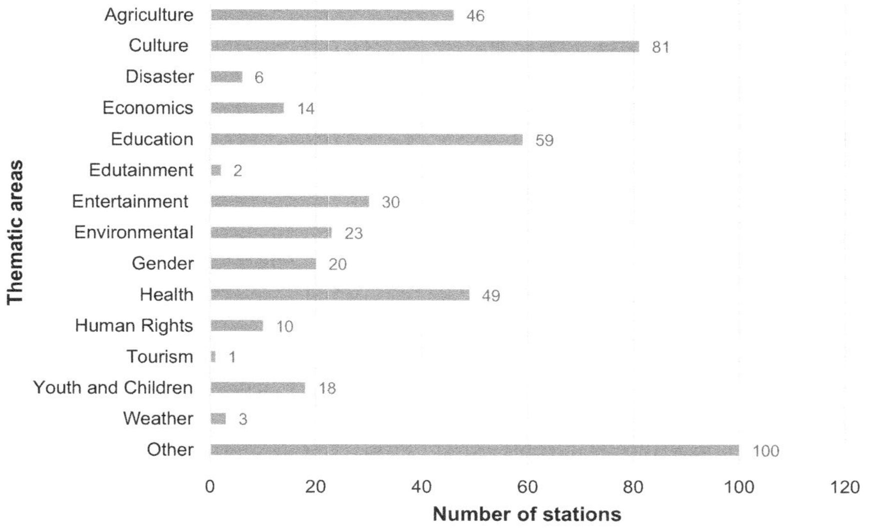

Fig. 5.11 Thematic areas for programming in CRS in Nepal (*Source*: Author's own illustration)

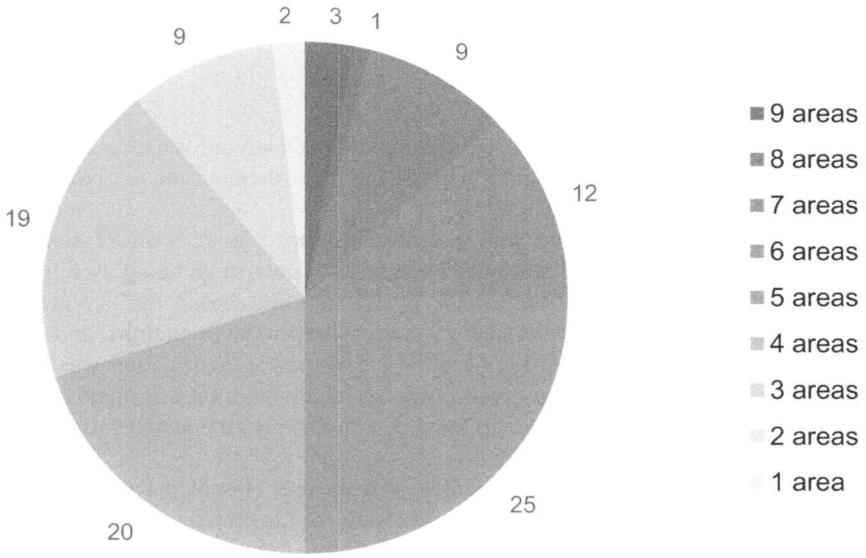

Fig. 5.12 Number of CRS catering to different amounts of thematic areas in programming (*Source*: Author's own illustration)

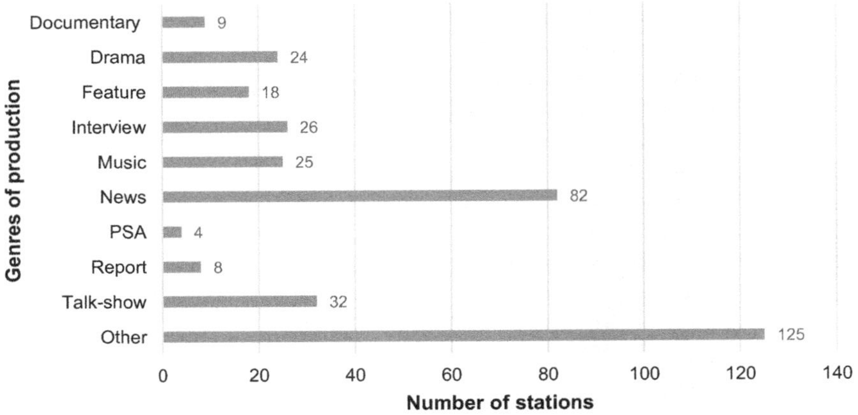

Fig. 5.13 Production genres used by CRS in Nepal (*Source*: Author's own illustration)

areas with *agriculture, culture, education, entertainment,* and *health* being the most popular themes with reference to the former and *culture* being the most popular with reference to the latter. Three stations highlighted nine areas with *agriculture, culture, economics, education, entertainment,* and *health* being the most popular. Finally, two stations highlighted one *other* area of focus, and one station highlighted eight thematic areas for programme production.

5.1.2.6 Production Genres

There were 152 stations (49.2% of 309 stations) that had any information about the genres[14] used to produce and present content on the above thematic areas. Figure 5.13 presents this information.

Of the 152 initiatives, *news* was the most produced genre with 82 stations utilising this format. This was followed by the *talk-show* format being used by 32 stations, *interview* by 26 stations, *music* by 25 stations, *drama* by 24 stations, *feature* by 18 stations, *documentary* by 9 stations, *report* by 8 stations, and *PSA* (public service announcement) by 4 stations. The *other* classification was used regarding 125 stations and represented instances where mention was made to programmes or content; however, due to language challenges, the actual format was not ascertained.

Apart from this, the production genres were further classified based on how many stations utilised different amounts of formats, as illustrated in Fig. 5.14.

Only one station of 152 stations with information showed utilisation of seven formats which included *documentary, drama, feature, interview, music, talk-show,* and *other*. There were three stations that utilised six formats with the most recurring

[14] These genres/formats reflect those common across the three countries, based on the literature review, while the "other" category addresses the unique formats.

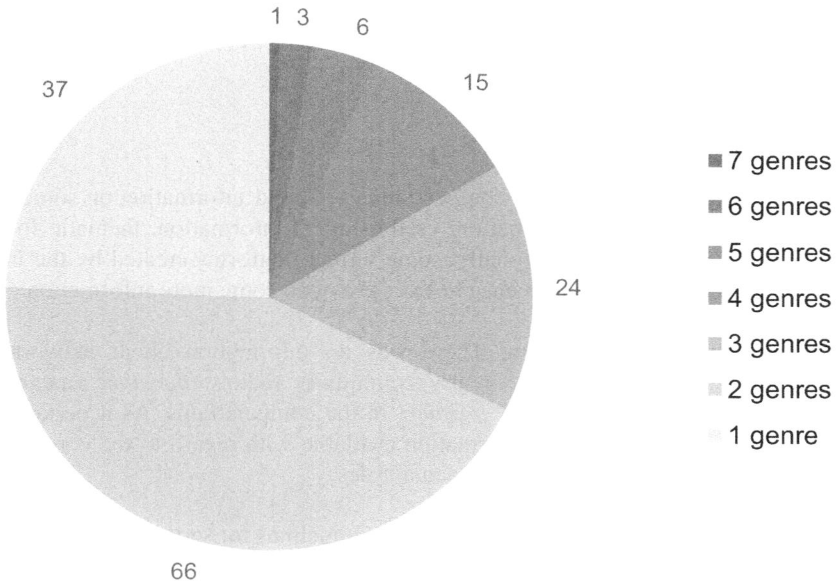

Fig. 5.14 Number of production genres used in programming by CRS in Nepal (*Source*: Author's own illustration)

ones being *feature, interview, music, news, talk-shows*, and *other*. Following this, 6 stations utilised five formats with *documentary, drama, interview, talk-show*, and *other* identified as the most popular formats; 15 stations utilised four formats with *drama, interview, music*, and *talk-show* being the most recurring; 24 stations utilised three formats with *music, news*, and *other* being the most popular; and 66 stations utilised two formats comprising *news* and *other*. Finally, 37 stations utilised at least one format.

5.2 India

India's Ministry of Information and Broadcasting (MIB) website had a list comprising 436 CRS categorised under three statuses as of December 2017. These categorisations were operational, LOI (letter of intent), and GOPA (grant of permission agreement). When this list was cross-referenced with Community Radio for Good Governance, 2015, and Community Radio in India, Towards Diversity, & Sustainability, 2016 (referred to as the compendiums), and all initiatives individually checked, there was data which supported a total of 193 operational CRS[15] in

[15] See *Appendix 5.1 Lists of active CRS in Nepal, India, and Bangladesh as of December 2017.*

India as of December 2017 across the 29 states and 8 union territories (CRFC, n.d.; List of Operational Community Radio Stations in India as on 31-05-2019, 2019).[16]

5.2.1 India Country Mapping

General Information The two compendiums provided information on some stations concerning contact information, establishment information, thematic focus, and a brief background. Additionally, some virtual platforms created by the individual initiatives and various licence holders provided some more information.

Management and Networking There was no information about networking among the stations beyond the yearly community radio *sammelans* (meaning: conference)[17] and mention of *key partners* in the compendiums. As it pertains to management, there was some information available with regard to the core teams within the stations but no mention of actual roles.

Policies and Guidelines There is the Policy Guidelines for setting up Community Radio Stations in India (n.d.) which was introduced in 2002[18] by the Government of India. It highlights (1) the basic principles, (2) eligibility criteria, (3) selection process and processing of the applications, (4) grant of permission agreement conditions, (5) content regulation and monitoring, (6) imposition of penalty/revocation of permission agreement, (7) transmitter power and range, (8) funding and sustenance, and (9) other terms and conditions for establishing a community radio station in India.

Apart from this CR-specific policy, there are other laws and regulations that govern mass media in India. These include the *Broadcasting Code of 1962*, the *Copyright Act 1957*, and the *Drug and Magic Remedies (Objectionable Advertising) Act of 1954* which apply to mainstream and community media (Basu, n.d.; History of mass media in India, n.d.).

---

[16] India's states are Andhra Pradesh, Arunachal Pradesh, Assam, Bihar, Chhattisgarh, Goa, Gujarat, Haryana, Himachal Pradesh, Jammu and Kashmir, Jharkhand, Karnataka, Kerala, Madhya Pradesh, Maharashtra, Manipur, Meghalaya, Mizoram, Nagaland, Odisha, Punjab, Rajasthan, Sikkim, Tamil Nadu, Telangana, Tripura, Uttar Pradesh, Uttarakhand, and West Bengal. The union territories comprise Andaman and Nicobar Islands, Chandigarh, Dadra and Nagar Haveli, Daman and Diu, Delhi, Lakshadweep, Ladakh, and Puducherry.

[17] The "community radio *sammelans*" are a yearly summit where key practitioners, activists, academics, and key stakeholders meet in New Delhi, India—normally around World Radio Day which is in February every year, for capacity sharing and building.

[18] The initial reading highlighted the 2002 Policy, however, further reading following data from the primary data collection phase revealed a 2006 Policy which is highlighted in Chap. 6: "Media Policy Environment."

Economic Sustainability The only information available pointed to some government funding regarding specific projects; but nothing more specific was found.

Community Apart from general descriptions about *catering to the marginalised*, specific information about the wider communities was not readily available. However, references were made to men, women, children, and youth communities in addition to some communities of interest such as farmers and students.

Programming From the limited information available, the content appears diverse and ranges from general community-based information to educational and entertainment themes. These were being produced in a variety of formats such as interview, talk-show, and music. Popular topics included health, education, culture, environment, agriculture, social awareness, and skills development.

Technology and Infrastructure Only some information regarding the transmitters for some of the initiatives was available.

5.2.2 India Initiatives' Mapping

5.2.2.1 Establishment Information

Figure 5.15 highlights the years of establishment for 159 stations (82.4% of 193 operational CRS) that had this information available. As can be seen, there is a steady increase in the number of operational stations from 2000 to 2014 with a peak in the 2012–2014 three-year period followed by a decline since then.

According to the data, *Anna Community Radio 90.4*—the first campus CRS, located at Anna University in Tamil Nadu—was the first initiative to be launched in

Fig. 5.15 Number of CRS established in India over 3-year periods (*Source*: Author's own illustration)

India on February 1, 2002. This was followed by *Sangham Radio 90.4*—the first rural CRS in India, being launched by the Deccan Development Society (DDS) located in then Andhra Pradesh (now *Telangana*), on October 15, 2008. Since then, 15 stations were launched during 2003–2005, 28 stations were launched during 2006–2008, 49 stations were launched during 2009–2011, 54 stations were launched during 2012–2014, and 13 stations were launched during 2015–2017. There was no information with regard to stations launched in 2017 available.

Concerning the overall goal, mission, aim, and objectives, only 127 stations (65.8% of 193 CRS) had information available. Note: while some stations explicitly stated their reasons for establishment, implications were ascertained by the author through descriptions on virtual platforms and the Genesis section of the 2016 compendium for others. Figure 5.16 illustrates the 227 instances where these 127 CRS identified reasons for establishment. It must be noted that some stations identified more than one reason.

The primary reason for the establishment of these initiatives in India was for *information and education* with 88 stations highlighting this area. This was followed by *advocacy and empowerment* which 67 stations highlighted, *documentation* which 14 stations highlighted, and *entertainment* which 10 stations highlighted. Of the 127 stations, 48 stations stated *other* reasons for establishment: 13 alluded to CRS being established to provide a voice for the voiceless; 8 stations each alluded to development reasons and access to various necessities such as basic services, skills development, and technology; 7 stations highlighted various societal reasons such as creating a sense of identity and dignity for the community and promoting diversity, freedom of expression, justice, social responsibility, and tolerance; 6 stations highlighted promotional purposes with five referencing local talent and one referencing rural entrepreneurship; 4 stations highlighted communication; 2 stations each alluded to improvements in agricultural production and quality of life, community focus such as the differently abled and heterogeneous community, and bridging generational gaps and those between the administration and community. Research, promotion of extracurricular activities, and self-employment generation

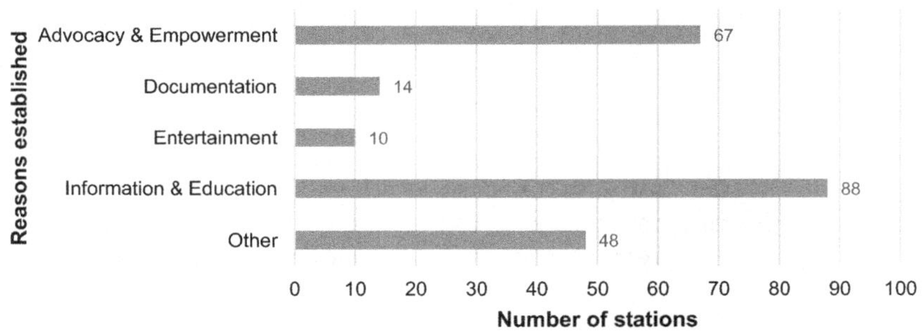

Fig. 5.16 Reasons for establishment of CRS in India (*Source*: Author's own illustration)

were also highlighted by stations. While some *other* reasons can be placed into one of the four identified categories, they were singled out because of their broad implications which cannot be specifically narrowed down to fit any of the identified categories.

With regard to the licence holders, 126 licences (65.3% of 193) were held by educational institutes: 116 were held by schools and universities, 66 were held by NGOs, 9 by agricultural institutes, and 1 each by a research-based institute and a religious organisation.

With regard to partnerships, 116 stations (60.1% of 193) identified 180 unique partners. This information is illustrated in Fig. 5.17.

Regarding the above, 60 partners were identified as being with educational institutions. This was followed by NGOs which accounted for 39 partners, government which accounted for 34 partners, businesses which accounted for 25 partners, trusts which accounted for 12 partners, INGOs which accounted for 9 partners, media entities which accounted for 6 partners, embassies which accounted for 3 partners, and CBOs which accounted for 2 partners. These partners were further classified based on their scale of operation which is visually presented in Fig. 5.18.

Of the 180 unique partners, 112 partners operated at the local level; this included educational institutes (schools, colleges, and universities), local government offices such as the Health Department and Agriculture Department, NGOs such as Barefoot College, and trusts such as *Bhai Kanhaiya Trust*. The second largest partnership category was at the national level with 53 partners which included government departments, ministries, and agencies along with some NGOs, trusts, and businesses; some of the most popular partnerships were with organisations such as the Society for the Promotion of Indian Classical Music and Culture Amongst Youth (SPIC MACAY), Ideosync Media Combine, *Maraa*, Ministry of Panchayati Raj,

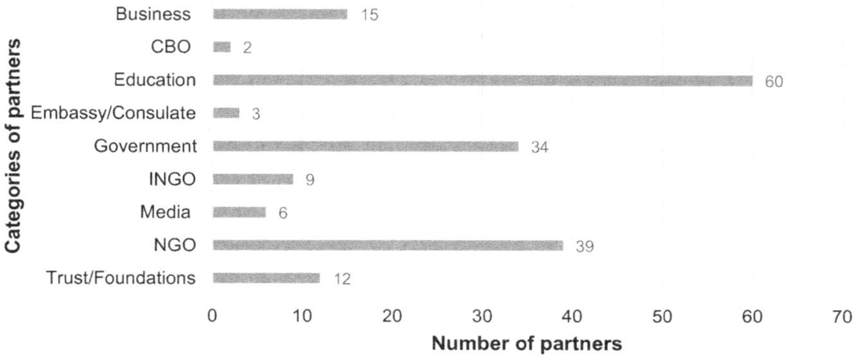

Fig. 5.17 Partners' classifications regarding CRS in India (*Source*: Author's own illustration)

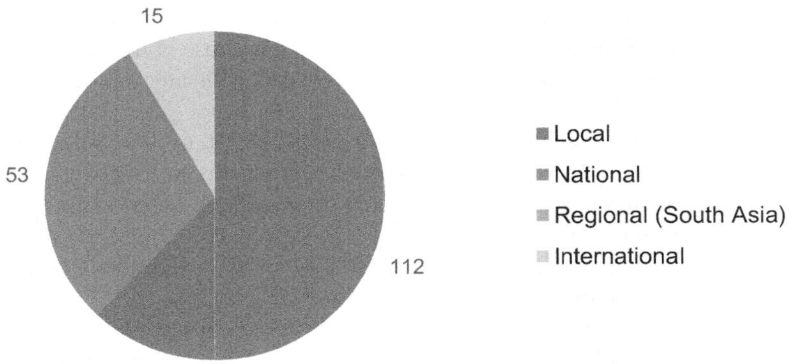

Fig. 5.18 Levels of operation regarding partner organisations in India (*Source*: Author's own illustration)

Ministry of Health and Family Welfare, the Government of Odisha, the Government of Karnataka, and National Health Mission. Finally, international partners accounted for 15 organisations and included INGOs, embassies or consulates, and international multilateral agencies such as the United Nations Children's Fund (UNICEF), United Nations Educational, Scientific and Cultural Organization (UNESCO), World Bank, BBC Radio World Service, and UNESCO Chair on Community Media. Apart from these identified partners, many stations referenced general groups of individuals and organisations such as village *panchayats* (meaning: council), agriculture organisations, professionals (teachers, bankers, doctors, social workers), and hospitals in addition to categories of community (such as children, youth, women, and farmers).

5.2.2.2 Location: States, Union Territories, and Environmental Classification

Figure 5.19 illustrates the categorisations of the active CRS within each state and union territory in India.

As can be seen, Tamil Nadu accounted for the majority of CRS in India with 29 stations while Delhi accounted for the most CRS in the union territories with 7 stations. With regard to states, Uttar Pradesh had the second highest number with 23 stations, followed by Maharashtra with 16 stations, and Karnataka and Madhya Pradesh each with 15 stations. The remaining stations and union territories accounted for 88 stations.

Figure 5.20 presents the environmental classifications of CRS in India based on rural, urban, peri-urban, and unknown.

Most CRS were in the urban areas of India which had 99 stations (51.3% of 193 stations); these were mostly owned by educational institutions in the larger towns and cities. The next environment was rural with 49 stations (25.4%), followed by

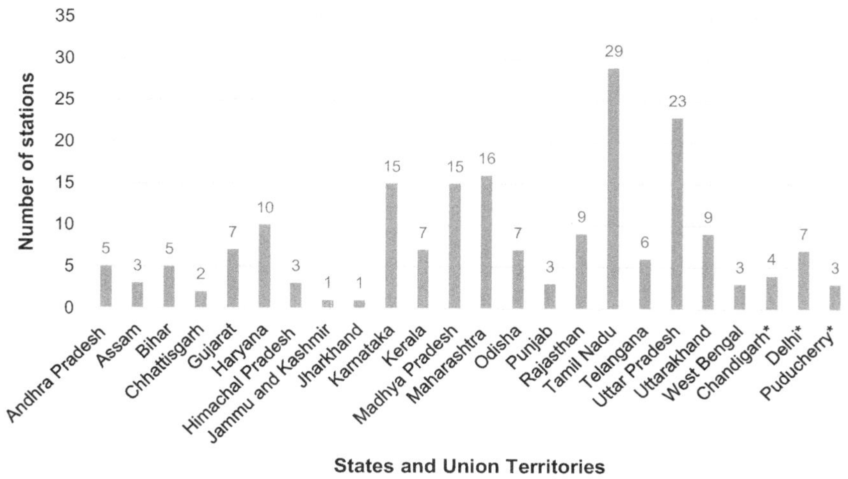

Notes: The following states and union territories of India did not have any CRS:

- *States:* Arunachal Pradesh, Goa, Manipur, Meghalaya, Mizoram, Nagaland, Sikkim, and Tripura
- **Union Territories:* Andaman and Nicobar Islands, Dadra and Nagar Haveli, Daman and Diu, and Lakshadweep

Fig. 5.19 Location of CRS in India with regard to states and union territories (*Source*: Author's own illustration)

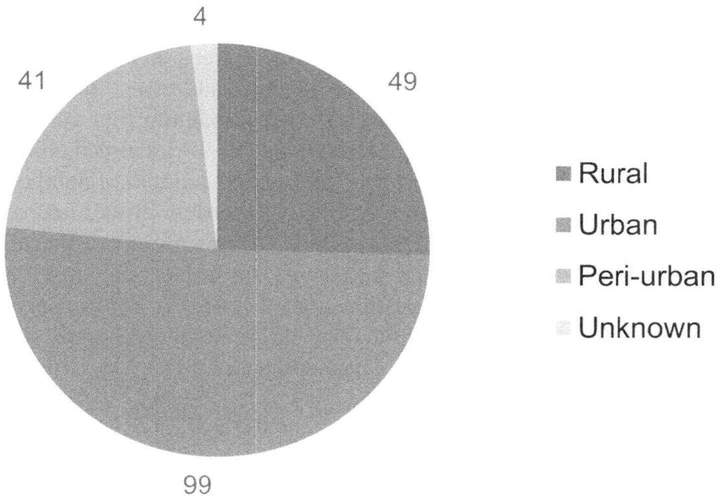

Fig. 5.20 Location of CRS in India according to environmental classification (*Source*: Author's own illustration)

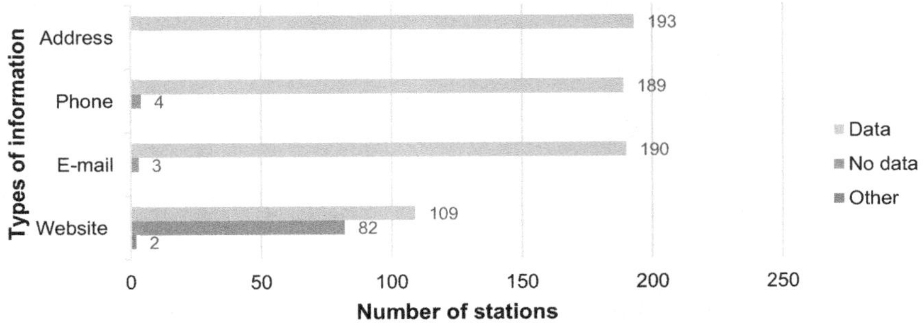

Fig. 5.21 Types of contact information available regarding CRS in India (*Source*: Author's own illustration)

peri-urban with 41 stations (21.2%). Of the 193 stations, the specific location for 4 stations (2.1%) was unknown even though information about the state was available. Overall, Madhya Pradesh had the most initiatives in rural areas with 9 stations (4.7%), while Tamil Nadu had the most initiatives in urban and peri-urban locations with 13 stations (6.7%) and 8 stations (4.1%), respectively.

5.2.2.3 Contact Information

The contact information regarding CRS in India was a mixture of both traditional and new media methods of communication. Figure 5.21 visually presents the types of contact information available for the 193 stations.

There was contact information available for all stations, in one form or another. While 193 stations had information regarding street addresses, only 189 stations (97.9% of 193) had complete addresses with the remaining four stations having only state-related information. Of the 189 stations (97.9%) that had contact phone numbers, one was inaccurate in that it had an excessive amount of numbers in relation to the format for phone numbers in India. Regarding e-mail addresses, 190 stations (98.4%) had this information available. It must be noted that the phone numbers and e-mail addresses found could have been further categorised into three types based on the (inferred) owner: station, licence holder, or contact person within the station. Finally, 111 stations (57.5%) had information relating to virtual platforms—there were 109 websites and 2 Facebook pages.

5.2.2.4 Community Profiles

Of the 193 stations, 146 stations (75.6%) had some information with regard to community; these different communities included children, LGBTQ, men, PWD, women, youth, and other. Figure 5.22 presents this information.

The most popular community was *women* which was addressed through programming in 75 stations. This group was followed by *youth* being catered to by 65 stations, *children* by 55 stations, *men* by 7 stations, *PWD* by 2 stations, and *LGBTQ* by 1 station. The *other* categorisation, identified by 125 stations (85.6%), was used

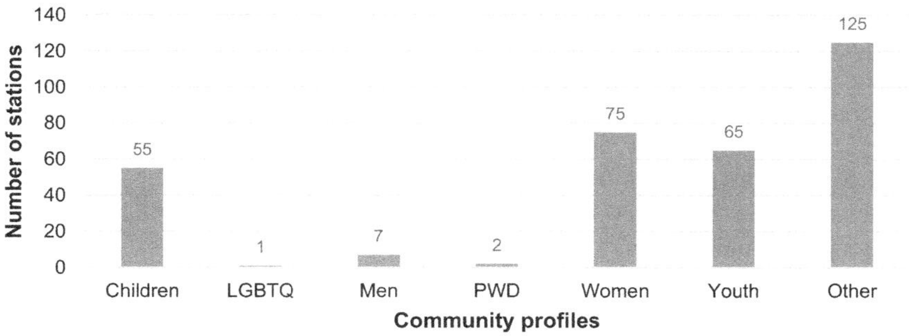

Fig. 5.22 Communities of CRS in India (*Source*: Author's own illustration)

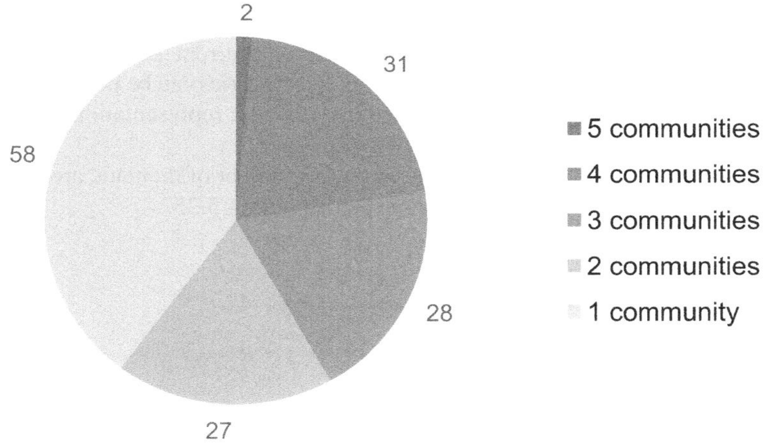

Fig. 5.23 Number of CRS catering to different amounts of communities in India (*Source*: Author's own illustration)

when references were made to the "community" or for specific communities of interest and included: apartment and boat dwellers, artists, drivers, ex-child labourers, farmers, fisherfolks, illiterate people, marginalised groups, migrants, parents and guardians, scientists, senior citizens, students, trainers, teachers, academicians, tribal groups, unskilled workers, and weavers.

Based on further analysis, the author was able to identify how many different communities each CRS catered to. This is visually presented in Fig. 5.23.

Of the two stations that catered to five different communities, both addressed *children, men, women, youth,* and *other*. Following this, 31 stations catered to four different communities with all 31 having programming for *women, youth*, and *other* while 29 catered to *children* and 2 catered to *men*. There were 28 stations that catered to three different communities: 21 catered to *children*, 1 to *LGBTQ*, 3 to *men*, 20 to *women*, 22 to *youth*, and 17 to *other*. Of the 27 stations that catered to two communities, 3 catered to *children*, 1 to *PWD*, 17 to *women*, 8 to *youth*, and 25 to *other*. Finally, there were 58 stations that catered to at least one identified community: 1 station highlighted *PWD*, 5 highlighted *women*, 2 highlighted *youth*, and the remaining 50 highlighted *other*.

5.2.2.5 Thematic Areas for Programming

There were 156 stations (80.8%) with data regarding the thematic areas addressed through programming; Fig. 5.24 reflects this.

The most popular thematic area identified was *culture* in which 116 stations were producing content. The next most popular thematic area was *education* which was catered to by 110 stations, *health* in 107 stations, and *agriculture* and *gender* each in 76 stations. All other identified thematic areas were reflected through programming with the *other* categorisation being used in relation to 114 stations, specifically about development, empowerment, social issues, entrepreneurship, laws and legalities, government and governance, peace and harmony, home management, media literacy, senior citizens, beauty and fashion, current issues, infotainment, comedy, and transportation. While some of these categories can be placed into existing areas, they were specifically identified to provide a representation of the wide variety of themes being addressed by CRS in India.

Programming was also classified based on the number of thematic areas used by CRS when producing content; this is represented in Fig. 5.25.

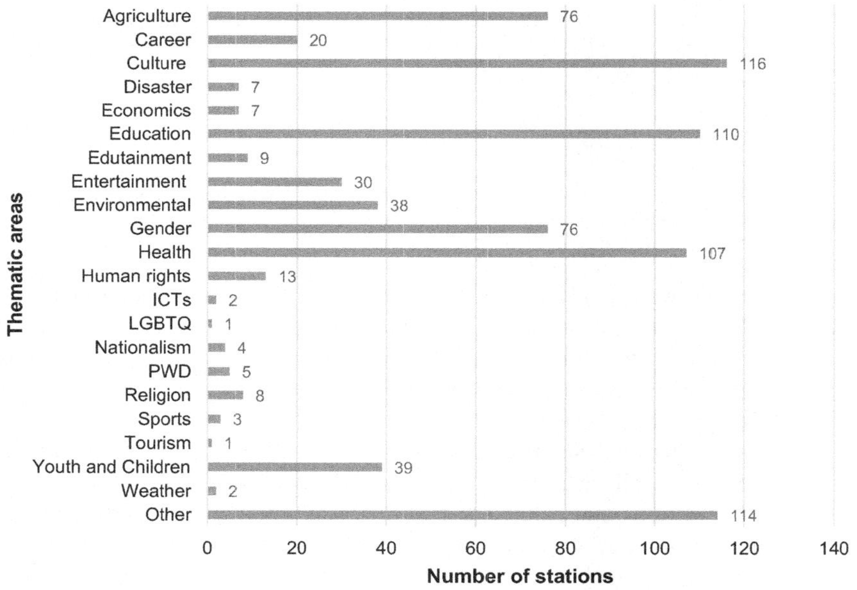

Fig. 5.24 Thematic areas for programming in CRS in India (*Source*: Author's own illustration)

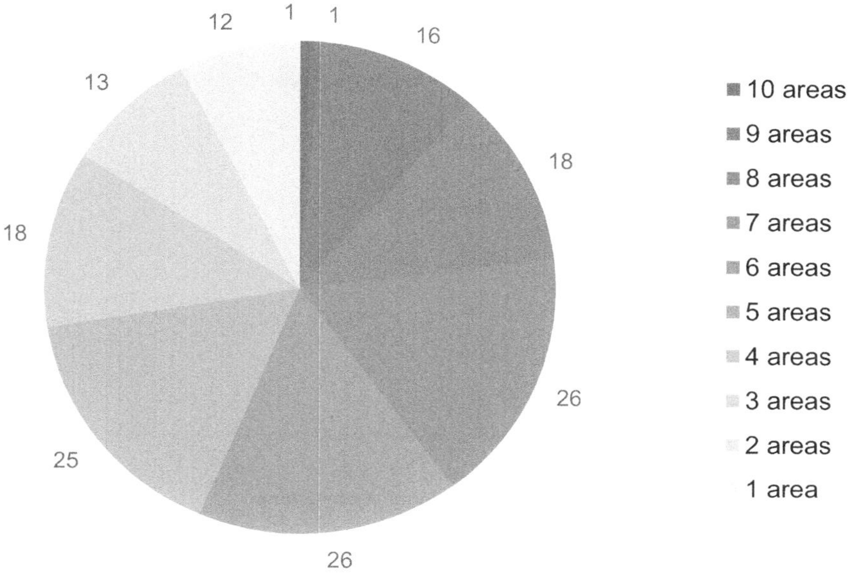

Fig. 5.25 Number of CRS catering to different amounts of thematic areas in India (*Source*: Author's own illustration)

Of the 156 stations that highlighted thematic areas for production, one station each highlighted ten and nine thematic areas where the recurring themes were *agriculture, career, culture, education, environment*, and *health*. Following this, 16 stations highlighted eight thematic areas with *agriculture, culture, education, entertainment, gender, health, youth and children*, and *other* being the most popular combination, and 18 stations highlighted seven thematic areas with *agriculture, career, culture, disaster, education, health,* and *other* being the most common combination. For those stations focused on six and five thematic areas, there were 26 stations each with the recurring themes being *agriculture, culture,* and *education*. Furthermore, there were 25 stations addressing four thematic areas, 18 stations addressing three thematic areas, 13 stations addressing two thematic areas, and 12 stations addressing at least one thematic area highlighted.

5.2.2.6 Production Genres

There were 101 stations (52.3% out of 193 stations) with information regarding the production genres utilised to present information on the above thematic areas. Figure 5.26 presents this information.

Of the 101 stations, the most popular genre of production was *drama* with 37 stations highlighting this format. This was followed by the *interview* and *live broadcast* formats being used in 28 stations each, *music* format in 25 stations, and *talk-show* in 16 stations. Other identified genres of production were documentary,

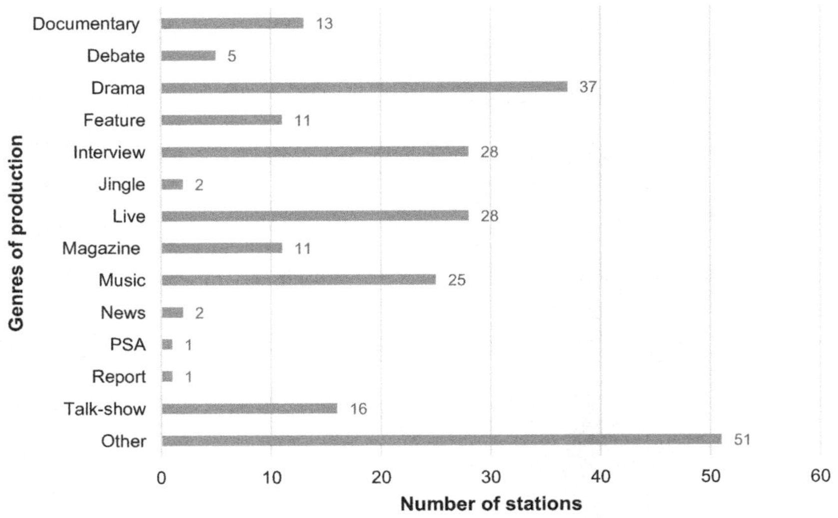

Fig. 5.26 Production genres used by CRS in India (*Source*: Author's own illustration)

feature, magazine, debate, jingle, news,[19] PSA, and report. Apart from these, 51 stations alluded to *other* formats used in production. The most popular were *phone-in* (and phone out incorporated in three instances) being used in 25 stations, *discussion* in 16 stations, and *vox populi* in 8 stations. Alternative formats not previously identified by the author but highlighted by these CRS included outdoor broadcast (live), competition and quiz, storytelling, expert talks, reality, alert (examinations), audio-collage, book reading, cartooning, commentary, diary, docu-drama, docu-feature, monologue, reporting, and street play. It must be noted that some of these alternative formats such as storytelling and cartooning can fit into broader categories such as drama while outdoor broadcast and commentary can be placed into live broadcast. However, due to the uniqueness of the formats, they were catalogued under other.

Apart from this, the formats were further classified based on how many stations utilised different production genres, as can be seen in Fig. 5.27.

One station each utilised eight and seven different formats for production while three stations utilised six formats; of these, the popular formats were *documentary, drama, feature, live, talk-show*, and *other*. There were 9 stations that utilised five formats (popular formats: *documentary, drama, feature, music, other*); 6 stations that utilised four formats (popular formats: *drama, interview, music, talk-show*); 16 stations that utilised three formats (popular formats: *interview, live, other*); 15

[19] The CR policy in India does not allow for the broadcast of "news" content from the CRS—they are not allowed to produce this type of content. Therefore, it must be noted that the CRS that identified news were not producing news bulletins but only sharing news-like content—such as the reading of the headlines in the daily newspapers on-air.

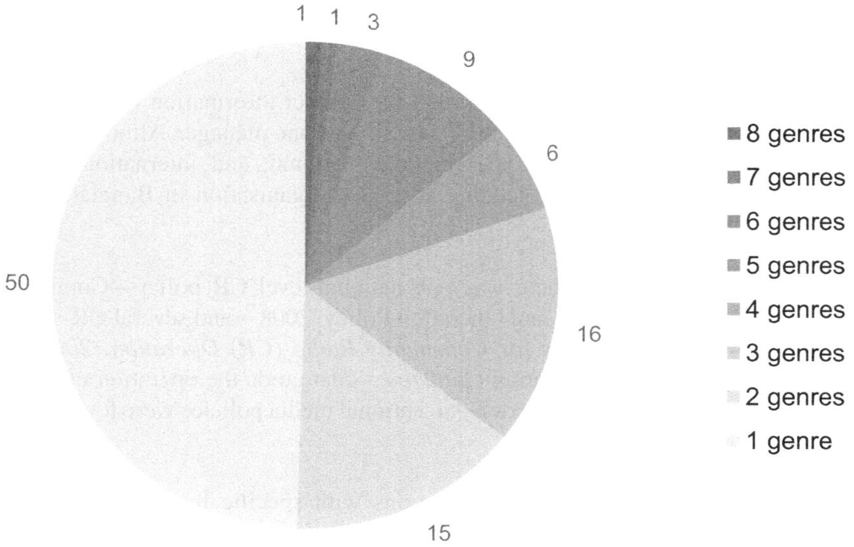

Fig. 5.27 Number of production genres used in programming by CRS in India (*Source*: Author's own illustration)

stations that utilised two formats (popular formats: *drama, live*); and 50 stations that utilised one format (popular format being *other*).

5.3 Bangladesh

Due to the relatively well-documented CR sector by the Bangladesh NGOs Network for Radio and Communication (BNNRC), it was easier for the author to ascertain the population of initiatives in this country. As of December 2017, there were 17 active CRS in Bangladesh, across the eight districts[20] with the first becoming operational in 2010 and the latest in 2016 (BNNRC, 2015; Community Radio in Bangladesh, n.d.).[21]

5.3.1 Bangladesh Country Mapping

General Information Most of the CRS operated in the rural areas of Bangladesh and were established near either coastal locations or inland water bodies. In general, concepts such as empowerment, working for rural people, creating awareness, edu-

[20] Bangladesh's districts are Barisal, Chittagong, Dhaka, Khulna, Mymensingh, Rajshahi, Rangpur, and Sylhet.

[21] See *Appendix 5.1 Lists of active CRS in Nepal, India, and Bangladesh as of December 2017.*

cation, assisting in their development, and combatting social ills were commonly mentioned in relation to CRS.

Management and Networking Through the contact information found for each station, it was deduced that each station has at least one manager. Although no specific networks were stated for the regional, national, and international levels, BNNRC was identified as the leading advocacy organisation in Bangladesh and operated at the national level.

Policies and Guidelines There was one national-level CR policy—Community Radio Installation, Broadcast and Operation Policy, 2008—and several CR-specific guidelines—*Code of Conduct for Community Radio (CR) Operation (2009)* and *Gender Equality and Socialization Guideline*—that guide the operation of CRS in Bangladesh. Due to language barriers, no national media policies were found during the desk review.

Economic Sustainability The only stations with specific financial information were *Radio Bikrampur* and *Radio Jhenuk* whose sources of funding were identified as being from subsidies. Based on the data, it can be deduced that the CRS were dependent on external funds, most of which were generated from donor projects (and sourced through the assistance of BNNRC).

Participation From the information found, it was clear that the CRS were supported by the communities in which they were located. Furthermore, there was some information available about the internal participants associated with several of these CRS. The following table, based on the data from BNNRC's website, reflects this (Table 5.1).

As can be seen, there were varying numbers of staff and volunteers within the 11 identified CRS. Also, data showed that the participants of *Radio Padma* and *Radio Sarabela* (34 individuals stated overall with no distinction between staff and volunteers) were paid either a salary or a stipend. Overall, it was also mentioned that there were 536 youth women and youths involved with CR in Bangladesh as rural broadcasters as of July 1, 2015. However, an article by the *Dhaka Tribune* in February 2016 has this number as 100 and a presentation by Rahman[22] (2015) states that there were 1000 youth women and youth involved in CR (BNNRC, n.d.).

Some other interesting information found about communities in CR in Bangladesh revolved around the "deficit of participation" of Dalits, as there were "inadequate institutional spaces for Dalit engagement in governance" (Rahman,

[22] AHM Bazlur Rahman is a community media activist and policy advocacy individual in Bangladesh with approximately 21 years of experience in this field. He is currently the CEO of BNNRC, an organisation he founded in 2000, which addresses community media development in the country (Rahman, personal interview, December 04, 2017).

Table 5.1 Quantity of staff and volunteers associated with CRS in Bangladesh according to the BNNRC's website in 2017

Station	Staff	Volunteers
Krishi radio	10	60
Radio Bikrampur	4	15
Radio Borendro	Not stated	96
Radio Chilmari	3	Not stated
Radio Jhenuk	Not stated	30
Radio Lokobetar	6	20
Radio Mahananda	10	20
Radio Mukti	12	105
Radio NAF	6	24
Radio Nalta	5	282
Radio Sagar Giri	5	30
Radio Sundarban	6	12

Source: Table based on author's own compilation

2015). As a result, CR is used to foster participation and engagement by ensuring access (Rahman, 2015).

Community *Radio Padma* and *Radio Pollikontho* were the only two CRS to have any explicit indication with regard to audience profiles with the former highlighting children, men, women, youth, and other while the later highlighted children, women, youth, and other specifically. Additionally, there was data regarding listeners for some stations: *Radio Bikrampur* had 800,000 listeners, *Radio Borendro* had 500,000 listeners, *Radio Chilmari* had 500,000 listeners, *Radio Jhenuk* had 200,000–300,000 listeners, *Radio NAF* had 200,000 listeners, *Radio Nalta* had 400,000 listeners, *Radio Pollikontho* had 400,000 listeners, and *Radio Sagar Giri* had 150,000 listeners. Overall, the audience reach was stated to be 4.6 million listeners for the first 14 stations established (Community Radio in Bangladesh, n.d.). Additionally, some stations identified some feedback methods: *Radio Borendro*, *Radio Mukti*, and *Radio Padma* identified the use of SMS; *Radio Sagar Giri* highlighted telephone calls; and *Radio Sundarban* highlighted SMS, telephone calls, and the use of village boxes.

What was interesting about CRS in Bangladesh was the use of listening groups (or clubs) which were formed by communities of interest to regularly listen to specific programmes together and provide feedback when necessary. The stations with data about these groups included: *Krishi Radio* (2 groups), *Radio Borendro* (5 school groups), *Radio Chilmari* (3 children's groups), Radio NAF (7 groups), *Radio Pollikontho* (769 groups), and *Radio Sundarban* (97 groups). A report by Rahman (2013) about the CRS affected by and which had reports about Cyclone Mahasen[23] mentioned that there were approximately 20,000 listeners' clubs with regard to six

[23] Cyclone Mahasen was a natural disaster that affected many communities in Southern Bangladesh in 2013.

stations—*Radio Nalta, Radio Sundarban, Radio Lokobetar, Radio Krishi, Radio NAF,* and *Radio Sagar Giri*—all of which assisted with the dissemination of disaster-related information.

Programming There was some information about the thematic areas and production formats used by CRS via the BNNRC's website. Apart from this, general information supplied by Rahman (n.d.) highlighted that CRS produce magazine programmes on Dalits' issues as well as news about this community via the Community Media News Agency.

Technology and Infrastructure Only a few stated any specific information concerning technology and infrastructure—all of which were indicated as being owned. Those with information included: *Krishi Radio* (recording studio and editing suite), *Radio Jhenuk* (four studios and seven rooms), *Radio Mahananda* (three studios, one transmission room, and one conference room), *Radio Padma* (three fully equipped studios), and *Radio Sagar Giri* (one studio). Apart from this, data revealed that one of the biggest challenges appeared to be stable electricity for some stations since CRS are unable to transmit at times due to power failures. However, according to Rahman (2013), during Cyclone Mahasen the staff, volunteers, and listeners' clubs found alternative power supply through generators to share vital information.

5.3.2 Bangladesh Initiatives' Mapping

5.3.2.1 Establishment Information

Figure 5.28 illustrates the years of establishment for the known 16 stations (94.1% of 17 operational CRS) in Bangladesh. As can be seen, there was the establishment and increase in the number of stations in 2009–2011 with a peak in 2012–2014 and then a decline in 2015–2017.

Radio Lokobetar was the first CRS to test transmission on May 27, 2010; however, *Radio Padma* was the first official licensed station to become operational on

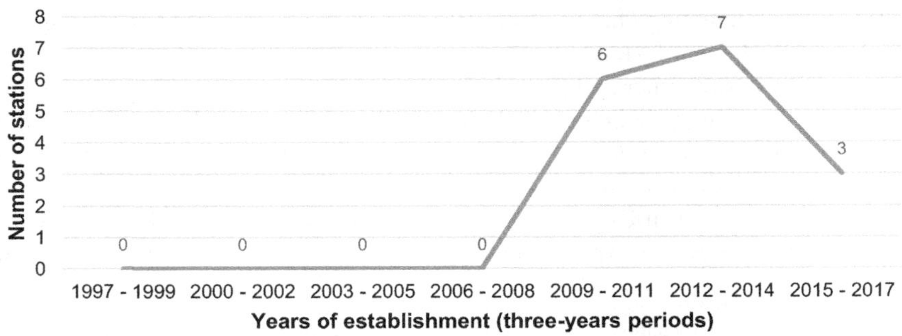

Fig. 5.28 Number of CRS established in Bangladesh over 3-year periods (*Source*: Author's own illustration)

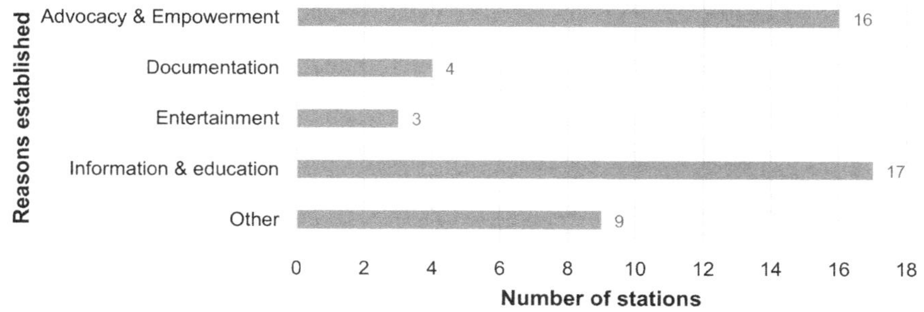

Fig. 5.29 Reasons for establishment of CRS in Bangladesh (*Source*: Author's own illustration)

July 22, 2011. These two were followed by the launch of four other stations in the 2009–2011 period which accounted for the establishment of a total of six stations in Bangladesh. Following this period, seven stations were established in the 2012–2015 period, and three stations were established in the 2017–2019 period.

Of the 17 stations, there was some information available concerning the overall goal, mission, aim, and/or objectives for their establishment. Figure 5.29 illustrates the reasons identified by the 17 CRS.

The main reason for the establishment of these initiatives in Bangladesh was *information and education* which all 17 stations identified. This was followed by 16 stations highlighting *advocacy and empowerment,* 4 stations highlighting *documentation,* and 3 stations highlighting *entertainment.* Additionally, nine stations highlighted *other* reasons for establishment which included disaster preparedness, community alerts, provision of companionship throughout the day, and addressing development-related issues.

Regarding legal ownership, 16 of the 17 stations highlighted that their mother organisations (a common term in Bangladesh used instead of licence holder) were NGOs while one station indicated that a government department held the licence.

With regard to partners, 9 stations (52.9% of 17 stations) had information highlighting 12 unique partners; this information is shown in Fig. 5.30.

Of the 12 identified partners, 8 partners were NGOs which included six development type organisations, one youth organisation, and one advocacy organisation. The one INGO partner was the United Nations Food and Agriculture Organization, while the one educational partner was the National Institute of Mass Communication (NIMCo). Furthermore, one government partner was with the Agriculture Information Service while one consulate partner was with the Embassy of Japan. These partners were further classified based on their scale of operation, as can be seen in Fig. 5.31.

Of the 12 unique partners, 3 partners operated at the local level, 7 at the national level, and the remaining 2 at the international level.

5.3.2.2 Location: Divisions and Environmental Classification

Figure 5.32 categorises the active CRS within each division in Bangladesh.

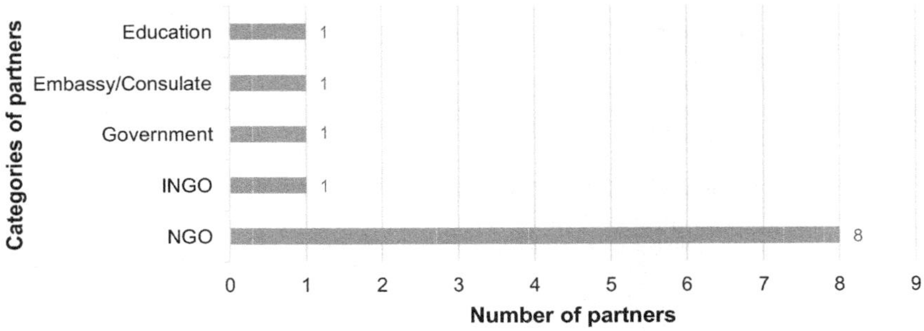

Fig. 5.30 Partners' classifications regarding CRS in Bangladesh (*Source*: Author's own illustration)

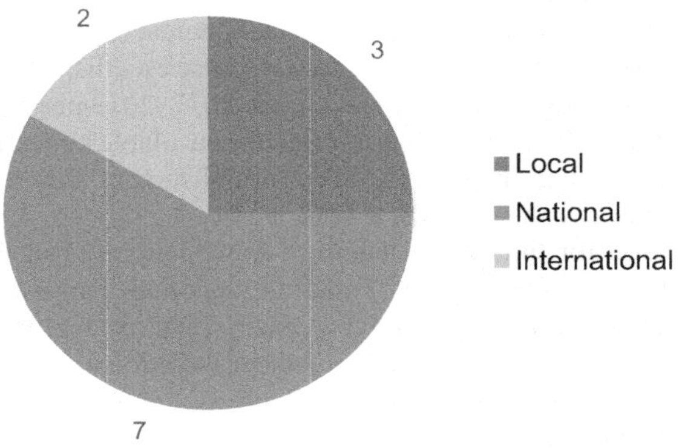

Fig. 5.31 Levels of operation regarding partner of CRS in Bangladesh (*Source*: Author's own illustration)

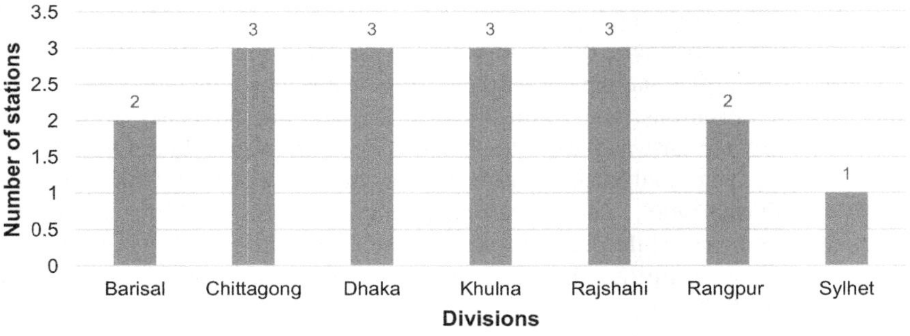

Note: The division of Mymensingh had no operational CRS so it was not included in Figure 5.32.

Fig. 5.32 Location of CRS in Bangladesh with regard to divisions (*Source*: Author's own illustration)

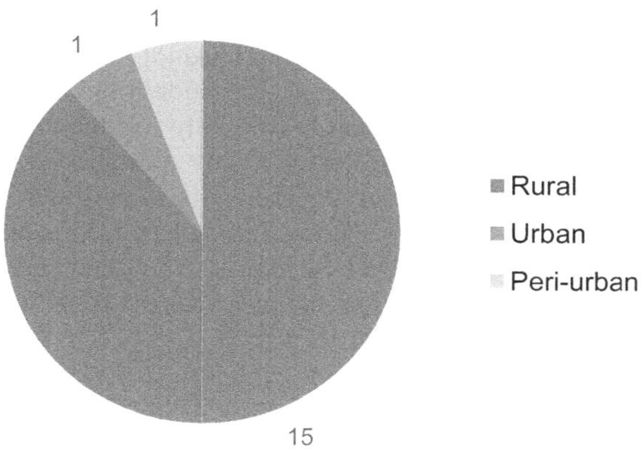

Fig. 5.33 Location of CRS in Nepal according to environmental classification (*Source*: Author's own illustration)

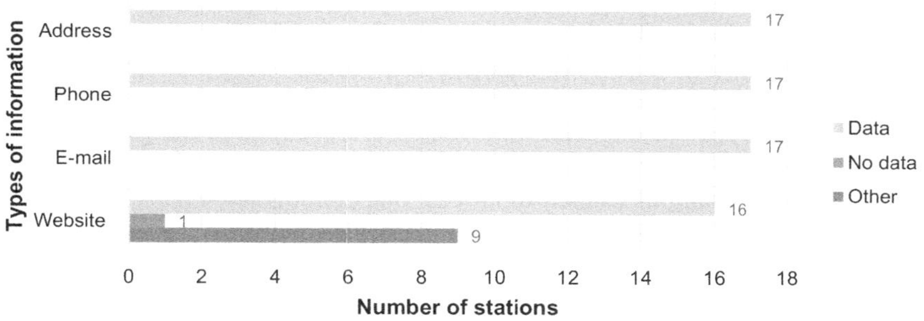

Fig. 5.34 Types of contact information available regarding CRS in Bangladesh (*Source*: Author's own illustration)

As can be seen, the Chittagong, Dhaka, Khulna, and Rajshahi Divisions each had three stations. This was followed by Barisal and Rangpur with two stations each, and Sylhet which had one station.

Furthermore, Fig. 5.33 visually depicts the environmental classification of CRS in Bangladesh.

As can be seen, 15 of 17 stations (88.2%) were in the rural environment which comprised mostly villages and farmlands. Of the remaining two stations, one each (5.9%) was in an urban area and a peri-urban area. Chittagong and Khulna each had three stations in rural areas, while Barisal, Dhaka, Rajshahi, and Rangpur each had two stations, and Sylhet had one station in this area. Dhaka had the only station in a peri-urban location, while Rajshahi had the only station in an urban location.

5.3.2.3 Contact Information

The contact information regarding CRS in Bangladesh was a mixture of both traditional and new media. Figure 5.34 is a visual representation of the types of contact information available for the 17 CRS.

All stations had information about their street address, phone contact, and e-mail contact available while only 16 stations (94.1%) had information relating to online platforms. Of the street addresses uncovered, 15 stations (88.2% of 17 stations) had complete information, while 2 stations (11.8%) only had the district and division information. Regarding the phone information, only six stations (35.3%) had accurate information with regard to format. Regarding the e-mail addresses, all stations had complete information. Finally, regarding the website information, only 7 of 16 stations (43.8%) had personal websites, 2 stations (12.5%) had Facebook pages, and the remaining 7 stations (43.7%) had profile pages via the BNNRC website.

5.3.2.4 Community Profiles

All stations had some information relating to the type of communities being catered to which included *children, men, women, youth, PWD*, and *other*. The *other* dynamic applied when the term "community" was used without any precise profiles being mentioned. Further to this, in Bangladesh reference is made to the third gender as opposed to *LGBTQ* due to the unique culture within the country. Figure 5.35 presents this information.

The most popular identified community was *women* with nine stations catering to them. This group was followed by *men* and *other* communities each with seven stations catering to them. *Youth* were catered to by six stations; *children* by four stations; and *PWD* by one station. While the *third gender* is recognised in Bangladesh, no station had any information regarding programming for this group specifically.

Overall, all 17 stations catered to at least one community; Fig. 5.36 shows the classification of the data about the number of profiles covered.

Of the two stations that catered to five different communities, both catered to *children, men, women*, and *youth*. Within the four stations that catered to four different communities, all stations addressed *children, women*, and *youth*. There was only one station that catered to three communities which included *women, youth*, and *other*. Of the four stations that catered to two types of communities, all had programming specific to *women*. Finally, the remaining six stations catered to *other* types of communities.

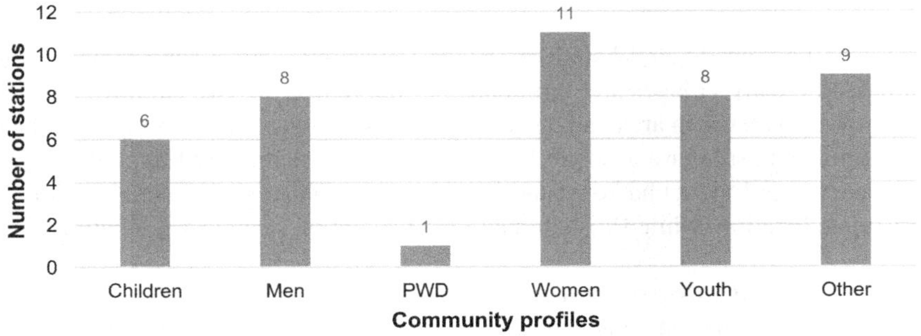

Fig. 5.35 Communities of CRS in Bangladesh (*Source*: Author's own illustration)

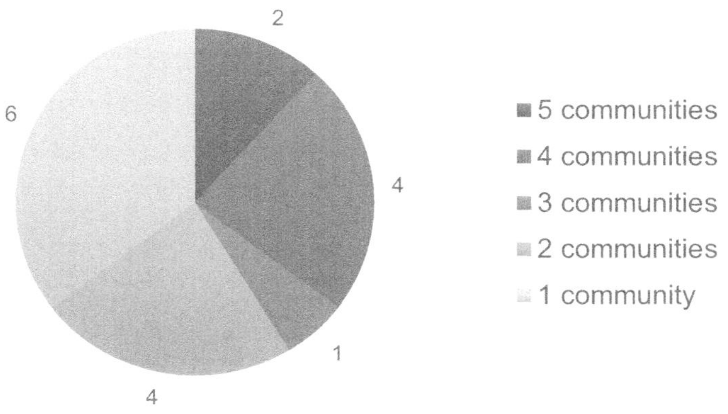

Fig. 5.36 Number of CRS catering to different amounts of communities in Bangladesh (*Source*: Author's own illustration)

5.3.2.5 Thematic Areas for Programming

Of the 17 stations, only 15 (88.2%) had any specific information with regard to the thematic areas covered through programming; this is illustrated in Fig. 5.37.

The most popular identified thematic area was *education* with 10 of the 15 stations producing programmes in this area. This was followed by *culture* being produced by nine stations, *health* by seven stations, and *environmental* topics by five stations. Additional identified thematic areas included agriculture, disaster, economics, edutainment, gender, human rights, ICTs, news, youth and children, and weather. The *other* category was used to encompass content such as disaster alerts, and communities of interest which included Dalits, farmers, labourers, and tribal people.

Programming was also classified based on the number of thematic areas used by CRS when producing content; this is represented in Fig. 5.38.

Of the 15 stations that had identified thematic areas, 3 stations each produced content on four and one thematic areas: the former highlighted *agriculture, education, gender,* and *health* as the most recurring areas, while the latter highlighted *education, culture*, and *other*. Following this, two stations each identified three and two thematic areas for production; the CRS catering to three areas had *gender, health*, and *disaster* as the most recurring themes, while there were no similarities within the stations that covered two thematic areas. Finally, there was one station each producing content which covered five thematic areas (*culture, environmental, gender, health,* and *other*); six thematic areas (*culture, disaster, economics, education, health,* and *ICTs*); seven thematic areas (*culture, economics, education, environmental, gender, health,* and *other*); eight thematic areas (*agriculture, culture, education, entertainment, health, other, weather,* and *youth and children*); and nine thematic areas (*agriculture, culture, economics, education, entertainment, environmental, health, human rights,* and *other*).

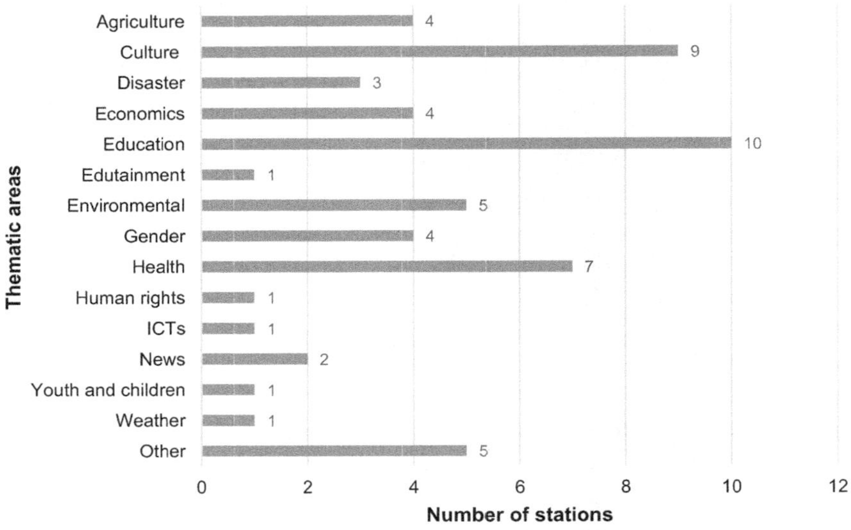

Fig. 5.37 Thematic areas for programming in CRS in Bangladesh (*Source*: Author's own illustration)

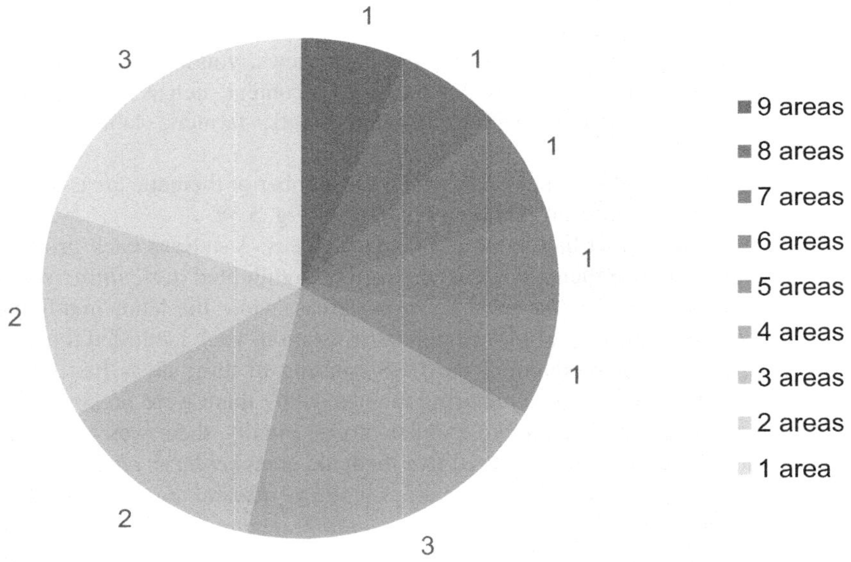

Fig. 5.38 Number of CRS catering to different amounts of thematic areas in Bangladesh (*Source*: Author's own illustration)

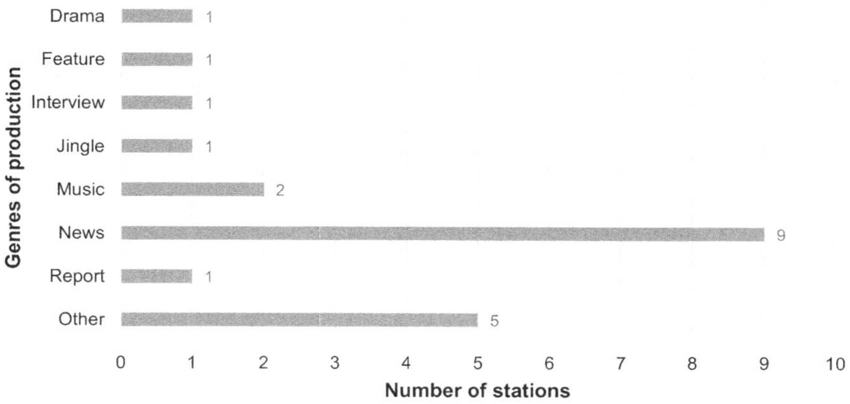

Fig. 5.39 Production genres used by CRS in Bangladesh (*Source*: Author's own illustration)

5.3.2.6 Production Genres

Out of 17 stations, there was information relating to production genres for ten CRS (58.8%); Fig. 5.39 presents this information.

Out of the ten stations, the most popular identified production format was *news* which was utilised by nine stations. This was followed by *music* which was used by two stations, and one station each identified *drama*, *feature*, *interview*, and *report* formats. For the *other* category, which was identified by five stations, only one station identified *jingles* as an alternative production format; the remaining stations mentioned production formats in general but did not explicitly identify any type being used.

Apart from this, the production genres were further classified based on how many stations utilised different production genres, as can be seen in Fig. 5.40.

Out of the ten stations, four stations mentioned utilising three formats while three stations identified two formats; the most recurring genres were *news* and *other*. Finally, three stations identified one format being utilised—all of which highlighted *news*.

5.4 Summary

Based on secondary data, there were 519 operational CRS in total in Nepal, India, and Bangladesh as of December 2017. The first country to enter the community media sector was Nepal with the launch of *Radio Sagarmatha* in 1997, followed by India in 2002 with the launch of *Anna Community Radio*, and Bangladesh in 2011 with the launch of *Radio Padma*. Of these 519 stations, Nepal had the most initiatives with 309 stations which accounted for over half (59.5% of 519 CRS) of the

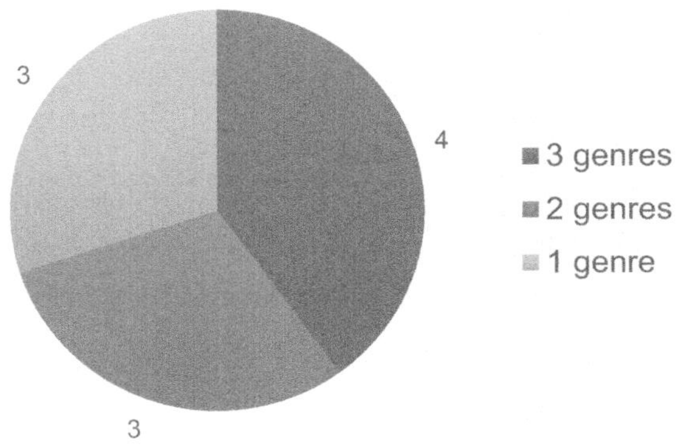

Fig. 5.40 Number of production genres used in programming by CRS in Bangladesh (*Source*: Author's own illustration)

active CRS; India had the next highest number with 193 stations (37.2%); and Bangladesh had the least amount with 17 stations (3.3%). There were 410 stations (79.0% of 519 CRS) with information about their dates of establishment. Of the 410 stations, the 2009–2011 period had the greatest number of CRS being launched with 126 stations (30.7% of 410 stations). Overall, there was a gradual increase in stations from 1997 to 2009, and from 2012 onwards, there was a noticeable decline across the three countries.

Regarding reasons for the establishment, data regarding 185 stations (35.6% of 519 CRS) were available for analysis. The most recurring reason was *information and education* purposes which 74 stations (40.0%) highlighted. This was followed by 59 stations (31.9%) highlighting *advocacy and empowerment*, 9 stations (4.9%) highlighting *documentation*, and 7 stations (3.8%) highlighting *entertainment*. Apart from these reasons, 48 stations (25.9%) stated *other* reasons ranging from development and persuasion to access to technology and communication. It must be noted that while some stations alluded to one main reason, others highlighted two or three reasons for establishment.

Of the 519 stations, only 215 stations (41.4% of 519 CRS) had any information about the licence holder. Overall, educational institutions had the licences to 116 stations (54.0% of 215 stations), NGOs had the licences for 85 stations (39.5%), agricultural institutions had the licences for 9 stations (4.2%), and CBOs had the licences for 2 stations (0.9%). Government, research, and religious organisations each had one licence (0.5% each).

Overall, there were 203 unique partners mentioned in the categories of business, CBOs, educational institutions, embassies or consulates, government offices and entities, INGOs, media, NGOs, religious organisations, and trusts or foundations. Educational institutions accounted for the highest number with 61 partners (30.0% of 203), followed by NGOs with 51 partnerships (25.1%), and government-related entities with 34 partnerships (16.7%). In Nepal and Bangladesh, the largest number of partners were NGOs, while in India educational institutions accounted for the largest number.

Regarding location, 273 initiatives (52.6% of 519 CRS) were in rural areas, followed by 139 initiatives (26.8%) in urban areas and 96 initiatives (18.5%) in peri-urban areas; there were 11 initiatives (2.1%) with unknown locations—7 from Nepal and 4 from India. Nepal and Bangladesh had most of their stations, 209 stations and 15 stations, respectively, in rural areas while India had the majority, 99 stations, in urban areas.

Regarding contact information, all stations had some sort of contact information whether in the form of a street address, phone number, e-mail address, or a virtual platform (website or Facebook page). Of the 519 stations, 517 stations (99.6%) had a street address; 512 stations (98.7%) had at least one e-mail address; 464 stations (89.4%) had a telephone number; and 402 stations (77.5%) had the address of a virtual platform.

There were 311 stations (59.9% of 519 CRS) with some information regarding the various communities involved with the initiatives. Of this, the most popular community was *women* which was mentioned in association with 229 stations (73.6% of 311 stations). The next most popular group was *men* which was mentioned with regard to 146 stations (46.9%), followed by *children* being mentioned by 135 stations (43.4%) and *youth* by 134 stations (43.1%). There were six stations (1.9%) that catered to *PWD* and five stations (1.6%) that catered to the *LGBTQ* community. Apart from the identified groups, 142 stations (45.7%) also catered to *other* communities and highlighted communities of interest such as artists, farmers, fisherfolks, senior citizens, tribal groups, and weavers.

With regard to thematic areas addressed in programming, 271 stations (52.2% of 519 CRS) had data available. The most popular thematic area for content production was *culture* which was addressed in 206 stations (76.0% of 271 stations). This was followed by *education* in 179 stations (66.1%) and *health* in 163 stations (60.1%). Additional identified thematic areas included agriculture, gender, environment, entertainment, youth and children, economics, human rights, career, disaster, edutainment, religion, weather, PWD, nationalism, ICTs, sports, news, tourism, and LGBTQ. Apart from these areas, *other* thematic areas were also addressed in 219 stations (80.8%) and included themes such as government and governance.

Finally, with regard to production genres used in programming, 263 stations (50.7% of 519 CRS) had information available. The most popular identified formats were *news* that was produced in 93 stations (35.4% of 263 stations), followed by *drama* in 62 stations (23.6%) and *interview* in 55 stations (20.9%). Additional identified production formats were documentary, debate, feature, jingle, live, magazine, music, PSA, report, and talk-show. Furthermore, the *other* categorisation was used with regard to 181 stations (68.8%) and comprised phone-ins/phone-outs, discussions, outdoor broadcasts (live), and vox populi, to mention the more popular formats.

Overall, CR in Nepal, India, and Bangladesh appeared to be vibrant and diverse across all three countries concerning thematic areas, programming, and community. While the information for Bangladesh was easier to source, due to the centralisation by the BNNRC, the information for the Indian initiatives was better organised in relation to the developed framework for analysis regarding this thesis. However, Nepal, seen as the most vibrant sector, had a paucity of information with regard to the various initiatives.

Even though there were challenges with sourcing secondary data, since most of these CRS operate at the grassroots level and are not concerned with broadcasting, the author was able to access sufficient information to create a foundation on which to build a physical database and create instruments for data collection. Though not perfect, through the use of Google Translate and Google Maps, the author was also able to better understand the data uncovered. Overall, the secondary data in the *South Asian Community Media Database (CMD) V.01* was adequate to work with and formed a solid foundation for primary data gathering.

References

ACORAB. (n.d.) *Members*. Retrieved November 30, 2017, from https://www.acorab.org.np/index.php?pagename=member&page=1

Basu, A. (n.d.). *Mass media laws*. Legal Service India—Lawyers. Retrieved November 30, 2019, from http://www.legalserviceindia.com/articles/media.htm

BNNRC. (2015). *Community Radio Station—Gender guidelines*. BNNRC.

BNNRC. (n.d.). *Community radio in Bangladesh*. Retrieved January 30, 2017, from http://www.bnnrc.net/

Community Radio for Good Governance [Compendium]. (2015). OneWorld Foundation.

Community Radio in India, Towards Diversity & Sustainability [Compendium]. (2016). OneWorld Foundation.

Community Radio Installation, Broadcast and Operation Policy 2008. (2008). Ministry of Information, People's Republic of Bangladesh.

CRFC. (n.d.). *List of CR station*. Retrieved April 30, 2016, from http://crfc.in/list-of-cr-station/

FM radio frequencies licenced in Nepal. (n.d.). *Nepal Radio*. Retrieved September 30, 2017, from http://www.nepalradio.org/p2_mhz_status.htm

History of mass media in India. (n.d.). *NIMC*. Retrieved December 30, 2017, from http://www.nimc-india.com/history-mass-media-india.php

List of Community and Commercial Radio Stations in Nepal. (n.d.). *Tech Sansar*. Retrieved September 30, 2017, from https://techsansar.com/ict/radios-in-nepal/

List of Operational Community Radio Stations in India as on 31-05-2019. (2019, May 31). *Ministry of Information and Broadcasting, India*. Retrieved October 30, 2019, from https://mib.gov.in/sites/default/files/List%20of%20251%20Operational%20CRS%20in%20India%20as%20on%2031-05-2019%28new%29.pdf

Media of Nepal. (n.d.). *Wikipedia*. Retrieved September 30, 2017, from https://en.wikipedia.org/wiki/Media_of_Nepal

Name List of All FM Radio Stations in Nepal. (n.d.). *I Am Nepal*. Retrieved September 30, 2017, from http://www.imnepal.com/list-radio-fm-stations-nepal/

Pavarala, V., Malik, K. K., Belavadi, V., Deshbandhu, A., & Raghunath, P. (2014). *Community radio continuous improvement toolkit: Version 2.0*. Commonwealth Educational Media Centre for Asia (CEMCA).

Policy Guidelines for setting up Community Radio Stations in India. (n.d.). *Ministry of Information and Broadcasting, India*. Retrieved September 30, 2017, from https://mib.gov.in/sites/default/files/c1_0.pdf

Radio Stations in Nepal. (n.d.). *Asia waves*. Retrieved September 30, 2017, from https://www.asiawaves.net/nepal-radio.htm

Rahman, B. (n.d.). *The Dalit voice in community radio—Experience, challenge and strategies in South Asia*. BNNRC.

Rahman, B. (2013, September 24). Community Radios in Coastal Bangladesh in addressing Cyclone Mahasen. *Social Good Summit*. Dhaka, Bangladesh.

Rahman, B. (2015, December 06–15). Community Radio: An Effective Mechanism for Community Education [PowerPoint presentation]. *Sub-Regional Workshop on Organizing and Managing Literate Environment*. Dhaka, Bangladesh.

Rampersaud, T. (2019). *Community Media Directory*. SANCOM. Retrieved July 30, 2019, from http://cmd.sancomonline.net/

6 Media Policy Environment

6.1 Nepal

In Nepal, the various constitutions adopted throughout the country's turbulent past guaranteed freedom of expression as a basic human right; however, in practice, this right was curtailed until the latest version of the constitution (Savada, 1991). Before this, at the start of the 1900s, there were 2048 constitutional provisions governing the operation of the press which resulted in very rigid controls by the government (Savada, 1991). With the establishment of private publications in the early 1980s, there were vocal protests from journalists against censorship from the government. Following the democratic revolution in the 1990s, some of the strict media controls were reduced and the right to distribute information was addressed in the *Constitution of the Kingdom of Nepal 1990*, the *Interim Constitution of Nepal* (2005), and *The Constitution of Nepal 2015*. Notably, "as politics have stabilised, pressure on journalists decreased" (*Nepal Profile*, n.d.) which has resulted in Nepal being categorised as "partially free" regarding freedom of expression and the media (*Nepal Profile,* n.d.). Apart from the constitution, there are several media policies (with subsequent acts, rules, and regulations) and codes of practice that provide legal and ethical frameworks for the operation of CR in Nepal, in lieu of a CR policy (*Nepal—Basic Data,* n.d.; *Nepal country profile,* n.d.; Savada, 1991).

Figure 6.1 visually represents the structure of the policy environment in Nepal as visualised by the author and includes the different constituents explained in this section.

6.1.1 Constitutional Provisions

The Constitution of Nepal 2015 ("2015 Constitution" for short) is the current governing document that guarantees freedom of the press, opinion, and expression. The Preamble establishes that the people of Nepal are committed to democratic norms

T. Rampersaud-Skorka, *Community Radio in South Asia*, Diversity and Inclusion Research, https://doi.org/10.1007/978-3-031-85201-5_6

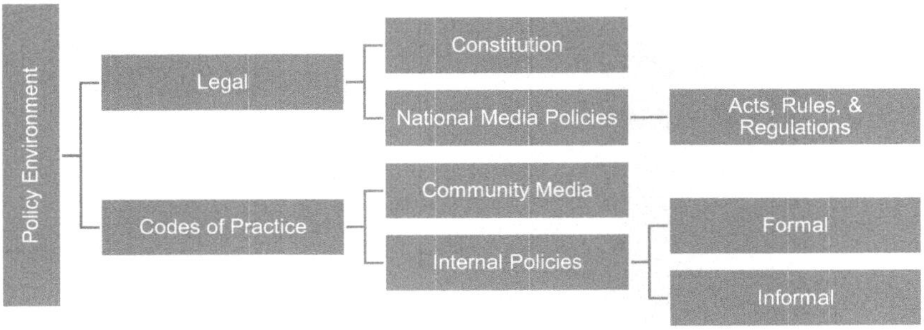

Fig. 6.1 Structure of Nepal's policy environment (*Source*: Author's own illustration)

and values to which freedom of the press applies (*The Constitution of Nepal [English translation] 2015,* 2015, pp. 1–2). However, while these freedoms are guaranteed by the 2015 Constitution, it is with the understanding that these can be suspended if there is a breach of national interest and security.

Specifically, "Article 17—Right to freedom," "Article 19—Right to communicate," and "Article 27—Right to information" relate directly to media. While Article 27 reaffirms the right to information by every citizen "on any matter of his or her interest or of public interest" (p. 19) with the provision that confidential matters shall be treated according to law, Articles 17 and 19 are more expansive. Article 17(1) states that "no person shall be deprived of his or her liberty in accordance with law" (*The Constitution of Nepal [English translation] 2015,* 2015, p. 9), while 17(2)(a) specifically highlights that every citizen has the freedom of opinion and expression (in addition to other freedoms). These clauses guarantee that individuals can express their opinions, however, within specific provisions. Article 17 specifically identifies restrictions regarding any act that undermines national interest or discrimination against different groups of people. Article 19(1) specifically highlights that media will not be censored if they do not share content that negatively affects national interest or discriminate against any groups within Nepali society (the same conditions applied to Article 17). Article 19(2) continues by highlighting that there will be no closure, seizure, or cancellation of registration for any media entity with the understanding that the media will not attempt to prevent any type of Act that will regulate "radio, television, online or any other form of digital or electronic equipment, press or other means of communication" (*The Constitution of Nepal [English translation] 2015,* 2015, pp. 13–14). Finally, Article 19(3) highlights that "no means of communication including the press, electronic broadcasting and telephone shall be interrupted except in accordance with law" (*The Constitution of Nepal [English translation] 2015,* 2015, p. 14)—that is, media entities can enjoy these freedoms as they operate within the defined parameters.

Although not as prominent as those discussed above, Article 51(b; 5), highlights that the State shall ensure there are policies "to make necessary provisions to make mass media fair, healthy, impartial, decent, responsible and professional" (*The Constitution of Nepal [English translation] 2015*, 2015, p. 30)—a clause that places the state as the watchdog for media, a moral compass that ensures media operate "properly." Although this is problematic, this clause also explicitly places the responsibility of enabling media policies in the hands of the government.

6.1.1.1 Social and Cultural Transformation and Development of Nepali Society

In addition to these specific media and communication clauses, the 2015 Constitution also addresses the need to ensure harmony and quality of life via Article 50(1) (*The Constitution of Nepal [English translation] 2015*, 2015, p. 27). Article 50(2) continues by highlighting protection from all forms of discrimination and injustice in the interest of developing social and cultural values for "national unity by maintaining social cohesion, solidarity and harmony while recognising cultural diversity" (*The Constitution of Nepal [English translation] 2015*, 2015, pp. 27–28). Article 51(c) addresses community development, specifically in clauses 3, 5, and 6 which highlight that policies should be developed to ensure the participation of the local communities, that there should be an end to discrimination, and that local cultures and artefacts should be protected (*The Constitution of Nepal [English translation] 2015*, 2015, pp. 30–31). While these are not media focused, they can be applied to the operation of media entities, particularly community radio (CR), since these specific clauses guarantee policies will focus on the importance of participation and inclusion of community members in processes of development—foundational elements of CR.

6.1.2 National Media Policy

As of May 2019, the Ministry of Communications and Information Technology's website had a total of 42 policies, acts, and regulations that govern the set-up and operation of print publications, broadcast media (radio and television), new media (internet), telecommunication service providers, and the production of movies in the country (*Laws and Rules*, n.d.; *Policy*, n.d.). Those relating to media, specifically CR, included the *National Communication Policy 1992 (2049 BS*[1]*)*, *National Broadcasting Act 1993 (2050 BS)*, *National Broadcasting Rules 1995 (2052 BS)*, *Working Journalists Act 1995 (2051 BS)*, and *Long-term Policy of Information and Communication 2002 (2059 BS)*.

While all these policies and their subsequent acts, rules, and regulations will not be addressed in detail, it was important to identify them since they provided a foundation for the 2016 policy. After years of planning and addressing problems with the

[1] BS (Bikram Sambat) is the unit of measurement for the date in Nepal which is 56 years and 8 months ahead of the Gregorian Calendar—represented by AD (*History of Bikram Sambat Nepali Calendar*, 2010). For this chapter, the date will be in AD format; however, where important, the BS equivalent will be stated also.

previous legislature, the *National Mass Communications Policy 2016* was introduced (Manali, in-depth interview, April 26, 2018); this policy is explained in detail below.

6.1.2.1 National Mass Communications Policy 2016 (2073 BS)

Learning from previous criticisms, there was more consultation and involvement of stakeholders and in-depth research conducted to ensure the *National Mass Communications Policy 2016* ("2016 Policy" for short) did not receive the same criticisms as its predecessor. As a result, it was crafted to support the values and norms of *The Constitution of Nepal 2015;* as Dahal and Sigdel (2016)[2] put it:

> The 2016 Policy has been formulated to develop a fair, dignified, responsible and accountable mass communication sector where they are accountable, responsible, independent, and fair. Media should work towards a society based on proportional inclusion and participation; for the protection of freedom and communication media; equitable development of all kinds of mass communication media with big, medium and small investment; and, access to information to all. (Dahal & Sigdel, 2016, p. 1)

According to Dahal and Sigdel (2016, p. 2), four of the nine objectives of this policy can be linked to political philosophies and address "political change, creation of a democratic society, promotion of governance, and creation of an equitable society based on principles of proportionality, inclusion and participation." They further stated that these four objectives address ideas about standardisation, regulation, and finances of mass media which specifically highlight reliable journalism, sustainability, self-regulation and self-assessment, and developing communication systems with information and communication technologies (ICTs) (Dahal & Sigdel, 2016, p. 2). There were also some objectives that addressed "enhancing access of all class, region, caste, language, gender and community to mass communication media as per the national policy of inclusion" and encouraging an active society, "thereby increasing representation of women, Dalit, indigenous nationalities, people with disability, Madhesi, marginalised community and backward region, class and community in mass community sector" (Dahal & Sigdel, 2016, p. 2). Based on the authors' analysis, this policy highlights the need for self-regulation and self-assessment as it encourages participation in media entities by the community.

It is important to note that the 2016 Policy specifically addresses freedom as it highlights "unrestricted exercise of freedom of the press and expression in line with established international value, norm and standards of freedom of opinion, expression and information flow as well as the principles enshrined in the Constitution of Nepal" (Dahal & Sigdel, 2016, p. 3). Additionally, the policy acknowledges three categories of sectoral broadcasting: public service broadcaster, private and commercial broadcasters, and community broadcasters. Further, as mentioned by Dahal and Sigdel (2016), "editorial independence" and "self-regulation" are explicitly

[2] The author relies on Dahal and Sigdel (2016) for information about the 2016 Policy since the original is in Nepali, and at the time of writing this thesis, their analysis was the only one in English to be found.

addressed as well as "media monopoly" and "media concentration." By highlighting these challenges that media face and making provisions for them, in addition to being specific about the freedom of the press as well as acknowledging community broadcasters, the policy provides a more fertile environment for CR in Nepal (Acharya, 2013; Dahal, n.d.; Dahal & Sigdel, 2016.)

6.1.3 National Codes

The *Community Radio Organisation Development Guidebook* by Mainali et al. (2004) was written specifically to guide community radio stations (CRS) through set-up and operations and to ensure their sustainability. Prepared using *Radio Sagarmatha* as a case, this text outlines specific codes that CRS can choose to implement within the existing policy environment regarding four sections: (1) organisational, (2) broadcasting, (3) financial, and (4) technical; these codes are highlighted in Table 6.1.

As can be seen in Table 6.1, the various codes address specific aspects of CR operation, albeit from a somewhat management perspective. However, as Mainali et al. (2004) highlight, the plans, policies, and procedures are an attempt for CRS to have clearer "long-term vision, mission, goal, objectives, and programs." By implementing these codes, CRS operate "with a focus on good governance to ensure transparency [since] only those organisations can survive which function under defined systems because they have vision, mission, policies, procedures, plans and programs" to guide them (Mainali et al. 2004, "Few Words" section). However, it is

Table 6.1 Ethical codes for CRS operation in Nepal as suggested by Mainali et al. (2004) in *Community Radio Organisation Development Guidebook*

Categories	Codes (plans, policies, procedures)
Organisational	i. Human resource plan of community radio ii. Documentation and knowledge management policy iii. Collaboration policy iv. Resource mobilisation policy and procedures v. Public consultation and maintenance of transparency policy and procedures vi. Human resource management policy and procedures vii. Volunteer mobilisation policy viii. Policy about trainees/interns ix. Dealing with competition plan x. Station management systems and procedures
Broadcasting	xi. Policy governing informative and educative programme
Financial	xii. General accounting principles and guidelines xiii. Accounting policies
Technical	xiv. Operational plan xv. Maintenance plan and procedure xvi. Technology upgrading plan

Source: Table based on author's own compilation
Note: Each of these codes is briefly described in *Appendix 6.1. Guidelines for CRS Operation in Nepal*

important to note that they are just that—codes and not enforceable by law; stations can choose to utilise them as they are, with slight alterations, or not at all.

6.2 India

One of the most famous quotes about freedom of the press in India was by Jawaharlal Nehru, the country's first Prime Minister, who stated, "I would rather have a completely free press with all the dangers involved in the wrong use of that freedom than a suppressed or regulated press" (Nehru cited in *India,* n.d.). Regardless of this idealistic view, freedom of the press and other media is not absolute as there are notable restrictions. International organisations have highlighted that while "privately-owned media are vigorous and diverse, authorities in India have used security, defamation, and hate speech to curb critical voices" (*India profile—Media,* n.d.). Furthermore, the safety of journalists and censorship of the press on sensitive issues, such as those in the state of Jammu and Kashmir, are existing challenges (*India profile—Media,* n.d.).

The media in India are guided by various policies at the macro level that regulate their operation. Figure 6.2 represents the structure of this policy environment as visualised by the author with explanations of the different constituents following.

6.2.1 Constitutional Provisions

The Constitution of India ("1949 Constitution" for short)—which was adopted in 1949—is the current macro-level legal document which supports the fundamental rights linked to media practices by citizens. Specifically, the preamble section states that there is security for all citizens regarding "liberty of thought, expression, belief, faith, and worship" as well as "equality of status and opportunity" (*The Constitution of India [English translation],* 2019, p. 22). Expanding on this ideal, Article 19 (1;

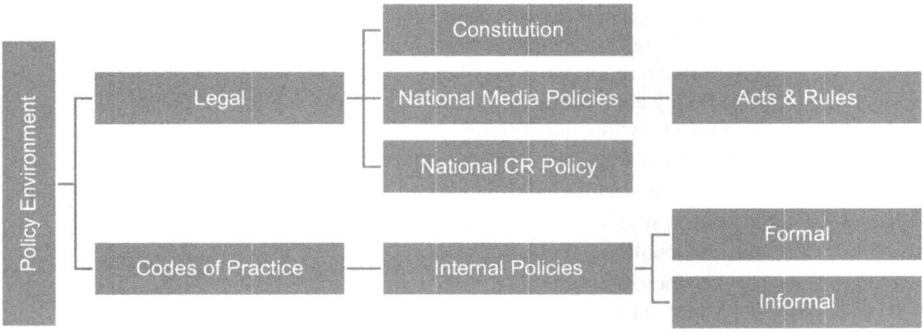

Fig. 6.2 Structure of India's policy environment (*Source*: Author's own illustration)

a) specifically states that "all citizens shall have the right to freedom of speech and expression" (*The Constitution of India [English translation]*, 2019, p. 27). However, this freedom is restricted regarding acts that negatively affect: the sovereignty, integrity, and security of the country; relationships with foreign states; public order, decency or morality; and general legalities such as contempt of court, defamation, or incitement to an offence (*The Constitution of India [English translation]*, 2019, p. 27).

As can be seen, freedom of speech and expression are constitutionally guaranteed; however, there are some conditional clauses. Furthermore, while the 1949 Constitution does not explicitly address media freedoms, this is implied through Article 19(a). Overall, several acts and rules have been passed into law about the media industry in India; those relating to CR are discussed below.

6.2.2 National Media Policies

According to Adukia (n.d., pp. 16–19, 41–42), there are over 80 different policies, acts, and rules relevant to the media sector in India which comprise print, television, film, music, radio, new media, and animation and visual effects. These laws, many of which have been in existence since pre-independent India, regulate the operation of media initiatives in the country. Some of the more pertinent laws, cited by Adukia (n.d., pp. 16–19, 41–42) in relation to broadcast media, include the *Right to Information Act, 2005*; *Right to Information Rules, 2005*; *Copyright Act, 1957*; *Copyright Rules, 1958*; *International Copyright Order, 1999*; *Electronic Media Advertisement Policy*; and *Protection of Identity of Children in Need of Care and Protection and Juveniles in Conflict with Law*. As can be seen, there are regulations which govern various areas that fall within media operation including the right to information, copyrights, advertisements, and the safety of children and juveniles.

Apart from these general regulations for the operations of media in India, Adukia (n.d., pp. 71–72) highlights that the *Indian Telegraph Act, 1885*, and the *Indian Wireless Telegraphy Act, 1933*, are key to the licensing and operation of radio stations in India. Furthermore, the author shares that the 1885 Act gives the government control over the licensing of initiatives while granting the Central Government the authority to take possession of any initiative "in cases involving public emergencies or public safety" (p. 71)—a broad generalisation that can be linked to the restrictions placed on freedom of speech and expression in Article 19(2). Adukia (n.d.) goes on to explain that this act also gives the government power to revoke licences for violation of any of the terms and conditions. Also, the 1933 Act regulates the licensing process and works in conjunction with the 1885 Act to ensure initiatives operate within approved rules and regulations.

Apart from these national policies for broadcast media, India has a CR-specific policy that is used to regulate the sector; this policy is discussed below.

6.2.3 National CR Policy

The *Policy Guidelines for Setting up Community Radio Stations in India* (n.d.) ("2006 Policy" for short) is the key document that governs the CR sector in India and is the second of its kind. The 2006 Policy builds on the 2002 Policy by opening up licensed ownership from *only* educational institutions to include non-profit agencies, such as civil society and voluntary organisations, that can prove service to the local community; agricultural institutes such as the State Agricultural Universities (SAUs), Indian Council of Agricultural Research (ICAR) institutions, and Krishi Vigyan Kendras; and societies, autonomous bodies, and public trusts registered under the *Societies Act* or any other relevant act (*Policy Guidelines for Setting up Community Radio Stations in India*, n.d., pp. 1–2). It should be noted that the 2006 Policy stipulates that these organisations should be registered for a minimum of 3 years before applying for CRS licences.

Regarding the specifics, the *Policy Guidelines for Setting up Community Radio Stations in India* (n.d.) includes nine main sections that govern the set-up and operation of CRS in India. These are as follows:

i. *Basic Principles* addresses the ideals that organisations desirous of setting up CRS must satisfy to be granted a licence. These broadly include a non-profit agenda focused on broadcasting educational, developmental, social, and cultural content that addresses the needs of a specific or well-defined community. Furthermore, the ownership and management structure should be reflective of the community and the organisation must be legally registered in India (p. 1.)
ii. *Eligibility Criteria* mentions the types of organisations allowed to apply for CRS licences. The 2006 Policy also clearly states that individuals, political parties and their affiliate organisations, entities with a profit motive, and organisations expressly banned by the union and state governments are not allowed to apply for CRS licences (p. 2.)
iii. *Selection Process & Processing of the Applications* highlights the entire procedure for application for a CRS licence under eight succinct points ranging from the details surrounding the commencement of applications and processing fee to a schedule for obtaining clearances and information on how the relevant departments scrutinise these submissions before a licence is granted. Two noteworthy points were: within one month of being issued a Letter of Intent, the applicants need to apply to the Wireless Planning and Coordination Wing for frequency allocation; and upon receipt of the Wireless Operating Licence, the permit holder needs to set up the CRS within three months and communicate a date of commissioning to the Ministry (pp. 2–3.)
iv. *Grant of Permission Agreement Conditions* addresses regulations permission holders have to follow to ensure the licence is not revoked. Some key points under this section include a non-transferrable 5-year licence; payment of the spectrum usage fee; cancellation of permission if the station is not operational within three months of receiving a licence or is closed for a period of more than three months; and only one licence per permission holder (p. 4).

v. *Content Regulation and Monitoring* specifies acceptable programmes for broadcast which include those that focus on development, agriculture, health, education, environment, social issues, community development, and culture—all of which should reflect the community's interest in the various CRS. Furthermore, there should be a minimum of 50% community participation; promotion of local language broadcasts; retention of broadcasts for three months; restrictions on news, current affairs, and other political content; and general constraints on content that could potentially cause societal unrest or disharmony and are discriminatory in nature (p. 5).

vi. *Imposition of Penalty/Revocation of Permission Agreement* highlights the penalties for violating any of the conditions outlined in the policy which range from temporary suspension of operation for one month for the first violation and up to three months for the second violation depending on the gravity of the situation, and revocation of permission completely for any subsequent violations. If the latter occurs, then the permit holder cannot apply for any other licence for a period of 5 years (pp. 6–7).

vii. *Transmitter Power and Range* specifies that CRS are licensed to cover a range of 5–10 km with the use of a transmitter that has a maximum of 100 W (watts). However, the transmitter power can be extended to 250 W if there is proof that the CRS needs to serve a larger area (pp. 7–8).

viii. *Funding and Sustenance* highlights the sources of funding CRS can have which include multilateral aid agencies, foreign agencies with necessary clearances, and government-sponsored content. Advertisements and announcements must be related to local events and be paid for by local organisations; also for every hour of broadcast, only five minutes of advertisements and announcements are allowed. This section further states that any revenue generated from these sources is to be used to cover operational expenses and capital expenditures; if there are excesses, then these can only be reinvested into the stations' activities through written permission from the MIB (p. 8).

ix. *Other Terms and Conditions* highlights miscellaneous points regarding the operation of CRS in India. Some of the more significant points include the need to ensure service to the community is the utmost priority, the permit holder will operate within the specified guidelines and provide information to the government upon request, and the involvement of any foreign person in the set-up, maintenance, and operation of the CRS needs prior clearance from the government (pp. 8–10).

As can be seen, while the 2006 Policy provides enabling elements for CR operation in India, it also has restrictive elements. The *Recommendations of the National Consultation on "Strengthening Community Radio"* (UNESCO Chair on Community Media, 2017, pp. 6–7) addresses these restrictions as it provides a detailed list of items that need to be redressed for a more enabling policy environment. Specifically, with regard to licensing, organisations not affiliated with any political parties or any government department with a dedication towards community service should be allowed to apply, even if they have been registered for less than three years. The argument can be made that regardless of the time registered, an organisation with the community's interest at heart will be focused on serving that community—which is the overall goal. Another key point highlighted in this document is the need to allow stronger transmitters, especially in mountainous regions, to ensure initiatives can reach their communities. Furthermore, regarding content, the document highlights that there is a need for the ban on news and current affairs programmes to be lifted, especially since it is the norm for international CRS to broadcast such content. In addition to these points relating to *licensing* and *content*, the document also highlights several recommendations that could potentially strengthen CRS operation in relation to *funding and monitoring* and *spectrum and technology*. These recommendations, which represent ideas from a variety of stakeholders, were made in the interest of ensuring that current initiatives are sustainable and that CRS, in the future, can operate within a more enabling policy environment.

6.3 Bangladesh

The policy environment in Bangladesh can be described as relatively free comprising media from the public, private, and community sectors. It is well developed and does not face any challenges once initiatives operate within the directives of the various official policies and codes of conduct (*Bangladesh profile—Media,* n.d.).

Figure 6.3 visually presents the structure of the policy environment in Bangladesh as visualised by the author with explanations of the different constituents following.

6.3.1 Constitutional Provisions

The *Constitution of the People's Republic of Bangladesh* ("1972 Constitution" for short), which was formally adopted on November 4, 1972, explicitly guarantees "fundamental human rights and freedom, equality and justice" (*Constitution of the*

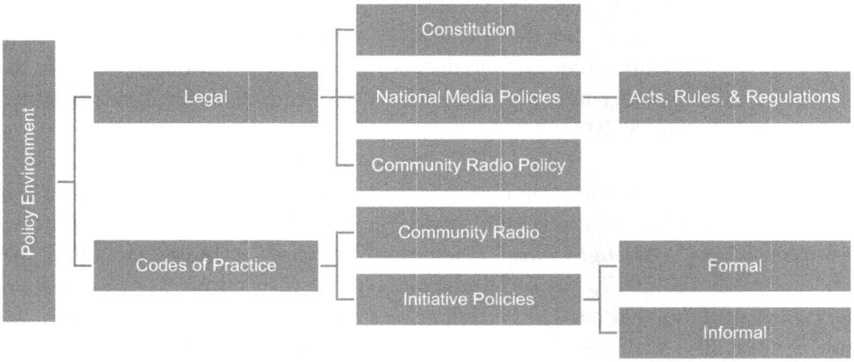

Fig. 6.3 Structure of Bangladesh's policy environment (*Source*: Author's own illustration)

People's Republic of Bangladesh [English translation], 1972, p. 1) for all citizens. Regarding the media sector, Article 39 guarantees "the right of every citizen of freedom of speech and expression; and, freedom of the press" (*Constitution of the People's Republic of Bangladesh [English translation],* 1972, p. 10). Thus, citizens are constitutionally guaranteed freedom to express themselves without fear of reprisal.

However, there are some restrictions which ensure that the exercising of these freedoms is done responsibly. Article 39 (*Constitution of the People's Republic of Bangladesh [English translation],* 1972, p. 10) also explicitly states that there are some "reasonable restrictions [which can be] imposed by law in the interests of the security of the State, friendly relations with foreign states, public order, decency or morality, or in relation to contempt of court, defamation or incitement to an offence." Therefore, should an individual or media house promote libel, defamation, or sedition, or produce content which poses a national security risk, they can be legally charged which could result in financial penalties or being jailed.

As a result of these constitutional provisions, there are several national-level policies that govern the set-up and operation of CR initiatives in Bangladesh.

6.3.2 National Media Policies

In a recent development that came a few years after the 2008 Policy of Bangladesh a revised and updated policy was approved by the Government of Bangladesh on August 4, 2014 (Azad, 2019); this resulted in the *Bangladesh Broadcast Act 2003*[3] (2016)—the most recent legislature to govern broadcast media.

This act cites the need "for the regulation of broadcasting services, including terrestrial, satellite and cable broadcasting, and to make provision for the establishment of an independent Authority to oversee broadcasting regulation with a view to promoting independent, pluralistic broadcasting in the public interest" (*Bangladesh Broadcast Act 2003*, p. 1). The author noticed that while the policy seems largely focused on the "Authority," it does take into consideration the positives of and need for diversity, plurality, and equality in addition to the practice of ethics and the need for morality when producing content for various audiences. Also, there are some restrictions highlighted, in keeping with Article 39 of the constitution, such as discouraging the broadcast of content which could encourage corruption, and ensuring advertisements are not discriminatory in nature (Azad, 2019; *Bangladesh Broadcast Act 2003*).

It is important to note that the act highlights aspects relating to community media very clearly. It clearly addresses *community broadcaster* by definition such as "a broadcaster which is controlled by a non-profit entity and operates on a non-profit basis, carries programming serving a particular community including by reflecting

[3]Though the Act was formally introduced in 2016, in the Preliminary Matters section, there is a specific clause highlight that it should so be referenced.

the special interests and needs of the community, and is managed and operated primarily by members of that community" (*Bangladesh Broadcast Act 2003*, p. 2). The presence of this definition and the later references to the same illustrate the acceptance of CR as part of the larger media landscape of Bangladesh.

Even though there is a strong policy environment, there are other laws used to govern media practitioners and entities such as the *Penal Code 1860*, the *Code of Criminal Procedure 1889*, the *Official Secrets Act 1923*, and *Law of Defamation* (Azad, 2019). Additionally, Bangladesh has a CR-specific national-level policy.

6.3.3 National CR Policy

With the formalising of the *Community Radio Installation, Broadcast and Operation Policy (2008),* 2008, the foundation for the establishment and operation of community media initiatives within Bangladesh was laid. This policy outlined the fundamental principles and eligibility criteria which govern the application for a CR licence. It has since been replaced by the *Community Radio Installation, Broadcast and Operation Policy 2017* ("2017 Policy" for short) which was made official on January 15, 2018. This updated policy was needed due to the changing media environment and the need for more enabling legislature to govern the same.

The 2017 Policy comprises 15 key sections: Concept of Community Radio; Fundamental Principles of Community Radio; Eligibility Criteria to Get Permission/ Licence to Establish and Operate Community Radio in Bangladesh; Licensing Process; Technical Structure; Broadcast-Related Terms and Conditions; Conditions for Advertisement; Other Instructions; Monitoring Broadcasting Activities; National Regulatory Committee; Technical Sub-committee of National Regulatory Committee; Central Monitoring Committee; Local Advisory Committee; Self-defence Opportunity; and Repeal and Protection (*Community Radio Installation, Broadcast and Operation Policy 2017,* 2018). As can be seen, these sections are quite comprehensive and address key aspects of CR. However, it is important to look at the 2008 Policy briefly, to understand the 2017 Policy.

Following the implementation of the 2008 Policy and the sector being active for the last decade, there were more comprehensive findings to ensure that the updated policy addresses specific areas and fills gaps which previously existed. Based on the author's analyses, the 2017 Policy expands on the concept of CR, providing a more detailed explanation. Also, it highlights specific guidelines for acquiring a licence, the technicalities for setting up and operating the station, the various committees that will monitor the operation of these stations, and how to address the cancellation of a licence.

While general clauses in the 2008 Policy were expanded upon and converted to entire sections in the 2017 Policy, the most notable change is the section addressing advertisements. The author noticed that CR initiatives were hampered by unfavourable clauses relating to advertisement in the 2008 Policy; due to challenges with regard to funding, the 2017 Policy allows initiatives up to 10% of the total broadcast content to be commercial advertisements now. However, there are some restrictions on the advertisements; for example, they should be focused on development matters, should not be discriminatory, and should not cause division among diverse groups of people within the community. (*Community Radio Installation, Broadcast and Operation Policy 2017,* 2018, p. 10).

Another noticeable change was the types of entities allowed to own CRS in Bangladesh. Apart from the previously allowed government research institutions, development organisations, and non-government development organisations, the 2017 Policy allows licensed ownership to any well-established organisation that caters to the development of marginalised communities which also includes research, educational, and training institutions, in addition to those mentioned before. Such research and educational entities need to be formally "certified by the proper authorities" while development NGOs must have "at least five years of experiences of working on poverty alleviation / mass media / information technology and development interventions at the community level." These NGOs also need to be legitimate and should be registered with the NGO Affairs Bureau in Bangladesh (*Community Radio Installation, Broadcast and Operation Policy 2017,* 2018, p. 3).

In addition to these criteria relating to licensing, the 2017 Policy also stipulates the creation of several committees and sub-committees, the formation of which is supervised by the Ministry of Broadcasting, to oversee various functions associated with the set-up and monitoring of CRS. Note: these committees are briefly explained in Appendix 6.2 (*Community Radio Installation, Broadcast and Operation Policy 2017,* 2018, pp. 3–4, 12).

Overall, the 2017 Policy highlights the acceptance of and the continuance of CR in Bangladesh by alluding to media diversification and liberalisation. However, the restrictions on licence holders and advertisements (though more relaxed now than in the 2008 Policy) and the rigid framework established for monitoring the sector can be interpreted as control mechanisms put in place by the government.

6.3.4 National Codes

Apart from the legally enforced policies above, there are several national codes which were collectively created and agreed to by practitioners and stakeholders.

6.3.4.1 Code of Conduct: Community Radio Operation in Bangladesh (2009)

With the establishment of 14 CRS, the *Code of Conduct for Community Radio (CR) Operation* (2009), comprising three sections with 41 guidelines, was agreed upon by these stations. The guidelines are categorised by "what community radio should do" and "what community radio should avoid." The general gist of the former is that CR should encourage the participation of the community in all aspects of the station, broadcast programmes which are of interest to the local community utilising their cultural references, and create a harmonious and truly representative environment for all. The latter section highlights that CR should not be used negatively to affect any specific group within society or broadcast content which can adversely

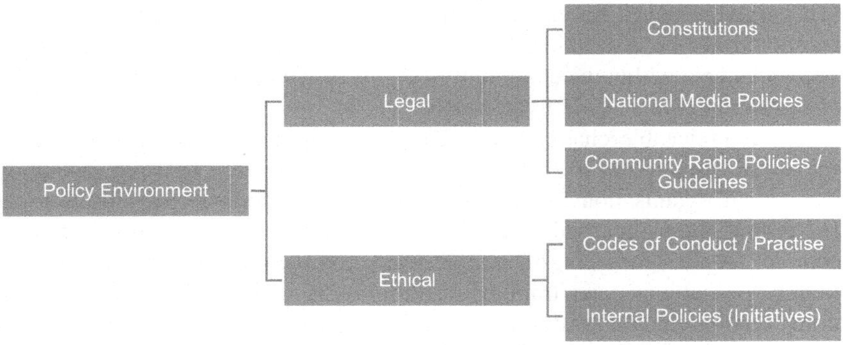

Fig. 6.4 The policy environment for CR in South Asia based on case studies (*Source*: Author's own illustration)

affect the general well-being of the public[4] (*Code of Conduct for Community Radio (CR) Operation*, 2009).

6.3.4.2 Gender Equality and Socialisation Guideline for Community Radio Stations (2012, 2013, 2015)

In keeping with the third target of the Millennium Development Goals (MDGs), which focuses on gender equality and women's empowerment, this guideline (of which the first edition was published in 2012 and the latest in 2015) ensures gender equality in the management, programming, and financial departments of CRS. It specifically highlights women's access and representation in radio, special representation of minority women, and financing and skill development for women in radio[5] (BNNRC, 2015).

6.4 Summary

In Nepal, India, and Bangladesh, the policy environments for CR initiatives comprise different elements relating to both legal and ethical procedures. Based on an analysis of the data gathered from the 11 case studies and in-depth interviews with key stakeholders, Figure 6.4 is a visual representation of the general policy environment in which these initiatives operate.

---

[4] This document was spearheaded by BNNRC with inputs from Mr Faroha Sudharowardi, Former Deputy Director, Bangladesh Betar, Dhaka, and Mr S. M. Shamim Reza, Assistant Professor, Department of Mass Communication and Journalism, Dhaka University, Dhaka, and prepared by the then 14 active CRS.

[5] BNNRC, through assistance from the European Union and Free Press Unlimited, used the initial guideline by the World Association of Community Radio Broadcasters (AMARC) and Women International Network Asia to create a Bangladesh-specific guideline in English and Bangla, with the first edition in 2012, followed by a second in 2013, and the latest in 2015 (BNNRC, 2015).

As can be seen in Fig. 6.4, the legal frameworks include each country's constitution along with their national-level media policies and the CR guideline and CR policy in the case of India and Bangladesh, respectively. The ethical frameworks, which are not enforceable by law, include national-level codes of conduct and initiative-specific internal policies.

Regarding the constitutions of the three countries, all three constitutions guarantee freedom of speech and expression as a fundamental right. However, the exercising of these freedoms has (reasonable) restrictions with the provisions that these rights will be expressed responsibly and not cause adverse effects, especially to national unity and the sovereignty of the countries. Specifically, articles in the constitutions address citizens' rights to freedom, communication, information, and of the press (*Constitution of the People's Republic of Bangladesh [English translation],* 1972; *The Constitution of India [English translation],* 2019; *The Constitution of Nepal [English translation] 2015,* 2015). Furthermore, *The Constitution of Nepal 2015* also has specific clauses that address the need to maintain and recognise cultural diversity in the social and cultural transformation as well as the development of Nepali society.

Based on these constitutions, each country has various national-level media policies that guide the operation of media entities. It must be noted that while Nepal only has general policies that oversee all media entities, India and Bangladesh have CR-specific national policies. Furthermore, all three countries have updated their policies within the last decade as stakeholders advocated for more enabling policy environments. Specifically, Nepal introduced the *National Mass Communications Policy 2016,* which has been lauded by Dahal and Sigdel (2016) as encouraging more self-regulation and self-assessment compared to the past policies. Bangladesh has introduced the *Community Radio Installation, Broadcast and Operation Policy 2017*—an updated version of the original policy, which was introduced in 2008, which has several noticeable changes of which the licensed owner of community radio stations (CRS) has been expanded to include any well-established organisations working for the development of marginalised communities. Also, the clauses relating to advertisements are more relaxed which allows for wider sourcing of funds for operation. India has had one policy update which occurred in 2006 with a key change being the opening of licensed ownership to include non-profit agencies, agricultural agencies, and organisations registered under India's *Societies Act*. Also, there have been several conversations surrounding key issues such as the ban on producing and broadcasting news via CRS and the lengthy licensing process which have caught the government's attention and resulted in over 100 Letters of Intent being granted for CRS to be set up in the country (118 new community radio stations to be set up: Union Minister Prakash Javadekar, 2019).

However, even with policies at the country level, there are noticeable gaps regarding ideals associated with the participatory approach to development - a foundation on which CR is built. As a result, there are national-level codes and initiative-specific regulations to fill these gaps; however, it is important to note that these codes are not enforceable by law as they are normative and are non-compulsory for CR practitioners to follow. Regarding Nepal, there are suggested 16 ethical guidelines for CRS based on the first CRS to be established in that country—*Radio Sagarmatha* (Mainali et al., 2004). These guidelines cover all key aspects of CRS operation from management functions to production functions and have been used as-is or adapted by various stations to suit station-specific needs. In the case of Bangladesh, there are two national-level guides—a Code of Conduct (2009) and a Gender Guidelines (2015)—which steer CRS on these topics.

As can be seen, the policy environment in South Asia has been in a state of evolution, albeit slow, which has resulted in CRS operating in more enabling environments today as opposed to a decade ago. With constitutions guaranteeing freedom of speech and expression—and alluding to the importance of diversity and harmony, the national-level media laws and CR-specific policies and guidelines have been updated to reflect these aspects; where there are gaps, codes of conduct have been used to supplement these legislatures. Overall, while the policy environment has restrictions in place, all three countries formally acknowledge CR as the third tier of broadcasting—especially for marginalised groups in society, which has resulted in over 500 stations in total across Nepal, India, and Bangladesh as of December 2017 (Rampersaud, 2019).

References

118 new community radio stations to be set up: Union Minister Prakash Javadekar. (2019, September 14). *India Today.* https://www.indiatoday.in/india/story/new-community-radio-stations-prakash-javadekar-1598948-2019-09-14

Acharya, P. (2013). The making and implementation of media policies in Nepal: Experiences of an emerging democracy [Policy Discussion Paper]. I *Alliance for Social Dialogue, Policy Research Fellowship Programme 2013*. November 2013. Kathmandu, Nepal: Alliance for Social Dialogue.

Adukia, R. S. (n.d.). *Media laws of India*. Ministry of Finance, India. Retrieved June 30, 2018, from http://www.caaa.in/Image/media_laws.pdf

Azad, M. A. K. (2019). *Bangladesh – Media Landscape*. European Journalism Centre (EJC).

Bangladesh Broadcast Act 2003 [English translation]. (n.d.). *ACE Project*. Retrieved May 30, 2019, from http://aceproject.org/ero-en/regions/asia/BD/bangladesh-broadcast-act-2003/view

Bangladesh profile – Media. (n.d.). BBC. Retrieved October 30, 2019, from https://www.bbc.com/news/world-south-asia-12650946

BNNRC. (2015). *Community Radio Station – gender guidelines*. BNNRC.

Code of Conduct for Community Radio (CR) Operation. (2009). SANCOM. Retrieved March 30, 2017, from http://www.sancomonline.net/wp-content/uploads/2015/02/Code-of-Conduct-CR-Operation-in-Bangladesh-English.pdf

Community Radio Installation, Broadcast and Operation Policy 2008. (2008). *Ministry of Information*, People's Republic of Bangladesh.

Community Radio Installation, Broadcast and Operation Policy 2017. (2018). Ministry of Information, People's Republic of Bangladesh.

Constitution of The People's Republic of Bangladesh [English translation]. (1972). Government of Bangladesh. Retrieved May 30, 2019, from http://hrlibrary.umn.edu/research/bangladesh-constitution.pdf

Dahal, T. (n.d.). *Nepal media policy and law update*. The Rising Nepal. Retrieved May 30, 2019, from http://therisingnepal.org.np/news/23865

Dahal, T., & Sigdel, S. (2016). *National mass communications policy 2016: A Review*. Freedom Forum.

History of Bikram Sambat Nepali Calendar. (2010, January 01). *Ashesh's Blog*. Retrieved May 30, 2019, from https://www.ashesh.com.np/bikram-sambat-nepali-calendar-history/

India. (n.d.). *Press reference*. Retrieved September 30, 2019, from http://www.pressreference.com/Gu-Ku/India.html

India profile – Media. (n.d.). *BBC*. Retrieved October 30, 2019, from https://www.bbc.com/news/world-south-asia-12557390

Laws and Rules. (n.d.). *Ministry of Communication and Information Technology, Nepal*. Retrieved May 30, 2019, from http://mocit.gov.np/detail/acts-and-regulations

Mainali, R., Chapagain, Y., & Subba, B. (2004). *Community radio organisation development guidebook*. CRSC/NEFEJ with support of Free Voice.

Nepal - Basic Data. (n.d.). *Press reference*. Retrieved September 30, 2017, from http://www.pressreference.com/Ma-No/Nepal.html

Nepal country profile. (n.d.). *BBC*. Retrieved April 30, 2019, from https://www.bbc.com/news/world-south-asia-12511455

Nepal Profile. (n.d.). *Freedom House*. Retrieved May 30, 2019, from https://freedomhouse.org/report/freedom-world/2018/nepal

Policy. (n.d.). *Ministry of Communication and Information technology*, Nepal. Retrieved May 30, 2019, from http://mocit.gov.np/detail/policy

Policy Guidelines for setting up Community Radio Stations in India. (n.d.). *Ministry of Information and Broadcasting, India*. Retrieved September 30, 2017, from https://mib.gov.in/sites/default/files/c1_0.pdf

Rampersaud, T. (2019). *Community media directory*. SANCOM. Retrieved July 30, 2019, from http://cmd.sancomonline.net/

Savada, A. M. (Ed.). (1991). *Nepal*. Country Studies. Retrieved May 30, 2019, from http://countrystudies.us/nepal/

The Constitution of India [English translation]. (2019). *Legislative Department, Ministry of Law and Justice, Government of India*. Retrieved October 2019, from http://legislative.gov.in/sites/default/files/COI-updated.pdf

The Constitution of Nepal 2015 [English translation]. (2015). *Ministry of Law, Justice and Parliamentary Affairs, Government of Nepal*. Retrieved May 2019, from https://www.wipo.int/edocs/lexdocs/laws/en/np/np029en.pdf

UNESCO Chair on Community Media. (2017). *National Consultation on "Strengthening Community Radio": Recommendations*. UNESCO.

Ownership and Management Philosophies

7

7.1 Nepal

The *National Mass Communications Policy 2016* highlights the need for laws that discourage media monopoly and concentration to ensure the development of "decent and dignified journalism" that limits the same person, family, or group owning and/or operating similar media entities (Dahal & Sigdel, 2016, p. 6). However, it does not specify who can apply for community radio station (CRS) licences—an aspect addressed by Lamichhane[1] (in-depth interview, April 27, 2018). He highlighted that there are provisions that enable co-operative organisations, comprising at least 25 members, and non-governmental organisations (NGOs)—both classified as community-based organisations (CBOs)—to apply for community radio (CR) licences. He stated that one challenge with these organisations is that their structure might not be truly representative of the communities. He added that if the management teams comprised elites from the community, then they could ultimately utilise the medium for their means and not necessarily for the community's benefits.

7.1.1 Approaches to Management and Communication

Based on the data from the three case studies (*Radio Sagarmatha, Radio Namobuddha,* and *Radio Sindhu*), the decision-making processes encompass horizontal, bottom-up, and top-bottom approaches. The horizontal approach is primarily used during inter-departmental meetings—such as when the programming department is planning the schedule for the next month, and during station meetings

[1] Dr. Ramchandra Lamichhane is the Executive Director, ACORAB, Nepal. He has been involved with development communication for approximately 26 years (since 1993) and CR for 7 years. Lamichhane is deeply motivated towards the continuity of CR since they are beneficial to communities (Lamichhane, in-depth interview, April 27, 2018).

T. Rampersaud-Skorka, *Community Radio in South Asia*, Diversity and Inclusion Research, https://doi.org/10.1007/978-3-031-85201-5_7

when the entire team discusses issues relating to the CRS. The bottom-up approach is evident when inter-departmental choices are communicated to the station manager by the department chiefs for final approval. In some instances, such as funding-related decisions, matters are forwarded beyond the manager to the radio operation committee[2] for their input. Finally, the top-bottom approach is apparent when either the operation committee or manager makes unilateral decisions and communicates this to the departmental chiefs, who then inform their teams. A point to note is that departments with few individuals, as is common with the accounts, marketing and public relations, and technical departments, normally include the station manager in decision-making (Shrestha,[3] in-depth interview, April 25, 2018; Srerestha,[4] in-depth interview, April 26, 2018; Syngtan,[5] in-depth interview, April 25, 2018).

Regarding communication methods, all case studies use both formal and informal procedures, and verbal and written techniques to share information. Specifically, *Radio Sagarmatha* highlights formal meetings and memos to communicate managerial information, while informal methods, such as chatting via social networking platforms, are used to communicate with each other on a more regular basis. Similarly, *Radio Namobuddha* identifies having formal meetings complemented by informal communication via group chats on social networking platforms such as WhatsApp. *Radio Sindhu*, on the other hand, highlights a mostly informal communication structure within the CRS where the entire team would sit together and make decisions since the team is "like a family" and less like an enterprise (Shrestha, in-depth interview, April 25, 2018; Srerestha, in-depth interview, April 26, 2018; Syngtan, in-depth interview, April 25, 2018).

According to the case studies, *Radio Sagarmatha* ensures consultation among all individuals before finalising important decisions while *Radio Namobuddha* relies mostly on the management individuals for final decisions, and *Radio Sindhu*, while ensuring participation of everyone involved at all times, leaves the final decisions to the paid staff (Shrestha, in-depth interview, April 25, 2018; Srerestha, in-depth interview, April 26, 2018; Syngtan, in-depth interview, April 25, 2018).

7.1.2 Internal Policies

According to the case studies, the formally recorded internal policies are introduced during the set-up of the CRS and are updated as the need arises. It was observed by the author that many of the internal policies are adaptations from the suggested codes highlighted in Table 6.1. Ethical codes for CRS operation in Nepal as suggested by Mainali et al. (2004) in *Community Radio Organisation Development*

[2] This is a board set up to oversee the CRS and ensure they are operating within internal policies created at the inception, according to the case studies.

[3] Ratna Prasad Shrestha is the Station Manager for *Radio Sindhu.*

[4] Sahah Man Srerestha is the Station Manager for *Radio Sagarmatha.*

[5] Bhakta Syangtan is the Station Manager for *Radio Namobuddha.*

Guidebook.[6] Another observation was that only *Radio Namobuddha* highlighted having codes of conduct for staff and paid volunteers. While all three case studies highlighted that while some policies are understood and communicated verbally, the more important ones are also placed around the station via notices. Apart from this, when new policies are implemented, handouts are circulated among station personnel (Shrestha, in-depth interview, April 25, 2018; Srerestha, in-depth interview, April 26, 2018; Syngtan, in-depth interview, April 25, 2018).

Regarding the types of internal policies, *Radio Sagarmatha's* station manager highlighted that the station follows 12 policies that are specific to its operations: marketing strategy; human resource plan; resource mobilisation policy and procedures; collaboration policy; documentation and knowledge management policy; station operation protocols; management systems and procedures; operation and maintenance of equipment; public consultation and maintenance of transparency policy and procedures; volunteer mobilisation policy; policy governing information and educative programmes; and finance policy. Also, there are three additional policies he felt the need to highlight. Specifically, there is a *Gender Policy* which, apart from addressing normal issues surrounding gender equality in the workplace, is unique in that it allowed for extended pregnancy leave for men so that they could support their partners; the *Language Use Guidelines* which oversees the need for balance in the variety of languages used by presenters of the various programmes; and the *Mixed Demographics Policy* which addresses the dynamics of staff composition especially about caste and gender representations (Srerestha, in-depth interview, April 26, 2018).

Similarly, *Radio Namobuddha* also has a *Gender Policy* which highlights 10–15 days leave for men when their partners are pregnant or have given birth. The station manager also singled out the *Style guide for broadcast* which highlights various sensitive areas that producers needed to be cognisant about such as appropriate use of languages and protocols for programmes, how to address people during interviews, and non-discrimination among individuals regardless of their position (whether the person is the president or a Dalit). Another unique policy highlighted was the *Education Policy* which addresses the need for educational programmes to be produced and broadcast and that educational content should be prioritised in any programme over other content. The other five internal policies of this CRS included Production Policy, Human Resource Management Policy, Finance Policy, Marketing Policy, and Technical Department Policy (Syngtan, in-depth interview, April 25, 2018.)

Radio Sindhu stated that there are internal policies that broadly addressed administration, advertising, programming, knowledge sharing, and technology and infrastructure. These broad areas are then broken down into more targeted areas which included staff mobilisation and responsibilities, marketing and advertisement, codes for news production and presentation, programme production, and resource selection. While these thematic areas addressed by the policies were mentioned, the

[6] See Chap. 6 for this table.

station manager did not expand on any specific content (Shrestha, in-depth interview, April 25, 2018).

Apart from the areas highlighted above, there are two specific aspects that needed individual foci: economic sustainability and editorial independence; these are addressed below.

7.1.3 Economic Sustainability

All three case studies highlighted that they operate on a non-profit basis with no extra money for reinvestments or savings. As a result, they explore multiple sources of funding to cover monthly expenditures. These sources of income and expenditures are highlighted in Fig. 7.1.

As highlighted in Fig. 7.1, the main source of income comprises advertisements; project-related funding from international non-governmental organisations (INGOs) and non-governmental organisations (NGOs)—these are sometimes classified as funding from multi-lateral development agencies (such as UNDP and UNESCO), and other individuals and entities. With regard to the latter, these comprise payments from production houses and media partners for work done by the CRS, local government funding, donations, financial assistance from the communities (though not regular), and payments to the stations for broadcasting public service announcements (PSAs) and other types of content such as programmes from third parties. The income is then used to cover the monthly expenses of the initiatives which include salaries for staff and stipends for (paid) volunteers; utilities including rent, telephone, internet, electricity, and water; and any miscellaneous spending (Shrestha, in-depth interview, April 25, 2018; Srerestha, in-depth interview, April 26, 2018; Syngtan, in-depth interview, April 25, 2018).

According to the case studies, the financial decisions are made by the senior staff with inputs from the radio operation committees, when needed. All the case studies highlighted that once recurring monthly expenditures are identified, staff are cleared

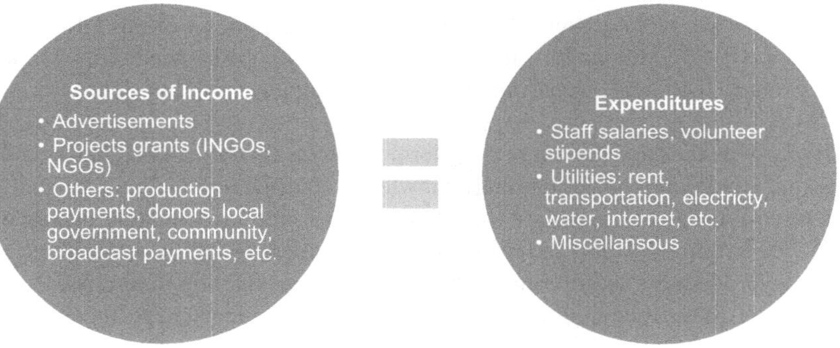

Fig. 7.1 Income and expenditures of the case studies in Nepal (Source: Author's own illustration)

to cover those; only when unusual or new amounts needed to be spent are the committees consulted. With monthly budgets that range from approximately USD $1400 to USD $4500 (NPR 150,000 to NPR 500,000), the case studies are mostly self-sufficient. Additionally, two CRS had special agreements to cover expenses. *Radio Namobuddha* provides a physical place for the transmission tower of their internet service provider who, in return, waives the internet costs. This station also trades on-air broadcast advertisement spots instead of paying for website creation and maintenance. While not a regular occurrence, *Radio Sindhu* had traded broadcast advertisement spots for use of signboards in the community, at times (Shrestha, in-depth interview, April 25, 2018; Srerestha, in-depth interview, April 26, 2018; Syngtan, in-depth interview, April 25, 2018).

Overall, all three initiatives are able to remain economically sustainable. However, due to multiple sources of funding, the case studies highlighted the need to ensure they remain independent and ensure funders do not influence the operations of the initiatives; the mechanisms employed are discussed below.

7.1.4 Editorial Independence

Each of the case studies had measures put into place to ensure editorial independence from their funders. These are explained through the examples below, which show how they remain independent and ensure the communities are their priority while being able to access the much-needed funds.

Radio Sagarmatha highlighted that in the past, there were instances where individuals and organisations that provided funding tried to have those projects take precedence over the needs of the communities. In those instances, the staff of the CRS reminded funders that the priority is always towards the needs of the communities and not to the funders. As a result, it became a practice to clearly state this from the beginning and enforce it through written documentation, such as a memorandum of understanding (MOU), which must be signed by all parties before any funds are exchanged (Srerestha, in-depth interview, April 26, 2018).

Radio Namobuddha has several measures and controls to address challenges to the station's editorial independence. Firstly, the station manager stated that it was a policy not to accept any type of funding from any questionable organisations—if there is uncertainty about individuals or organisations, then background checks are done to ensure their integrity and credibility before finalising any agreement. Secondly, the needs of the individuals and/or organisations providing funds are discussed in detail before committing to a project to ensure that there are no conflicts of interest which could cause future challenges; this ensures funders have similar objectives to the station. Also, this CRS has a general policy that states no funding is accepted from or in relation to products and services relating to multi-national corporations, tobacco, or alcohol manufacturers and suppliers, and human resource companies (referred to as *sucat shops* locally) where labour is exploited; there is a preference for local people and businesses over outsiders (Syngtan, in-depth interview, April 25, 2018).

Radio Sindhu's operational mandate is to clearly state that the station is independent, and this is always the priority. It was highlighted in the interview that before accepting any funds, the expectations are thoroughly addressed to ensure the funders, and the CRS has the same objectives. Also, the station manager highlighted that it is a practice to always research prospective funders to ensure there are no hidden agendas with regard to the funds. In doing so, station personnel are proactive and ensure their independence (Shrestha, in-depth interview, April 25, 2018).

Overall, the case studies appeared to be aware of the challenges associated with funding and have implemented measures to ensure their independence is not compromised while seeking finances to ensure continuity as they serve their communities.

7.2 India

Apart from the permit holder, "ownership" can also be attributed to the communities and participants. According to Nagarajan[7] (in-depth interview, June 18 and 19, 2018), in many instances, from the initial stages of setting up a CRS, it is communicated to the community that everyone owns the station, anyone can use it—especially in instances where the life of the CRS extends beyond development projects. He highlighted that the ideals surrounding ownership do have influence as involved individuals become empowered and make tough decisions regarding matters affecting them. While Dutta[8] (in-depth interview, March 23, 2018) agrees with Nagarajan, he shared a challenge regarding campus CRS. He stated that when these initiatives broadcast beyond the academic community, they need to ensure the inclusion of the non-academic members of the community. He highlighted that, in many cases, the community is not represented in the various committees and, as a result, do not claim ownership. To overcome this, he posits that the management committees for campus CRS should reflect community diversity.

Regarding the case studies (*Sangham Radio, Tilonia Radio, Radio Luit,* and *Waqt ki Awaaz*), it was clear to the author that those actively involved with these initiatives are generally encouraged to feel like owners. This is supported by the data presented in the following four sub-sections which highlight aspects of inclusivity, independence, and motivation to participate.

[7] Mr. Ramakrishnan Nagarajan, Executive Director, Ideosync Media Combine, India, and member of the Community Radio Forum (India), who has been working in the development communication field for approximately 24 years and specifically with CR for 19 years. He assists CRS in setting up and becoming operational, training activities for CRS, lobbying for CRS in India, and networking with other stakeholders for the betterment of CR in India and South Asia (Nagarajan, in-depth interview, June 18 and 19, 2018).

[8] Dr. Ankurran Dutta has been working in the development communication field for approximately 13 years. As a media teacher and work various experiences with organisations such as CEMCA (India), he is focused on promoting the use of community media in India since they allow the common people to be producers of their own stories (Dutta, in-depth interview, March 23, 2018).

7.2.1 Approaches to Management and Communication

Based on the data gathered from the case studies, their decision-making processes comprise two approaches: horizontal (which is more inclusive as it allows all participants to contribute) and top-bottom (which is more hierarchical and involves management making decisions and passing these down to others). The choice of the structure is dependent on the issue being addressed. Furthermore, while there are two distinct approaches to management and communication, all case studies highlighted that all internal participants are normally involved in the process with regard to programming decisions.

Specifically, *Sangham Radio* highlighted that outside of the station, the director of the Deccan Development Society (DDS) oversees the general operation of the initiative as per the permit holder's role and responsibilities. However, this individual allows the staff[9] latitude in operating the station on a daily basis due to the trust he has in them. The staff take the lead on decision-making since they are intimately aware of every aspect, especially those regarding programme production. However, in some instances, they approach the director for assistance when a situation needs more input (General Narsamma,[10] in-depth interview, April 06, 2018).

Similarly, the other three case studies highlighted that the smaller, daily decision-making, especially those relating to programming, are made by the staff of the initiatives. However, contrary to *Sangham Radio*, major decisions, such as those regarding funding and hiring of staff, are taken by the licence holders and then communicated to the staff. Specifically, *Tilonia Radio* is guided by three committees constituted within the licence holder NGO and comprise coordinating, procurement, and management. These committees make relevant decisions and set up internal policies for the CRS and communicate these to the staff. *Radio Luit* has an advisory committee that makes decisions about significant issues, such as finances. Finally, *Waqt ki Awaaz* highlighted that issues such as those relating to technology and infrastructure are forwarded to the NGO for decision-making (Aarti Devi,[11] in-depth interview, March 07, 2018; Acharjya,[12] in-depth interview, February 05, 2018; Shukla,[13] in-depth interview, March 08, 2018).

Regarding communication methods, the author was able to deduce that the four CRS use both formal and informal methods comprising written and verbal techniques. However, it appears that informal communication is preferred among participants, especially since many of these individuals are friends with each other. Aarti Devi (in-depth interview, March 07, 2018) highlighted that due to high levels of comfort with each other, the two staff of *Tilonia Radio* can have some flexibility

[9] The differentiation between staff and volunteers are made under the "Community" section of this chapter.

[10] General Narsamma is the station manager for *Sangham Radio* and a key figure in the CR movement in India.

[11] Aarti Devi is the station manager for *Tilonia Radio*.

[12] Bhaskar Jyoti Acharjya is the programme executive of *Radio Luit*.

[13] Radha Shukla is the coordinator (instead of the title station manager) for *Waqt ki Awaaz*.

regarding job responsibilities since both women will cover for each other should one be absent. These sentiments were also inferred by General Narsamma. Shukla (in-depth interview, March 08, 2018) went one step further and stated that *Waqt ki Awaaz* is like a home for those who work there; she stated that teamwork is the focus, and there is an open-door policy—anyone can approach another for assistance.

While the three rural CRS are mostly informal with each other, *Radio Luit* highlighted almost equal formal and informal communication among the staff and volunteers. Acharjya highlighted that weekly and monthly meetings[14] are mostly formal in nature, while the use of virtual platforms, such as WhatsApp, fosters more informal sharing of information (Acharjya, in-depth interview, February 05, 2018).

The mixed approaches to management and communication within the case studies have been reported as being effective so far. As a result, none of the CRS highlighted having any inclination to change any aspects of these approaches.

7.2.2 Internal Policies

These approaches to management and communication are reflected in the internal policies of the case studies. Through a focus on station management, advertising, content (production, sharing, ownership), funding, and technology and infrastructure, internal policies (both formally and informally recorded and shared among the participants) fill gaps present in the policy environment for CR initiatives. These policies are normally written and shared during orientation sessions via handouts, meetings, notices around the stations, and workshops in addition to being verbally shared from participant to participant.

With specific reference to case studies, General Narsamma (in-depth interview, April 06, 2018) highlighted that *Sangham Radio* has several key internal policies which include no broadcasting of politics, caste, or religious content; no encouragement of advertisements, especially from profit-motivated enterprises; no broadcast of any type of paid programming; no production work by the radio team for personal events such as weddings; and no production of programmes for monetary benefits. She highlighted that these self-imposed restrictions are there to ensure *Sangham Radio* produces programmes that only "benefit the village people and are not for monetary benefits."

Aarti Devi (in-depth interview, March 07, 2018) highlighted that there is a policy to *only* broadcast positive messages at *Tilonia Radio*. As a result, she stated that interviewers are cognisant of the slangs used by community people and ensure that negative messages are removed before broadcast to ensure no groups are offended by any message. Furthermore, Aarti Devi highlighted that any information broadcast regarding political parties during elections are done so in an objective manner which puts the station in a neutral position; that is the CRS remains unaffiliated with

[14] Meetings are indicative of in-person communication, whether interpersonal, small group, or larger group.

any political group. Finally, she stated that there is respect regarding copyright—the station will only broadcast information for which permission is given.

Shukla (in-depth interview, March 08, 2018) stated that *Waqt ki Awaaz* has a maintenance policy regarding the studio and equipment. Also, she stated there are policies for fieldwork, management of the CRS in general, and production—which includes programming, scheduling, and timing. However, details were not provided regarding the specifics of these internal policies. Similarly, no internal policies, apart from guidelines regarding the use of the studio, were identified for *Radio Luit* (Acharjya, in-depth interview, February 05, 2018).

As can be seen, all four case studies have some initiative specific internal policies to guide their operations. The initiative specific policies do appear to support the positive aspects of community radio in the wider mediascape of India.

7.2.3 Economic Sustainability

All four case studies highlighted that they operate on a non-profit basis where monthly funds are normally sufficient to cover expenditures; Fig. 7.2 highlights the sources of income and expenditure.

As can be seen in Fig. 7.2, there are multiple sources of income and expenses per month across the four CRS. The sources of income include advertisements, contributions and donations from the community, funds from multi-lateral agencies, state funding, and other sources which include money from the licence holder and payments for minor production work done. The monthly expenditures include salaries for staff, honorariums for (paid) volunteers, and utilities such as electricity, transportation, and logistics. On rare occasions, there are costs associated with staff development such as travel, accommodation, and food for participants attending seminars and workshops (Aarti Devi, in-depth interview, March 07, 2018).

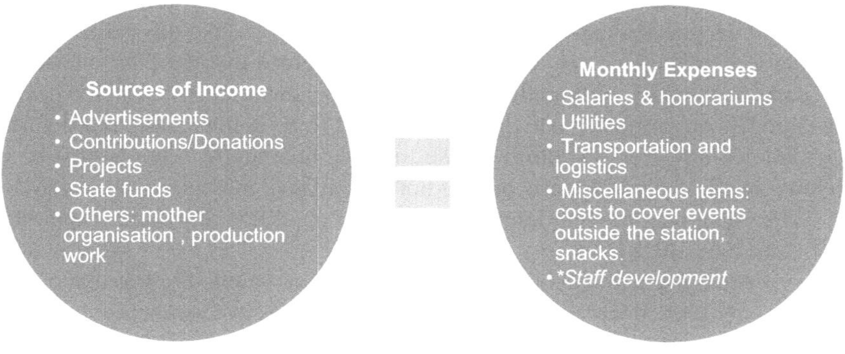

Fig. 7.2 Monthly sources of income and expenses of the case studies in India (Source: Author's own illustration)

Based on an analysis of the funding data shared by each case, it appears that only *Sangham Radio* was the only CRS not to fully depend on the mother organisation for funding. This station relies on yearly donations from the community, project-related funds, and payments for documentation and production services rendered to remain viable (General Narsamma, in-depth interview, April 06, 2018).

Tilonia Radio, on the other hand, relies on the licence holder to cover monthly expenses, as does *Waqt ki Awaaz*. In the past, *Tilonia Radio* had receive a government grant which supplemented the mother organisation's contribution for a year. *Radio Luit* was the only station to highlight receiving DAVP (Directorate of Advertising and Visual Publicity) advertisements in addition to funds received from the University (Aarti Devi, in-depth interview, March 07, 2018; Acharjya, in-depth interview, February 05, 2018; Shukla, in-depth interview, March 08, 2018).

In addition, there were some "special agreements" regarding monthly expenditures. *Tilonia Radio* highlighted that there is no payment for electricity since solar panels are in use—a point also highlighted by *Waqt ki Awaaz*. *Radio Luit* shared that there are no costs for rent, phone (landline), or electricity since the station is in a university building and the licence holder pays these (Aarti Devi, in-depth interview, March 07, 2018; Acharjya, in-depth interview, February 05, 2018; Shukla, in-depth interview, March 08, 2018).

With monthly operational costs ranging from approximately USD $200 to USD $900 (INR ₹10,000 to INR ₹60,000), all four initiatives stated that they are normally able to cover their costs.

7.2.4 Editorial Independence

All four CRS highlighted that they have policies in place that ensure funders do not have any opportunity to influence the stations.

Specifically, *Tilonia Radio* highlighted that the CRS would not associate with any funds that have conditions attached which are contrary to the station's objectives; if the objectives are not similar, then no partnership is formed. Likewise, *Radio Luit* ensures that prospective funders' objectives are like the station's before entering into any agreement. *Waqt ki Awaaz* highlighted that there has never been any issue in the past surrounding editorial independence of the CRS, especially since funders are normally individuals who want to be donors without any further expectations; however, should this arise then the community's needs will be the deciding factor if funds are accepted or not (Aarti Devi, in-depth interview, March 07, 2018; Acharjya, in-depth interview, February 05, 2018; Shukla, in-depth interview, March 08, 2018).

The general gist expressed by the case studies, some implicitly, was that partnerships are only formed when there are similar objectives between prospective funders and the CRS' operational mandates. Additionally, comments by interviewees highlighted that the stations' communities are the ultimate priority; thus, only funds that focus on them and their positive social change are accepted.

7.3 Bangladesh

The physical ownership of CRS in Bangladesh is guided by the 2017 Policy, which highlights licence ownership by educational institutes, research organisations, and NGOs. However, even though the licence is held by formally registered organisations with years of experience, the communities these stations serve are also seen as owners as they dictate how the stations should be operated, the broadcast content, and the participants. Thus, the day-to-day operations of the stations fall within the purview of the staff and volunteers—who are from the communities being catered addressed. They, with guidance from the committees, are responsible for ensuring the station is sufficiently sustained to fulfil their operational mandates.

7.3.1 Approaches to Management and Communication

The decision-making processes within the case studies (*Radio Padma, Borendro Radio, Radio Bikrampur,* and *Radio Sarabela*) are mostly horizontal in nature and include the staff and volunteers; however, there are instances of top-bottom and bottom-up decision-making being implemented. The horizontal process occurs when staff and volunteers sit and discuss key aspects of the stations; the communication of information from departmental meetings to the various committees is indicative of the bottom-up flow, and decisions made by the committees and passed down to the stations is the top-down approach. Additionally, although decisions are made by these key groups, consultation and feedback from the external communities which the initiatives cater to and recommendations from the advisory committee are taken into consideration and incorporated when applicable (Parveen,[15] in-depth interview, December 10, 2017; Salahin & Pallobi,[16] in-depth interview, December 09, 2017; Sarkar,[17] in-depth interview, December 09, 2017; Sutradar,[18] in-depth interview, December 09, 2017).

Specifically, *Radio Padma* has a chief coordinator who oversees the policy-making for internal rules and regulations, human resources management, and general management of the station. The station manager is the person tasked with the daily operation of the initiative along with her team, under the guidance of the coordinator. However, there are instances where the management committee and/or only the senior staff in this initiative sit and make decisions—an effective technique since getting over 80 individuals together for decision-making is not always possible; however, the larger meetings that include everyone do occur at least twice a year. While there are clearly defined jobs within this CRS, with some individuals having more responsibilities than others, the hierarchy is not there in practice since everyone has equal opportunities to participate, whether through face-to-face

---

[15] Shahana Parveen is the Station Manager for *Radio* Padma.

[16] M.D. Musfiqur Salahin, Senior Producer, and Israt Pallobi is a Producer at *Radio Bikrampur*.

[17] Shubrata Sarkar is the Station Manager for Radio *Borendro*.

[18] Santa Rani Sutradar is the Station Manager of *Radio Sarabela*.

meetings and informal meetups or social networking platforms such as WhatsApp (Parveen, in-depth interview, December 10, 2017).

Radio Borendro highlighted that while the management and other committees for the CRS do have input, the operation of the initiative is left to the staff and volunteers. The CR team is responsible for making all decisions and has found that a more informal and inclusive approach is best. There are monthly staff meetings for normal matters where everyone sits together and discuss ideas before making any final decisions. However, in some instances, there have been emergency meetings when issues needed immediate attention, and the external committees were consulted afterwards. The station manager highlighted that due to the high level of participation, there are normally many ideas shared and arriving at a consensus is sometimes difficult—in such instances, the team finalises decisions taking into consideration the station's objectives. Whether communicating in meetings or through mediated platforms, the approaches to management and communication were described as being effective for this CRS (Sarkar, in-depth interview, December 09, 2017).

Radio Bikrampur highlighted that decisions are made at the monthly meetings based on experiences by staff and volunteers, feedback from listeners (the listeners' clubs included), and the mother organisation (Ambala Foundation)—all of which are indicative of the horizontal approach. However, with regard to new concepts, the volunteers and staff will get together and create a consolidated list of ideas and present them to Ambala Foundation for approval (which can be a bit challenging as it takes about 2 to 3 days to receive a response). However, the overall inclusive approach has encouraged participation from the staff and volunteers and resulted in a multitude of fora being used from meetings to text messages and social networking (Salahin & Pallobi, in-depth interview, December 09, 2017).

Radio Sarabela has both formal and informal methods of decision-making including meetings, text messages, and social networking, depending on the issues. The station manager is in charge and operates the initiative with inputs from all staff and volunteers—which are normally shared at the monthly meetings. The station manager highlighted that teamwork is most effective as it is easier to discuss ideas together and then finalise decisions instead of having one person make a unanimous decision and delegate to others. There is also flexibility regarding decisions made—if an idea finalised during the monthly meeting is not possible then it is not implemented. In such instances, the station manager will decide if it is important to address at once or wait for the monthly meeting to discuss with the team (Sutradar, in-depth interview, December 09, 2017).

This general preference for and implementation of horizontal, inclusive communication has resulted in a high level of comradery among the staff and volunteers. During the visits to the case studies, the author noticed that everyone would contribute to the questions—some in English and most in Bangla which their peers translated; however, it was observed that the station manager would present the final consolidated answer in most cases. It must be noted that this was not due to hierarchy but more out of respect to that person's job. Overall, the current approaches are effective for decision-making within the case studies in Bangladesh.

7.3.2 Internal Policies

The various initiatives have their own formal and informal policies for operation. Regarding all four case studies, there are some general *do's and don'ts* that are communicated informally which everyone is aware of such as logging their in and out times in the register and not eating in the recording studio. Additionally, practitioners are aware of ethics which are important when dealing with various situations such as how to behave with each other and different groups in society, especially when recording content, not to collect monies for covering issues, and the general need to ensure the communities are the priority in the story and no other entity. Apart from these, each station also had some more initiative specific codes of practice (Parveen, in-depth interview, December 10, 2017; Salahin & Pallobi, in-depth interview, December 09, 2017; Sarkar, in-depth interview, December 09, 2017; Sutradar, in-depth interview, December 09, 2017).

Radio Padma identified a *chain of command* that is followed within the station. While the station does position itself within aspects of representative, participatory communication, due to the amount of volunteers and the need to ensure effective management of the station, the internal hierarchy (chain of command) is followed. It is important to note that this has been decided to ensure there is no miscommunication or confusion and that everyone is aware of what is happening within the initiative; it was not designed to enforce any control mechanisms (that suppress people) (Parveen, in-depth interview, December 10, 2017).

Radio Borendro identified that the *by-laws* created at the time the station was established are important. These can be found in a formal document that guides the operation of the management committee as well as specifies the roles and responsibilities of participants. It ensures that everyone is aware of how the station should be operated. Note: the author could not peruse this document personally as a copy could not be found in the station (Sarkar, in-depth interview, December 09, 2017).

Radio Bikrampur highlighted four policies. It was pointed out that the *Ambala Foundation Human Resource Policy* was adopted by the CRS, and it guides decisions relating to volunteer management, financial management, and office rules and regulations. The other policies comprised: *Official Guidelines for RJs* which was created by the station manager with inputs from staff and volunteers and covers the behaviour of the team when on-air or recording programmes; a *Sensitive Programming Guideline* which provides points on what and what not to communicate in programmes and how to behave when dealing with vulnerable individuals in order to ensure nobody feels victimised or marginalised; and a *Security and Safety Policy* that addresses various methods to ensure participants are protected at all times (Salahin & Pallobi, in-depth interview, December 09, 2017).

Similarly, *Radio Sarabela* has also adopted some policies from SKS Foundation, which include the *Human Resources Policy* and *Economic Policy*. Though detailed information was not provided, it was highlighted that these two policies were important to ensure that staff and volunteers are treated appropriately within the CRS environment and that the finances are managed efficiently—both of which are important to the station's continuity (Sutradar, in-depth interview, December 09, 2017).

These internal policies of the case studies are used in conjunction with those at the national level to ensure the stations can operate efficiently and effectively to fulfil their mandates.

7.3.3 Economic Sustainability

It was observed by the author that the case studies operate on a not-for-profit basis; therefore, their focus is on ensuring their incomes are equal to their expenditures from month to month. There are no savings or reinvestments since excess funding is not a common occurrence. Figure 7.3 visually highlights the sources of income and monthly expenditures, which are discussed below.

As can be seen in Fig. 7.3, with monthly operational costs ranging from as little as US $720 (BDT 60,000) to as much as US $3600 (BDT 300,000), the case studies identified sources of funds as being from projects, licence holders/mother organisations, and development advertisements, as well as some small amounts of donations from various benefactors. *Radio Padma* and *Radio Borendro* receive their funds from project grants and development advertisements, with the majority regarding *Radio Padma* being directed to specific programmes and activities by the funding agencies. *Radio Bikrampur* and *Radio Sarabela* receive the bulk of their funding from their mother organisations and some from project grants. *Radio Borendro* also receives additional funding from development advertisements and donors (Parveen, in-depth interview, December 10, 2017; Salahin & Pallobi, in-depth interview, December 09, 2017; Sarkar, in-depth interview, December 09, 2017; Sutradar, in-depth interview, December 09, 2017).

These funds are spent on salaries for full-time staff, stipends for volunteers, and utility expenses such as electricity, phone, and internet. Also, there are miscellaneous expenses of which *Radio Bikrampur* identified entertainment costs (which include snacks for guests and minor maintenance of equipment), and *Radio Sarabela*

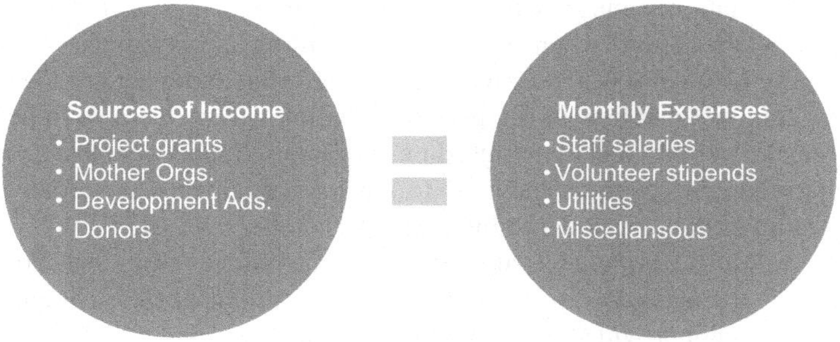

Fig. 7.3 Monthly sources of income and expenditure of the case studies in Bangladesh (Source: Author's own illustration)

identified honorariums for guests on their programmes. None of the monthly expenditures is subsidised by any utility company—all initiatives pay for their electricity, water, internet, and telephone (Parveen, in-depth interview, December 10, 2017; Salahin & Pallobi, in-depth interview, December 09, 2017; Sarkar, in-depth interview, December 09, 2017; Sutradar, in-depth interview, December 09, 2017).

With regard to expenditures, major spending decisions are made by the management committees as staff and volunteers are not always equipped to make these decisions. In some instances, the team will simply state what their needs are, and this information is forwarded to the management committee for decision-making. Specifically, the chief coordinator makes the funding decisions at *Radio Padma*, with necessary inputs from the management committee. *Radio Borendro* refers all funding decisions to the management committee, as does *Radio Bikrampur;* however, with the latter, the station manager is consulted before decisions are finalised. *Radio Sarabela* has a slightly different system—major funding decisions, such as salary and stipends for staff and volunteers, and costs relating to infrastructure and technology are undertaken by the mother organisation, while minor funding decisions, such as guests' honorariums, are made by the station manager (Parveen, in-depth interview, December 10, 2017; Salahin & Pallobi, in-depth interview, December 09, 2017; Sarkar, in-depth interview, December 09, 2017; Sutradar, in-depth interview, December 09, 2017).

7.3.4 Editorial Independence

All the case studies highlighted having a memorandum of understanding (MoU) which governs interactions between the initiatives and those who provide funding. This document clearly outlines the collaboration process and restricts interference from the external funding agencies with regard to the operation of the CRS. Normally, these agreements are discussed with funders before undertaking any projects to ensure all parties are fully aware of and agree to the processes involved in the collaboration and that no problems occur later on (Parveen, in-depth interview, December 10, 2017; Salahin & Pallobi, in-depth interview, December 09, 2017; Sarkar, in-depth interview, December 09, 2017; Sutradar, in-depth interview, December 09, 2017).

Each case study highlighted various aspects of this agreement. *Radio Padma* shared that there is a specific clause stating that the station will retain editorial independence. *Radio Borendro* highlighted that the radio team will only work with external agencies after the MoU has been discussed and all parties are of the same understanding and agreement; only at this stage will there be any exchange of money. *Radio Bikrampur* emphasised the importance of funding agencies understanding that once the concept has been agreed upon and the work has been planned, the agency will not interfere in the production process. Finally, *Radio Sarabela* added that there are external audits done so that funders know that there is no internal corruption and, therefore, do not see a need to interfere (Parveen, in-depth interview, December 10, 2017; Salahin & Pallobi, in-depth interview, December 09,

2017; Sarkar, in-depth interview, December 09, 2017; Sutradar, in-depth interview, December 09, 2017).

7.4 Summary

When one hears the terms *ownership* and *management*, ideas contrary to the ideals of participatory communication come to mind—expertise, sophistication, and control are prominent, which are not in line with de-professionalising initiatives. However, based on the case studies, it is clear that there are management aspects that are in sync with the so-called utopian views associated with CR. Having categorised the management functions under approaches to management and communication, internal policies and guidelines, economic sustainability, and editorial independence, a summary across Nepal, India, and Bangladesh is provided below. However, it is first important to understand how *ownership* is used with regard to CRS in the region.

7.4.1 Ownership of CR Initiatives

Several thinkers in the field have pointed out that it is important for CR initiatives to be owned, operated, and managed by the members of the communities (Atton, 2001; AMARC, n.d.; Carpentier, 2016; Malik, 2011; Rodríguez, 2001). As Manali[19] (in-depth interview, April 26, 2018) highlighted, CR should be about 10–20% technology and the rest should be the community—a position strongly echoed by practitioners and activists such as Dutta (in-depth interview, March 23, 2018), who was previously referenced for pointing out that mainstream media are *for* and *about* us, but not *by* us—a situation that CR addresses. Sutradar (in-depth interview, December 09, 2017) stated it best when she highlighted that the idea behind *Radio Sarabela* is that it should be 10% radio and 90% community—a practice that has been implemented and can be seen through the level of community involvement. As a result, individuals see the CR as "our radio." Keeping this in mind, Fig. 7.4 provides a visual representation of the ownership of these initiatives, as visualised and interpreted by the author based on the 11 case studies.

As can be seen in Fig. 7.4, there are three levels of ownership: licence holder, CR team, and community. The licence holders are the individuals and/or organisations granted legal permission to establish and operate a CRS. Their ownership philosophies guide the internal management of these stations. As a result, all organisations

[19] Raghu Mainali is a community media activist who has been an advocate for and a key stakeholder of the community media sector in Nepal and South Asia for approximately 26 years, since the early 1990s. He has been involved in the development communication field for approximately 31 years. Mainali was involved in the set-up of *Radio Sagarmatha* and, today, continues his activism with CRSC and NEFEJ (Mainali, in-depth interview, April 26, 2018).

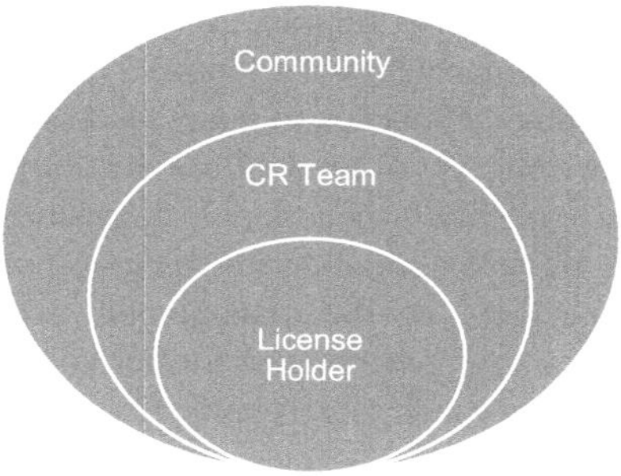

Fig. 7.4 The ownership environment for CR in South Asia based on case studies (Source: Author's own illustration)

with a focus on community development are the choice entities to hold these types of licences (this was highlighted in the CR policies of India and Bangladesh and by stakeholders in Nepal). Apart from this, in keeping with the ideals surrounding community ownership, the CR team is normally encouraged to feel like they own the station and, as such, should feel comfortable to be more active in the operational aspects of these initiatives. Finally, while it is desired that entire communities actively participate in the stations, this is not an achievable reality. As a result, to ensure that there is a sense of community ownership, the CRS reminds their peers that the station is there for their benefit and the content broadcast is based on their communicated needs. Besides, they are always reminded that they can become active participants in daily activities whenever they have the desire to do so. Overall, the metaphorical feeling of ownership over the station is stronger in the CR team than the wider community; however, the wider community is reminded regularly that the CRS is "their own."

7.4.2 Approaches to Management and Communication

Apart from these ideas surrounding licensed and metaphorical ownership of CRS in Nepal, India, and Bangladesh, the approaches to management and communication within these initiatives are also indicative of the type of ownership philosophies implemented. Overall, the author was able to categorise these based on the decision-making processes which include horizontal, top-down, and bottom-up. Ideally, a horizontal approach to decision-making is encouraged as this is representative of a more inclusive process that does not stick to the traditional organisational hierarchy. However, upon closer inspection, it was found that all three methods are utilised within the case studies simultaneously—the approach used would be determined by the issue being addressed.

Major decisions, such as those relating to funding and hiring of staff, are addressed in a top-down manner where the licence holder and/or the management committee have the most input. However, in many instances, these decisions are not made in isolation and are reflective of inputs from the daily CR teams. The bottom-up approach is normally applicable when there is departmental decision-making (in the larger stations) with the final agreements being communicated from the departments to the station managers, to the management committees, and so forth. However, overall, there is a strong preference for horizontal decision-making since this is the most inclusive approach and is reflective of the ideals of CR. Teams accomplish this by ensuring everyone is made aware that their opinions and thoughts are important and welcome; in situations where some might remain quiet in bigger groups, senior staff and volunteers ensure their participation by asking targeted questions.

In addition to these approaches to communication, the CRS highlighted the use of both formal and informal methods of communicating with each other. The more formal methods, such as official meetings and professionally written communication, are used for the more important and policy-relevant information since these need to be properly recorded. On the other hand, there are informal means of communication, especially with social networking platforms such as WhatsApp and Facebook, to share general ideas and receive feedback from each other. In such instances, individuals are more inclined to propose ideas for the stations (especially programmes) and receive feedback on feasibility and/or how to strengthen concepts and implement them. Overall, the case studies shared that there is a high level of comradery among the team members.

7.4.3 Internal Policies, Economic Sustainability, and Editorial Independence

Another key aspect under ownership and management, as highlighted above, includes the internal policies of these initiatives—which also encompass economic sustainability and editorial independence. While there are macro-level national policies and guidelines, these are not specific to the diversities found in CR initiatives. As a result, each of the 11 case studies highlighted various internal policies implemented to guarantee these stations operate as efficiently and effectively as possible while ensuring their communities are the priority. What is interesting to note is that the CRS in Nepal highlighted internal policies and guidelines that address both management and production aspects while those in India and Bangladesh appear to focus more on production-related aspects. This could be attributed to the fact that the guidelines outlined by Mainali et al. (2004) for Nepal had a bit more of a business approach as opposed to a community-focused approach apparent in the Indian and Bangladeshi CRS. However, all case studies highlighted the need to ensure that the community is served.

Finally, while economic sustainability and editorial independence are especially important aspects of CRS, the way they are addressed are guided by internal policies and guidelines. Regarding economic sustainability, this is a challenge highlighted by all 11 case studies since they operate on a non-profit basis—the key element that defined how these initiatives were identified as CR. As a result, general sources of funding include project grants, donations, funds from the licence holder (also referred to as mother organisations), and some amounts from advertisements. Monthly expenditures include salaries for staff, stipends for (paid) volunteers, and utilities such as rent, telephone, electricity, and internet. In an attempt to ensure economic sustainability, some case studies highlighted that they had utilised bartering in the past (such as broadcasting an advertisement on-air in exchange for the use of a billboard in the community and providing space for an internet service provider's antenna in exchange for website building and maintenance), but this is not a regular practice and funding remains a challenge.

Regardless of the scarcity of funds for CR initiatives, a key aspect highlighted by the case studies was that funds that would result in disempowering or marginalising the communities or select groups in the communities or are from individuals or organisations that have contrary views to the stations' objectives are not accepted. This ensures that the initiatives keep editorial independence and prioritise their communities over everything else. What is important to note is that case studies in Nepal, India, and Bangladesh highlighted that before accepting any type of funds, all parties involved are clear as to what is expected of each other. This ensures that there is no miscommunication, and external funders are aware that the CRS will not compromise on their values.

References

AMARC Asia-Pacific. (n.d.). *Homepage*. Retrieved May 31, 2018, from http://amarc-ap.org/.

Atton, C. (2001). *Approaching alternative media: Theory and methodology*. Napier University.

Carpentier, N. (2016). Community media as rhizome: Expanding the research agenda. *Journal of Alternative and Community Media, 1*(1) Retrieved July 31, 2019, from https://www.researchgate.net/publication/312020956_Community_media_as_rhizome_Expanding_the_research_agenda

Dahal, T., & Sigdel, S. (2016). *National mass communications policy 2016: A review*. Freedom Forum.

Mainali, R., Chapagain, Y., and Subba, B. (2004). *Community radio organisation development guidebook*. CRSC/NEFEJ with support of Free Voice.

Malik, K. K. (2011). Community radio: Guidelines on management and ownership. In UNESCO. *Ground Realities, Community Radio in India*. UNESCO.

Pavarala, V., Malik, K. K., Belavadi, V., Deshbandhu, A., & Raghunath, P. (2014). *Community radio continuous improvement toolkit: Version 2.0*. Commonwealth Educational Media Centre for Asia (CEMCA).

Rodríguez, C. (2001). *Fissures in the Mediascape: An international study of citizens' Media*. Hampton Press.

8 Community Radio Practitioners

It is important to note that the categorisations used regarding the community practitioners are based on the level/type of participation by individuals. These classifications do not attempt to address the various cultural underpinnings as the project focuses on mapping at a macro level in order to foster some understanding of similarities and differences regarding community radio (CR) across the South Asia region. Overall, the participants from the case studies can be generally classified into either "internal" or "external" participants with various sub-communities attributed to each.

8.1 Nepal

The case studies (*Radio Sagarmatha, Radio Namobuddha,* and *Radio Sindhu*[1]) identified their communities by both interests and geographic reach. However, regarding the *LGBTQ* (lesbian, gay, bisexual, transgender, queer) community, there were no confirmed participants since Nepal is conservative and individuals are not comfortable to openly identify as being part of this community (Syngtan,[2] in-depth interview, April 25, 2018).

8.1.1 Types of Participants

As can be seen in Fig. 8.1, members of the internal community can be placed into categories comprising staff, volunteers and trainees, community journalists, and management committee. Members of the external community can be placed into categories comprising resource persons, audiences, and the general community. Both main categories are discussed in the following sub-sections.

[1] See *Chap. 4: Profile of Case Studies* for in-depth information of each initiative.

[2] Bhakta Syngtan is the Station Manager for *Radio Namobuddha.*

T. Rampersaud-Skorka, *Community Radio in South Asia*, Diversity and Inclusion Research, https://doi.org/10.1007/978-3-031-85201-5_8

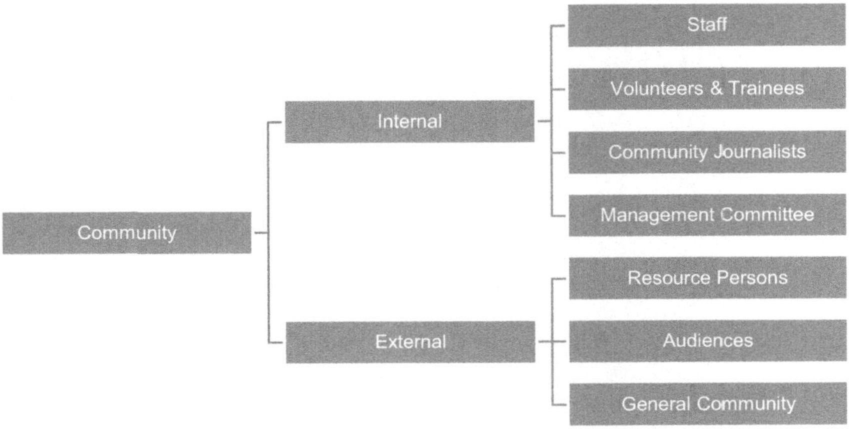

Fig. 8.1 Classification of community in Nepal based on case studies (Source: Author's own illustration)

8.1.1.1 Internal Community

Regarding the case studies, there are four types of participants comprising the internal community: staff, volunteers and trainees, community journalists (CJs), and the management committee. Staff, whether full-time or part-time, are salaried employees with specific jobs within each station; they are the essential personnel. Volunteers, on the other hand, are present for specific programmes and purposes; in many instances, they are referred to as "paid volunteers" since they receive stipends or reimbursements for basic costs incurred such as transportation to foster content production. There are also CJs—individuals who function as interfaces between a community radio station (CRS) and its community. Finally, the management committee oversees the CRS operations but is not involved in the daily tasks. Overall, according to the case studies, all internal participants receive money or other acknowledgements for their contributions and are generally enthusiastic about being affiliated with the initiatives.

With this general understanding, Fig. 8.2 and the subsequent explanations provide more detailed data regarding the internal participants. Note: the management committee was excluded from analysis as they are not part of daily operations.

Figure 8.2 illustrates that *Radio Sagarmatha* has 22 staff and 12 volunteers; of the 34 individuals, approximately five staff have management responsibilities while the remaining participants undertake production roles. *Radio Sagarmatha* highlighted that the decision to have staff and volunteers came from experience—staff are more committed because they receive a regular salary for fulfilling their duties. The station manager added that volunteers are not compelled to complete their tasks, as this is not their main source of income, and their participation is based on their interests and availability; as a result, they are not necessarily relied upon to ensure continuous production of content (Srerestha,[3] in-depth interview, April 26, 2018).

[3] Sahah Man Srerestha is the Station Manager for *Radio Sagarmatha.*

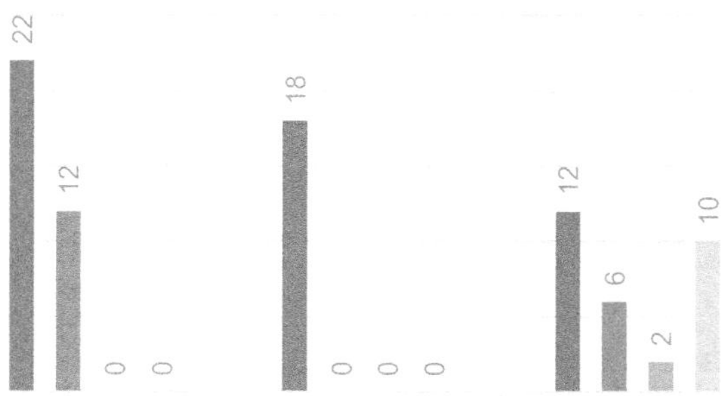

	Radio Sagarmatha	Radio Namobuddha	Radio Sindhu
Staff	22	18	12
Volunteers	12	0	6
Trainees	0	0	2
Community Journalists	0	0	10

Fig. 8.2 Staff and volunteers within each case study in Nepal (Source: Author's own illustration)

Radio Namobuddha does not have any internal volunteers but does differentiate between full-time and part-time staff. Of the 18 staff, 7 are full-time, and 11 are part-time. Seven of the eighteen staff undertake management tasks while 11 undertaking production tasks.[4] The station manager thought it important to share that there was a decrease, and eventual end, in volunteers following the 2015 earthquake in Nepal—the resulting tragedy realigned volunteers' priorities and the station has since not regained this resource (Syngtan, in-depth interview, April 25, 2018).

Radio Sindhu has 12 staff, 2 trainees, 10 CJs, and 6 volunteers. Of the 24 paid individuals (staff, trainees, CJs), 10 undertake management responsibilities and 14 undertake production responsibilities. Further analysis revealed that all CJs and volunteers undertake production tasks while one trainee each had management and production responsibilities. The decision to pay staff was to ensure individuals are always involved in the daily operations of the CRS since volunteers include mostly teachers—people who already have a career which bore a higher priority (Shrestha,[5] in-depth interview, April 25, 2018).

Further to these general categorisations, the internal community was classified according to *men*, *women*, *youth*, and *PWD* (persons with disabilities).[6] The most popular group was *women* who accounted for 55.6% of the known gender

[4] There is no correlation between the seven staff in management roles and the seven full-time staff. The 7 full-time staff perform both management and production roles as is the case with the 11 part-time staff.

[5] Ratna Prasad Shrestha is the Station Manager for *Radio Sindhu.*

[6] See *Chap. 5: Descriptive Mapping of CR in SA* for an explanation as to why these categories were identified.

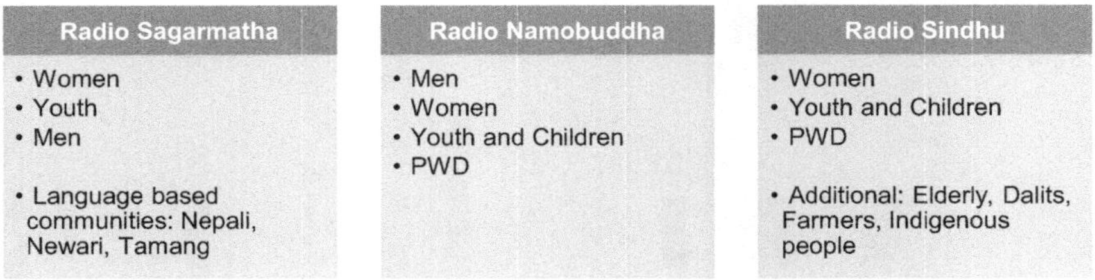

Fig. 8.3 Classification of the external community of each case study in Nepal (Source: Author's own illustration)

representations (40 out of 72 individuals—not counting the 10 CJs[7]). With regard to *youth*, this category represents 26% of the internal participants (including the CJs who were all identified as such); the remaining 74% were individuals over the age of 30 years. Finally, there was one *PWD* participant identified for *Radio Sindhu*—a man with visual impairments who holds a master's degree (Shrestha, in-depth interview, April 25, 2018; Srerestha, in-depth interview, April 26, 2018; Syngtan, in-depth interview, April 25, 2018).

8.1.1.2 External Community[8]

While there is much known about the internal community associated with the case studies, not much is known about their external community; however, interviewees were able to provide enough information which give some idea about these groups.

According to *Radio Sagarmatha's* station manager, this CRS caters to the Kathmandu Valley in general—an area including 4.5 million people of which there is support from approximately 6% of this population. *Radio Namobuddha's* station manager identified their audience as being approximately half a million within a 17 km radius, while *Radio Sindhu's* station manager identified the external community comprising approximately one million people within a 57 km radius of which one-third provides general support to the station. Figure 8.3 is a visual representation of the types of the external community (not mutually exclusive but as communicated to the author by the stations) for the three CRS.

As can be seen in Fig. 8.3, all three case studies have *women* and *youth* as identified external participants; *Radio Sagarmatha* and *Radio Namobuddha* also identified *men*; and *Radio Namobuddha* and *Radio Sindhu* identifying *PWD* participants. Apart from these classifications, *Radio Sagarmatha* identified three language-based groups comprising Nepali, Newari, and Tamang while *Radio Sindhu* revealed that they focus on several traditionally marginalised groups in the society comprising the elderly, Dalits, farmers, and indigenous people. These communities were ascertained based on the target audiences for programming (Shrestha, in-depth interview,

[7] The genders of the ten CJs at *Radio Sindhu* were not provided as there was some disagreement among the CR team. Therefore, the information regarding genders does not reflect this.

[8] Members of the internal community are also part of the wider, external community.

April 25, 2018; Srerestha, in-depth interview, April 26, 2018; Syngtan, in-depth interview, April 25, 2018).

Further, the case studies highlighted that while the participation from all communities is good, there is always a need to increase the number of participants. Specifically, *Radio Sindhu* expressed an interest in expanding the reach to include scavengers and riverain people; however, since this would be an expensive process, it has not yet been undertaken. While the other two case studies did not identify specific groups, they expressed a need to expand the geographic reach so that more people can have access to the content being broadcast. However, while there are challenges to physical expansion, the CRS engages in other methods aimed at increasing community engagement; these are addressed in detail in the following section (Shrestha, in-depth interview, April 25, 2018; Srerestha, in-depth interview, April 26, 2018; Syngtan, in-depth interview, April 25, 2018).

8.1.2 Motivation and Mobilisation

Radio Sagarmatha highlighted the need for increased participation, especially from the youth community, as does *Radio Namobuddha,* which highlighted the need for overall increased participation from the community. Alternatively, *Radio Sindhu* highlighted that the current participation is sufficient taking into consideration the station's resources; however, there is a need to ensure that this is sustained. As a result, all three case studies implement various methods to attract participants for both the internal and external communities (Shrestha, in-depth interview, April 25, 2018; Srerestha, in-depth interview, April 26, 2018; Syngtan, in-depth interview, April 25, 2018).

Regarding *Radio Namobuddha*, the CRS team has been trying to increase community involvement to re-establish its volunteer population. However, this has not garnered positive results beyond participation during live programmes. As a result, there is a plan to create radio centres in the various villages to teach individuals about CR and how to produce programmes in the hope that this type of community outreach would encourage greater participation through awareness creation. The station manager also highlighted that while there is a great deal of enthusiasm during the conceptual stage for programme production, due to the effort it takes actually to produce the programmes for broadcast, this enthusiasm diminishes over time which has resulted in many ideas disappearing (Syngtan, in-depth interview, April 25, 2018).

With regard to *Radio Sagarmatha* and *Radio Sindhu*, motivation is not a major challenge since participants are more self-motivated. *Radio Sagarmatha* highlighted that the youth want to gain knowledge on various aspects of radio production. As a result, they join the team to learn and gain exposure. *Radio Sindhu* highlighted that most of their internal participants want to give back to the community and find the CRS as an ideal medium for doing this. Also, the station manager highlighted that through production work, the team can interact with various members of their communities, present information using their mother tongues (their main language), and represent their communities—all of which are empowering for participants (Srerestha, in-depth interview, April 26, 2018; Shrestha, in-depth interview, April 25, 2018).

Apart from these initiative specific techniques, all three CRS identified advertisements, awareness creation campaigns, and encouragement of walk-ins through on-air broadcasts and interpersonal interactions as mobilisation methods. Together, these methods ensure some station visibility with regard to motivation and mobilisation and encourage participation from the wider community (Shrestha, in-depth interview, April 25, 2018; Srerestha, in-depth interview, April 26, 2018; Syngtan, in-depth interview, April 25, 2018).

8.1.3 Capacity Building and Sharing

In each case study, all members of their internal community have access to capacity building and sharing opportunities—these are accomplished through orientation or introductory sessions and continuous training with regard to theme-based programmes and production techniques. All individuals receive training depending on the needs of the station—both old and new staff, volunteers, trainees, and CJs (Shrestha, in-depth interview, April 25, 2018; Srerestha, in-depth interview, April 26, 2018; Syngtan, in-depth interview, April 25, 2018).

Radio Sagarmatha highlighted that there are regular theme-based training sessions for staff and volunteers on topics such as child marriages and the right to information (RTI). *Radio Namobuddha* also highlighted a focus on theme-based training sessions that address areas such as agriculture, child rights, and disaster recovery. *Radio Sindhu* also identified having training sessions and added that these are encouraged as much as possible since they help with the sharpening of existing skills and learning of new ones. What is interesting to note is that *Radio Sagarmatha* personnel also provide training for other CRS from time to time. However, the station manager stated that this has posed challenges in the past such as transportation to outlying stations. Additionally, sometimes there are miscommunications about the needs of the CRS requesting training and when *Radio Sagarmatha's* team arrives, they realise they are not fully prepared (Shrestha, in-depth interview, April 25, 2018; Srerestha, in-depth interview, April 26, 2018; Syngtan, in-depth interview, April 25, 2018).

Overall, *Radio Sagarmatha* highlighted that these kinds of sessions are appreciated, especially since they give rise to innovative ideas as well as increase existing knowledge. *Radio Sindhu* supported this position and added that these sessions are welcome, especially since an increase in knowledge would mean better programmes. Contrary to the other two CRS, *Radio Sindhu's* station manager highlighted that their internal community wished there were more training since there are insufficient opportunities to ensure continuous elevation to deal with evolving issues promptly (Shrestha, in-depth interview, April 25, 2018; Srerestha, in-depth interview, April 26, 2018; Syngtan, in-depth interview, April 25, 2018).

8.2 India

Based on the case studies (*Sangham Radio, Tilonia Radio, Radio Luit,* and *Waqt ki Awaaz*), communities are identified using generalised categories comprising *men, women, youth,* and *children* within reach of the stations—a description that shows communities are classified by geography. Further, details supplied, such as identifying distinct groups being catered to including tribal groups, housewives, and cleaners, alluded to these CRS also classifying their communities by interests. This information is key to remember as the categories are presented below.

8.2.1 Types of Participants

As can be seen in Fig. 8.4, members of the internal community can be placed into categories comprising staff and paid volunteers, in addition to the management committees formed to guide the CRS. Members of the external community can be placed into categories comprising volunteers, resource persons, audiences, and the general community. Both main categories are discussed in the following sub-sections.

8.2.1.1 Internal Community

While staff are full-time individuals paid to ensure operation of the CRS, paid volunteers are part-time individuals who are given monetary compensations for their contributions. Regarding the paid volunteers of *Sangham Radio,* they are called reporters and produce programmes for the CRS in their free time since they are the full-time staff of the Deccan Development Society (DDS). In the case of *Radio Luit,* their paid volunteers are referred to as Radio Activists (RAs) and comprise the

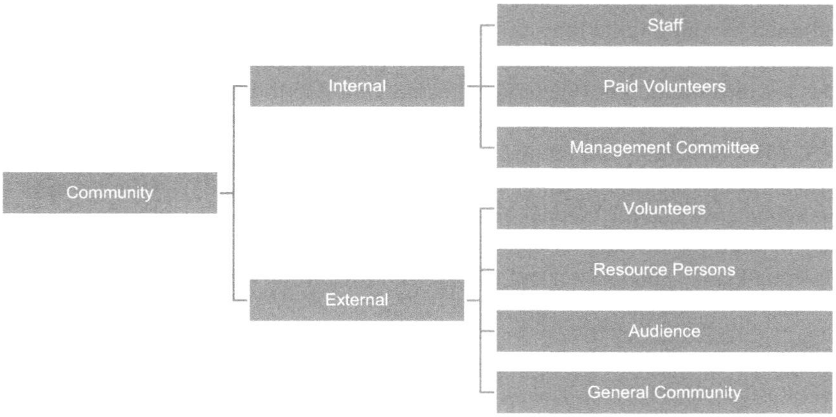

Fig. 8.4 Classification of the community with regard to the case studies in India (Source: Author's own illustration)

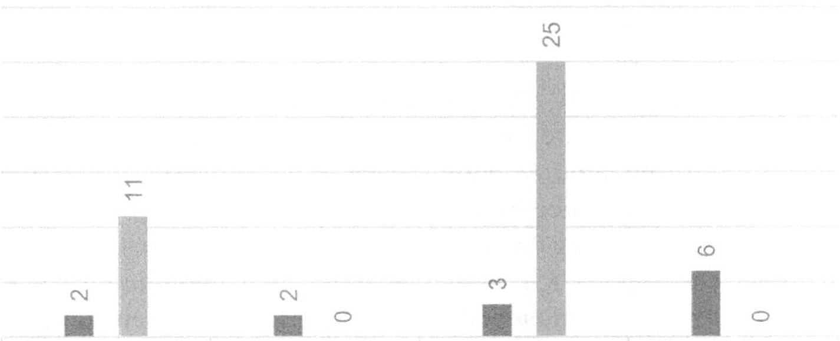

	Sangham Radio	Tilonia Radio	Radio Luit	Waqt ki Awaaz
Staff	2	2	3	6
Volunteers	11	0	25	0

Fig. 8.5 Staff and volunteers within each case study in India (Source: Author's own illustration)

media and communication students at the Gauhati University. All internal participants receive some financial compensation—whether as a regular salary, honorarium, or stipend (Aarti Devi,[9] in-depth interview, March 07, 2018; Acharjya,[10] in-depth interview, February 05, 2018; General Narsamma,[11] in-depth interview, April 06, 2018; Shukla,[12] in-depth interview, March 08, 2018).

With these broad categories in mind, Fig. 8.5 visually represents more specific data regarding internal participants for each of the case study.

As can be seen in Fig. 8.5, *Sangham Radio* has 2 staff and 11 volunteers; of these individuals, both staff members undertake management and production aspects (even though the assigned roles are station manager and producer) while all volunteers undertake production-related functions. The station manager highlighted that even though they have 11 volunteers, their loyalty is to the mother organisation first as they are full-time employees of DDS—a non-governmental organisation; only when they have some free time will they produce programmes for the CRS. She continued by stating that the staff are more invested in the continuity of the station due to their very personal links to advocacy for the initiative and the benefits it provides for the community (General Narsamma, in-depth interview, April 06, 2018).

Tilonia Radio has two staff who undertake all operational aspects of the CRS. Like *Sangham Radio*, the staff of this CRS multi-task in their roles and responsibilities regarding management and production functions. However, the station manager is also the creative person who does the actual programmes for broadcast, in addition to station management, while the producer undertakes more conceptual tasks and less technical tasks with regard to productions. The presence

[9] Aarti Devi is the station manager for *Tilonia Radio*.

[10] Bhaskar Jyoti Acharjya is the programme executive of *Radio Luit*.

[11] General Narsamma is the station manager for *Sangham Radio* and a key figure in the CR movement in India.

[12] Radha Shukla is the coordinator (instead of the title station manager) for *Waqt ki Awaaz*.

of these two paid staff ensures that the station is continuously producing and broadcasting content to the community (Aarti Devi, in-depth interview, March 07, 2018).

Radio Luit has 3 staff and 25 volunteers; of the three staff, two are involved in the daily operations of the station as programme executive and transmission operator—one each undertaking management and production functions, while the volunteers undertake production functions only. Regarding the third staff, this person holds the title of station manager by default due to being the director of the Institute of Distance and Open Learning (IDOL), Guwahati University—the title is more symbolic as the programme executive undertakes all the responsibilities normally assigned to a station manager. Additionally, the two daily staff receive salaries from the CRS while the station manager does not receive a salary—as director his responsibilities include oversight of the CRS. The decision to have paid staff within the station was made approximately 4 months after the launch of the CRS due to the need to have regular staff to undertake daily tasks (Acharjya, in-depth interview, February 05, 2018).

Finally, regarding *Waqt ki Awaaz,* of the six staff, one undertakes management functions as the station coordinator while the remainder conduct production functions relating to technical aspects and production tasks. Even though the interviewee mentioned volunteers, these are not involved in the operation of the station and are therefore addressed in detail under the external community (Shukla, in-depth interview, March 08, 2018).

The author was also able to analyse data as per the generic classifications. Specifically, *women* participants were significantly higher than *men* with 82% of internal participants belonging to this group (18 out of 22 individuals—not including youths as the gender for this category was not provided by the case studies). As per the age classification, 55% comprised *youth* participants (27 out of 49 internal participants) with the remainder being adults.

All four case studies highlighted that there was no difference between the performances of staff and paid volunteers. Individuals involved with the CRS tend to work towards the success of the CRS. However, all four case studies stated that there is a need to have staff within these initiatives to ensure the stations are in continuous operation; the paid volunteers are complimentary to the staff in that they are not depended upon to manage the CRS—they mostly carry out production functions.

8.2.1.2 External Community

While the case studies were able to provide detailed information about the internal community, this was not extended to the external community. However, the author was able to classify the members of the external community into four main categories: volunteers, resource persons, audience, and the general community. While the first three categories comprise active participants, the latter encompasses individuals not involved in any CR activity but are within reach of the station.

Concerning the geographical reach of the stations, *Sangham Radio* caters to 150 villages (an actual number was not possible to ascertain), *Tilonia Radio* caters to 30 villages (comprising approximately 60,000 people), *Radio Luit* caters to the campus population and surrounding areas (over 5000 people), and *Waqt ki Awaaz* caters to

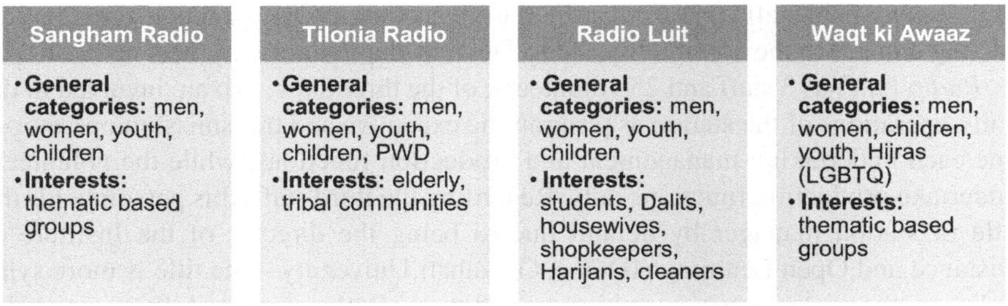

Fig. 8.6 Classification of the external communities of each case study in India (Source: Author's own illustration)

303 villages (comprising approximately 300,000 people) (Aarti Devi, in-depth interview, March 07, 2018; Acharjya, in-depth interview, February 05, 2018; General Narsamma, in-depth interview, April 06, 2018; Shukla, in-depth interview, March 08, 2018).

Furthermore, the interviewees provided insight regarding communities of interest within the external community of their CRS; Fig. 8.6 depicts this data.

As can be seen in Fig. 8.6, regarding the generic categories, all four case studies cater to *men, women, youth*, and *children* communities. Additionally, *Tilonia Radio* has programmes that target the *persons with disabilities (PWD)* community while *Waqt ki Awaaz* has programmes that target *Hijras* (who are considered as members of the *LGBTQ* community). As per other types of external communities, both *Sangham Radio* and *Waqt ki Awaaz* highlight that through thematic areas (such as agriculture, environment, culture, health, and gender), they cater to various groups; however, they did not specify any particular community of interest. *Tilonia Radio* and *Radio Luit*, on the other hand, identified catering to various interest groups such as tribal groups, students, housewives, shopkeepers, Dalits, and cleaners (Aarti Devi, in-depth interview, March 07, 2018; Acharjya, in-depth interview, February 05, 2018; General Narsamma, in-depth interview, April 06, 2018; Shukla, in-depth interview, March 08, 2018).

All four case studies highlighted sufficient support from their communities; however, there is always the desire to increase participation; as a result, the techniques used by the case studies to foster an increase in participation are addressed below.

8.2.2 Motivation and Mobilisation

Due to the lack of sufficient financial motivation for non-staff individuals, it is difficult to attract new participants as many individuals cannot commit to more responsibilities if they cannot earn some money as it is a matter of survival for them. As a result, the case studies rely on various incentives to ensure current participants are encouraged to continue contributing.

Sangham Radio highlighted their ability to provide monthly prizes of USD 7 (INR ₹500) for each volunteer who produce programmes containing one song, one story, one interview, and one discussion. Another motivator is the sentimental feelings individuals have by being associated with initiatives that focus on social change. General Narsamma (in-depth interview, April 06, 2018) stated that there is a dedication by the staff to continue working with the CRS since they have been there since establishment; they have strong sentiments for the CRS. Likewise, Acharjya (in-depth interview, February 05, 2018) highlighted that the "feel good factor" is a strong motivator as individuals who are able to participate in their developments are empowered to continue doing this. Another reason was knowledge seeking—people want to learn how to produce programmes for broadcast, how to operate these initiatives, and, generally, about the various thematic areas highlighted in content production. Finally, individuals are encouraged to thinking of the CRS as "our radio"—if they do not use it then no-one else will (Aarti Devi, in-depth interview, March 07, 2018; Acharjya, in-depth interview, February 05, 2018; General Narsamma, in-depth interview, April 06, 2018; Shukla, in-depth interview, March 08, 2018).

In addition to the above self-motivating factors, CRS utilises capacity building and sharing activities to sustain participation of the internal community.

8.2.3 Capacity Building and Sharing

All four case studies highlighted that there are training sessions available for both new and old internal participants. These sessions are facilitated by internal and external personnel—depending on the needs of the CRS and the prospective facilitators' knowledge, experiences, and availability. While some sessions utilise a workshop format, there is also the use of on-the-job training; Shukla (in-depth interview, March 08, 2018) jokingly highlighted that practical situations are necessary as workshop trainings tend to stay in the workshop.

Sangham Radio highlighted that their staff are now the facilitators of training sessions since there has not been any new internal participants for some time. The staff facilitate training as a result of the years of combined experiences and knowledge gained over time. The station manager explained that one of the key reasons why they facilitate CR sessions in their community is because outsiders normally have a challenge communicating in the local language. As a result, it is easier for them to train their community members. However, the staff do attend training sessions organised by other organisations to ensure they are continuously learning (General Narsamma, in-depth interview, April 06, 2018).

Tilonia Radio and *Waqt ki Awaaz* highlighted that training is done on a needs basis since there has not been any meaningful change in staff over the years. Regarding the latter, inexperienced staff are given on-the-job training from seasoned, more experienced staff. However, should the staff of these two CRS find they are lacking knowledge in any area, they arrange training sessions to fill such gaps (Aarti Devi, in-depth interview, March 07, 2018; Shukla, in-depth interview, March 08, 2018).

Radio Luit is unique in that it is a campus CRS with internal participants changing every year since they are media and communication students. As a result, there are formal training sessions conducted every year. While some of these sessions occur in the classroom setting, there are also sessions in the CRS on various production tasks such as scripting, recording, and editing (Acharjya, in-depth interview, February 05, 2018).

8.3 Bangladesh

Based on the case studies (*Radio Padma, Borendro Radio, Radio Bikrampur,* and *Radio Sarabela*), programmes are geared towards *women, men, youth,* and *children* communities who are identified by geography. Also, interests-based groups including farmers, tribal groups, drug addicts, Dalits, students, fishermen, beauticians, housewives, labourers, people with disabilities, and the third gender.

8.3.1 Types of Participants

8.3.1.1 Internal Community

According to the case studies, and as can be seen in Fig. 8.7, the internal community includes staff, (paid) volunteers, and the management committee. While staff are paid a monthly salary, in some instances, volunteers are also given a stipend to compensate for the time spent undertaking station activities instead of a job. These stipends are not enormous amounts and are used to cover expenses such as travel (Parveen, in-depth interview, December 10, 2017; Salahin & Pallobi, in-depth interview, December 09, 2017; Sarkar, in-depth interview, December 09, 2017; Sutradar, in-depth interview, December 09, 2017).

With this in mind, Fig. 8.8 provides more in-depth information regarding the internal community.

As can be seen in Fig. 8.8, *Radio Padma* has 10 staff (including 5 management and 5 production persons) and 72 volunteers (who perform production-related tasks). The decision to have staff and paid volunteers was made by the chief coordinator of the CRS. While staff ensure daily operation of the station, the volunteers—who are mostly university students—help whenever they have the time instead of undertaking a part-time job with the stipend acting as a motiving factor (Parveen, in-depth interview, December 10, 2017).

Radio Borendro has three staff comprising management and production persons and 31 volunteers—all of whom are in the programming department. While the station manager receives a salary, the two project-related staff are paid through the project funds; volunteers are given stipends based on the work performed. The decision to pay stipends to the volunteers was made following the establishment of the CRS as financial challenges faced by volunteers became visible (Sarkar, in-depth interview, December 09, 2017).

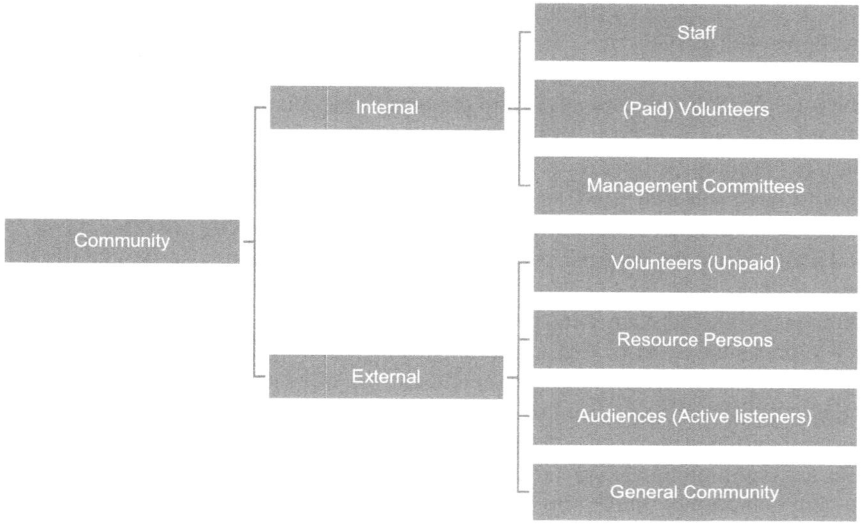

Fig. 8.7 Classification of community with regard to the case studies in Bangladesh (Source: Author's own illustration)

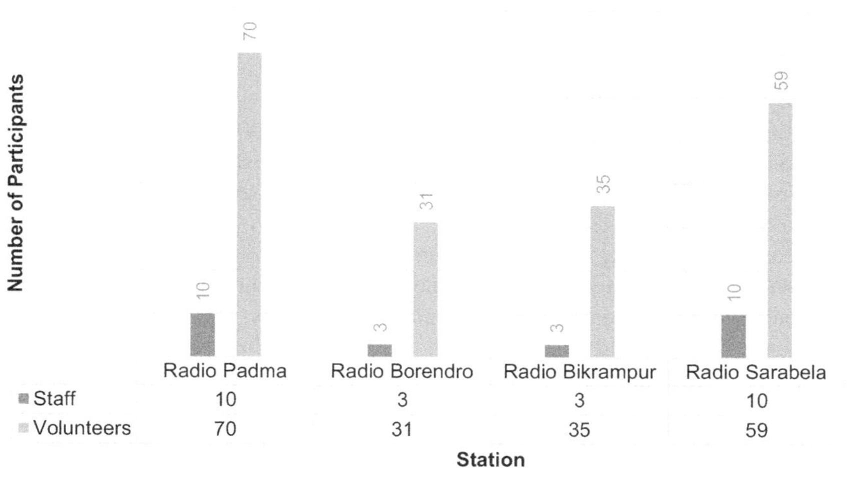

	Radio Padma	Radio Borendro	Radio Bikrampur	Radio Sarabela
Staff	10	3	3	10
Volunteers	70	31	35	59

Fig. 8.8 Staff and volunteers within each case study in Bangladesh (Source: Author's own illustration)

Radio Bikrampur has three staff and 25 volunteers with the staff comprising the station manager, office assistant, and senior producer and all volunteers undertaking production roles. While there is no standard stipend for volunteers, their travel allowances, as well as any other costs associated with production, are normally covered. The decision to have full-time staff and to cover basic expenses incurred by volunteers was taken by the licence holder (Salahin & Pallobi, in-depth interview, December 09, 2017).

Radio Sarabela has ten staff, of which five are in management and five in production; all 59 volunteers are in the programming department. While the project-related staff are paid from the project funder, the remaining staff are paid by the station's funding; volunteers also receive a stipend for their productions. This decision to have full-time staff and to pay the volunteers stipends was implemented from the beginning (Sutradar, in-depth interview, December 09, 2017).

Furthermore, the internal community of the case studies can be classified by *men, women, youth* and *children*, and *PWD* (persons with disabilities). Regarding the latter, while there are some programmes for this group, only *Radio Sarabela* has one representative from that community as a volunteer. Additionally, while the *LGBTQ* community is recognised based on the *third-gender* classification, there were no self-identified participants in any of the case studies. As for the other categories mentioned above, *youth and children* classification includes over 75% of the internal communities across all case studies, with many of them being from the student community. Interestingly, both *Radio Borendro* and *Radio Sarabela* identified children participants who do undertake production functions for children-specific programmes; however, they are not regular volunteers. Regarding the male-female dynamics, these are almost equal in the number regarding the four case studies (Parveen, in-depth interview, December 10, 2017; Salahin & Pallobi, in-depth interview, December 09, 2017; Sarkar, in-depth interview, December 09, 2017; Sutradar, in-depth interview, December 09, 2017).

8.3.1.2 External Community

These three CRS cater to approximately 600,000–700,000 people in general, with *Radio Sarabela* catering to 200,000 people (due to the island layout of the area). Apart from this, the case studies were able to share some specifics, which are represented in Fig. 8.9.

As can be seen in Fig. 8.9, groups comprising *men, women, youth and children*, and *PWD* are being catered to by all the case studies through their programmes while only two CRS cater to the *third gender*. Additionally, *Radio Padma* also caters to students, farmers, and fishermen while *Radio Borendro* caters to tribal groups, farmers, and drug addicts; *Radio Bikrampur* caters to Dalit communities, which comprise smaller groups such as the sweeper community and snake charmers; and *Radio Sarabela* caters to local entrepreneurs, such as beauticians and shop owners, in addition to farmers, labourers, housewives, and Dalits. A unique point to note is that each of these CRS has numerous *listeners' clubs* across the communities the broadcast to. These groups are normally associated with specific programmes and would religiously listen and supply important feedback to the production team regularly (Parveen, in-depth interview, December 10, 2017; Salahin & Pallobi, in-depth interview, December 09, 2017; Sarkar, in-depth interview, December 09, 2017; Sutradar, in-depth interview, December 09, 2017).

Apart from the listeners' clubs, other engagement techniques of the external community have been stated as being "satisfactory" by the case studies, but there is always the desire to get more people involved.

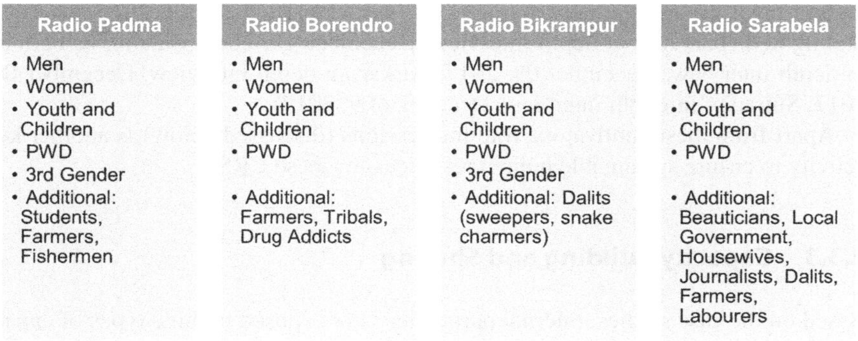

Fig. 8.9 Classification of the external communities of each case in Bangladesh (Source: Author's own illustration)

8.3.2 Motivation and Mobilisation

Participation from the communities is described as "good"; however, to ensure that the initiatives are sustained, there is a need for new people to become more actively involved in the initiatives. As highlighted in several case study interviews, the idea behind CR is for there to be *10% radio and 90% community* (Parveen, in-depth interview, December 10, 2017; Salahin & Pallobi, in-depth interview, December 09, 2017; Sarkar, in-depth interview, December 09, 2017; Sutradar, in-depth interview, December 09, 2017).

Radio Padma has several strategies in place to get more individuals involved such as approaching specific members from the community to become guests on the various programme. In such instances, the friends and families of these individuals listen to the programme and sometimes become regular listeners. One such programme is *Amader Gunijon* (meaning: Our Heroes), which focuses on outstanding members of the community. Further to this, the team at *Radio Padma* makes a directed effort to ensure that marginalised women are involved either directly, through various jobs, or indirectly, as unpaid volunteers, with the station (Parveen, in-depth interview, December 10, 2017).

At *Radio Bikrampur*, producers would physically visit resource persons and record them in the field in order to ensure that these individuals are included in the programmes since many do not have time to visit the CRS, as does *Radio Sarabela*. Additionally, audience members are encouraged to use text messages or phone calls to share information. There are occasions when the CR team, equipped with cell phones, visit the people, and allow them to send text messages or make phone calls as programmes are broadcast live (Salahin & Pallobi, in-depth interview, December 09, 2017; Sutradar, in-depth interview, December 09, 2017).

Apart from these techniques, the case studies highlighted that individuals become internal participants because they see themselves as becoming voices for their communities (which also makes them into mini-celebrities due to their radio personality status, as one participant highlighted). Additionally, the self-development aspect of getting involved and the networking opportunities participation created were also highlighted (Parveen, in-depth interview, December 10, 2017; Salahin & Pallobi, in-depth interview, December 09, 2017; Sarkar, in-depth interview, December 09, 2017; Sutradar, in-depth interview, December 09, 2017).

Apart from these motivators, training sessions (discussed below) is another key activity to ensure sustainable human resources for these CRS.

8.3.3 Capacity Building and Sharing

Based on the case studies, internal participants are exposed to three types of capacity building and sharing sessions: orientation, introductory, and continuous. Mostly, inexperienced staff and volunteers participate in the orientation and introductory sessions while the latter is open to all (Parveen, in-depth interview, December 10, 2017; Salahin & Pallobi, in-depth interview, December 09, 2017; Sarkar, in-depth interview, December 09, 2017; Sutradar, in-depth interview, December 09, 2017).

At the national level, various agencies, such as Bangladesh NGOs Network for Radio and Communication (BNNRC), National Institute for Mass Communication (NIMCo), Press Institute of Bangladesh (PIB), and Campaign for Popular Education (CAMPE), provide multiple opportunities for interactive sessions over the course of the year. These can range from six to ten sessions in total and are held for both new and old internal participants. While all organisations provide learning opportunities related to content production and becoming stronger CR practitioners, BNNRC also facilitates sessions about advocacy (Parveen, in-depth interview, December 10, 2017; Salahin & Pallobi, in-depth interview, December 09, 2017; Sarkar, in-depth interview, December 09, 2017; Sutradar, in-depth interview, December 09, 2017).

Internally, *Radio Padma* has at least one introductory session for inexperienced staff and volunteers per year; however, it is also open to older participants so they can refresh their knowledge. *Radio Borendro* has a weekly in-house session which is conducted by their chief programme producer. This session is for both old and new staff and volunteers and covers production-related information, both thematic and technical in nature. Whenever the need arises, activists, journalists, and professionals are also invited to these sessions for their inputs. *Radio Bikrampur* has a continuous internal training system in place where there is always information being shared among practitioners as they produce programmes. Further to this, there is at least one training sponsored by Ambala Foundation yearly at the local level, and staff and volunteers conduct orientation sessions for newcomers. Finally, *Radio Sarabela* has a Community Media Class, which occurs every Friday at the station. During these sessions, information relating to every aspect of radio production are shared. Individuals are encouraged to discuss the challenges they face and to help each other with possible solutions. The agenda for these sessions is normally open-ended and focuses on challenges with the previous week's broadcasts; however, if individuals request something specific, then this is arranged. Overall, training is welcomed by staff and volunteers as they provide opportunities for the development of new skills and knowledge or to build on previous skill sets (Parveen, in-depth interview, December 10, 2017; Salahin & Pallobi, in-depth interview, December 09, 2017; Sarkar, in-depth interview, December 09, 2017; Sutradar, in-depth interview, December 09, 2017).

8.4 Summary

Regarding community ownership, the next logical question is: *"who are part of the communities?"* Before addressing the generalisations across the region, it is important to restate the categories within the broad rubric of community; these were identified by the author based on analysis of data from the 11 case studies and are visually represented in Fig. 8.10 as it pertains to the South Asian region comprising Nepal, India, and Bangladesh.

As can be seen in Fig. 8.10, the community for a CR initiative can be further subdivided into internal and external—based on their associations with the initiative. The internal community comprises the staff and paid volunteers who ensure that the station is operational daily while the external community comprises all other individuals associated with the CRS.

While the ideal is to have a variety of daily volunteers from the (external) community, the reality is that many of these groups are underprivileged and, as a result, their time is spent working to earn a salary and support themselves and family. Therefore, to ensure that these stations are still operating with the interest of the community, individuals from those communities are given opportunities to learn how to manage, operate, and produce content for radio broadcast and are hired as

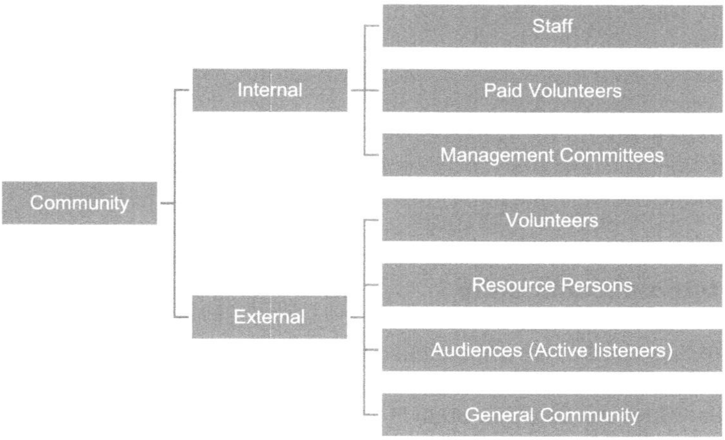

Fig. 8.10 Classification of communities in CR in South Asia based on the case studies (Source: Author's own illustration)

staff. However, due to funding challenges, it is not possible for the CRS to hire everyone as a full-time staff. To ensure there are enough human resources available for operation, paid volunteers are a complimentary element to the staff. The term paid volunteer indicates that these individuals do not receive a salary for the duties undertaken but are at least given a stipend or some sort of compensation for their time. This has been a large motivating factor as interested individuals who cannot dedicate their full energies towards the operation of these initiatives are at the very least able to cover some incurred expenses such as transportation. With regard to Nepal, these paid volunteers are also classified as trainees and community journalists. It must be noted that while members of the management committees of CRS are part of the internal community—do influence the operation of the stations on a daily basis, due to their overseer like function—they are not discussed in detail.

Regarding the external community of an initiative, there are individuals who act as an interface between the station and the people being served (general community)—they are referred to as volunteers and assist the internal community (CR team) with information about upcoming events, organising meetings, acting as guides during fieldwork for production, and even assisting with minor aspects when in the field. Some CRS will try to provide a small monetary stipend for the time volunteers spend with the team, but this is not always a reality. Apart from the volunteers, the resource persons are considered as part of the external community—these individuals do sometimes act as talent or provide information for programming. However, the most important group comprises the active listeners—those individuals who would provide feedback to the CRS about the different programmes stating what they liked, did not like, and their current needs. They are the ones who ensure the stations are operating in the interest of the community. Finally, the general community comprises those within reach of the station—they might be listening but are not actively engaged with the programme, CRS, or CR team.

Overall, while the ideal is to have full participation from the community being served, this is not possible due to circumstances. As a result, CRS have implemented the staff aspect from mainstream media; however, this has not affected the stations since the objectives are clearly stated and staff respect and support this operational mandate. Furthermore, any member from the external community could become a part of the internal community at any point in time—they simply need to communicate this to the CR team and move forward from there.

8.4.1 Internal Community

Overall, the case studies have highlighted that these initiatives can be operated comprising an internal community comprising as little as 2 people to as much as 80 people. Based on the data from the 11 case studies, there are a total of 91 staff (25.9%) and 251 volunteers (74.1%)—of which the specifics for each country are shared in Fig. 8.11.

As can be seen in Fig. 8.11, while India and Bangladesh have larger numbers of paid volunteers, Nepal has more staff than paid volunteers. This could be a result of the fact that the Nepali CR sector is a bit more sophisticated than the other two

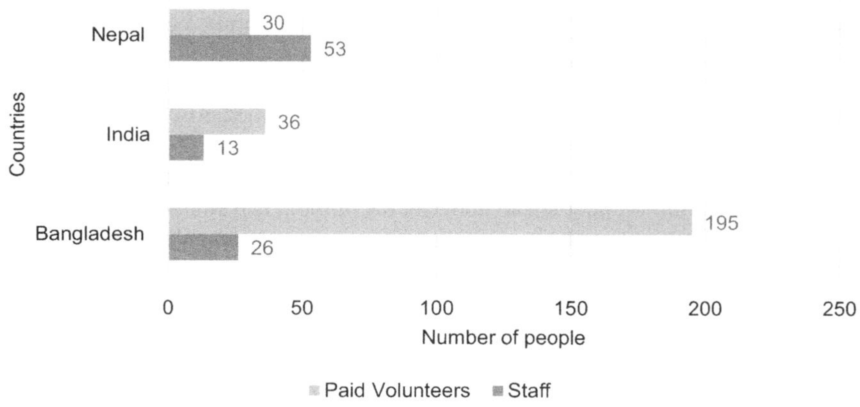

Fig. 8.11 Internal communities in South Asia based on the case studies (Source: Author's own illustration)

countries. As a result of not having a CR policy, the initiatives in Nepal are able to operate as other media entities, which means they are operated more like a business. Therefore, while they are community-focused and identify as CR initiatives, they are also operated similar to commercial FM stations. Regarding the high number of volunteers for CRS in Bangladesh as opposed to the other two countries, this could be attributed to the fact that there was a significantly higher youth participant percentage in Bangladesh, which is 75%, while India had 55% and Nepal had 26%. The assumption is that youth have more time to volunteer as opposed to adults—who need to have careers that can support their families financially. As for the gender dynamics, there appear to be more women participants who account for over 60% of the internal community.

Further to these specifics of internal communities, there were some minor representations of communities of interest which included PWD and LGBTQ. What is important to note is that in Bangladesh the LGBTQ are not acknowledged by this full label but as people with a third gender. In Nepal, while there is an acknowledgement that there might be representatives from this group in the internal community, there was no-one who openly identified as an LBGTQ person due to the conservative society. Finally, in India, while secondary data does reveal the presence of LGBTQ participants in the internal community of some CRS, none of the case studies had any.

8.4.2 External Community

Regarding the external community, this was harder to classify as different stations cater to various communities. Furthermore, there is no emphasis on market research which would provide concrete information such as all the different groups within the external community and amount of people. However, the case studies were able to provide some information regarding this community. It must be noted that while the term "external" is used, this was done for categorisation purposes and not to disassociate these individuals from the CRS—they are still very much part of the initiatives' communities but are not directly involved in the daily operations of the stations.

Specifically, Nepal had larger transmitters ranging from 100 W to 1000 W, which catered to half a million people and above. CRS in India had smaller allowances for broadcast range even though their transmitters were on average of 100 W—these CRS catered to approximately a 12-km-radius reach. Finally, Bangladesh had transmitters comprising 100 W and 250 W, which allowed each of the case studies to cater to approximately 200,000 people and more within a 17 km to 34 km radius. What was consistent is that all the case studies showed that the rural CRS had smaller communities while the urban and peri-urban CRS had larger communities with Bangladesh having the largest reach due to the population density and topography of the country.

Apart from this, there was some information regarding the communities of interest. In addition to the men, women, youth, children, PWD, and LGBTQ, CRS in Nepal, India, and Bangladesh cater to various other groups of which the popular recurring ones were farmers, fisherfolks, tribal and indigenous peoples, Dalits, housewives, cleaners, and the elderly. Overall, there was a focus on the common people more—those who were traditionally marginalised by mainstream media.

8.4.3 Motivation and Mobilisation

Apart from these dynamics regarding the internal and external community, there are a variety of techniques employed in an attempt to attract more participants, both internal and external. Overall, there are capacity building and sharing sessions organised for internal community members so that they can learn new skills and improve existing knowledge to ensure a continued upward movement of persons. Regarding the external community, a variety of outreach activities are done to ensure these individuals are also given opportunities to participate. Some of these include having the CR team physically visit individuals to record their stories so that those people do not have to take time off their work to visit the station, having call-in segments on live broadcasts, and promoting the stations as being the communities' stations and everyone is welcome to participate.

Overall, while the current staff and volunteers are reportedly sufficient for the operation of the initiatives and the interactions with the external communities was described as being good enough to ensure community-focused content, there is always a desire to increase participation—both internally and externally. However, funding challenges have resulted in creative aspects of community engagement and involvement.

Community Radio Programmes 9

One of the key indicators if a radio station could be classified as a community radio station (CRS) is the types of programming produced and broadcast. This chapter addresses specifics relating to programming including the thematic areas used in programming and the production genres that guide programme production. Further, it highlights the processes for selecting and producing content.

9.1 Nepal

In all three stations visited (*Radio Sagarmatha, Radio Namobuddha,* and *Radio Sindhu*[1]), it was highlighted that they produce the majority of programmes broadcast. Specifically, *Radio Sagarmatha* and *Radio Sindhu* highlighted that they produce approximately 80% of their content while *Radio Namobuddha* produces approximately 70%. While there is outsourcing ranging from 20% to 30% on average, the stations did share that this is not a regular activity. Also, all three case studies highlighted that they utilise virtual fora to share their programmes in addition to on-air radio broadcasts. In particular, all three highlighted the use of websites while *Radio Sagarmatha* and *Radio Sindhu* also identified the use of Facebook Pages. Additionally, *Radio Sagarmatha* identified the station's YouTube Channel and SoundCloud platforms. Apart from these aspects, there are other similarities about the thematic areas for programme production, production genres, and content selection and production—all of which are discussed in the following sub-sections (Shrestha,[2] in-depth interview, April 25, 2018; Srerestha,[3] in-depth interview, April 26, 2018; Syngtan,[4] in-depth interview, April 25, 2018).

[1] See *Chap. 4: Profile of Case Studies* for in-depth information of each initiative.

[2] Ratna Prasad Shrestha is the Station Manager for *Radio Sindhu.*

[3] Sahah Man Srerestha is the Station Manager for *Radio Sagarmatha.*

[4] Bhakta Syangtan is the Station Manager for *Radio Namobuddha.*

T. Rampersaud-Skorka, *Community Radio in South Asia*, Diversity and Inclusion Research, https://doi.org/10.1007/978-3-031-85201-5_9

9.1.1 Thematic Areas

All three case studies highlighted a multitude of thematic areas used for content production which show similarities in general foci as well as differences; these are highlighted in Table 9.1.

As can be seen in Table 9.1, all three case studies produce content on all thematic areas except PWD and LGBTQ. Regarding the "other" thematic area highlighted by two stations, *Radio Sagarmatha* identified thematic content production on social issues, sustainable energy, climate change, and sex education. While the latter three themes can fit into existing categories of environmental, gender, and health, the station manager separated them due to their importance with regard to Nepali society—a need for them to be treated as individual items and not sub-sets of existing themes. *Radio Namobuddha* highlighted the broadcast of public hearings from the communities—which accounts for approximately 10–12 programmes per year, as their "other" classification. The station manager explained that occurrences at these public hearings are important matters to the community; as a result, the CRS records as well as broadcasts them live so that those who cannot attend in-person would still be informed (Srerestha, in-depth interview, April 26, 2018; Syngtan, in-depth interview, April 25, 2018).

Additionally, even though *Radio Sagarmatha* and *Radio Namobuddha* highlighted that there is a need for more thematic areas to be addressed in programme production, no further information was provided with regard to this. *Radio Sindhu,* on the other hand, stated that these thematic areas are sufficient for now as they cover all the topical issues necessary with regard to their community (Shrestha,

Table 9.1 Thematic areas for programme production in the case studies in Nepal (Source: Table based on author's own compilation)

Thematic Areas	*Radio Sagarmatha*	*Radio Namobuddha*	*Radio Sindhu*
Agriculture	✓	✓	✓
Culture	✓	✓	✓
Disaster	✓	✓	✓
Education	✓	✓	✓
Entertainment	✓	✓	✓
Edutainment	✓	✓	✓
Environmental	✓	✓	✓
Gender	✓	✓	✓
Health	✓	✓	✓
LGBTQ (lesbians, gay, bisexuals, transgender, queer)			
PWD (persons with disabilities)			
Youth and children	✓	✓	✓
Other	✓	✓	

in-depth interview, April 25, 2018; Srerestha, in-depth interview, April 26, 2018; Syngtan, in-depth interview, April 25, 2018).

9.1.2 Production Genres

According to the case studies, a variety of genres (or formats) are used to produce programmes on the above thematic areas; Table 9.2 highlights this.

As can be seen in Table 9.2, each case study highlighted at least ten different formats used in programme production with features, interviews, magazines, music, news, public service announcements (PSAs), reports, and talk-shows being common in all three CRS. Regarding additional formats utilised, *Radio Sagarmatha* highlighted the use of the game show format; *Radio Namobuddha* highlighted phone-ins, SMS (short message service) programmes, and request-based programmes; and *Radio Sindhu* highlighted community discussions (live broadcasts). In the case of *Radio Namobuddha's* other formats, although they can also fit under the live format, due to their uniqueness, the station manager thought it important to single them out. Similarly, the discussion format identified by *Radio Sindhu* is a live broadcast, but the manager wanted to highlight it (Shrestha, in-depth interview, April 25, 2018; Srerestha, in-depth interview, April 26, 2018; Syngtan, in-depth interview, April 25, 2018).

While *Radio Namobuddha* highlighted that these formats are sufficient for now, *Radio Sagarmatha* and *Radio Sindhu* voiced a resounding "no" to this question as

Table 9.2 Production genres for content creation in the case studies in Nepal (Source: Table based on author's own compilation)

Thematic Areas	*Radio Sagarmatha*	*Radio Namobuddha*	*Radio Sindhu*
Documentary	✓	✓	
Drama	✓		✓
Debate			
Feature	✓	✓	✓
Interview	✓	✓	✓
Jingle			
Live		✓	✓
Magazines	✓	✓	✓
Music	✓	✓	✓
News	✓	✓	✓
Promo			
PSA	✓	✓	✓
Report	✓	✓	✓
Talk-show	✓	✓	✓
Other	✓	✓	

they think more formats would attract more listeners; however, considering the resources, *Radio Sindhu* added that they are satisfied with the current formats utilised (Shrestha, in-depth interview, April 25, 2018; Srerestha, in-depth interview, April 26, 2018; Syngtan, in-depth interview, April 25, 2018).

Regarding the time it takes to produce different programmes, all three case studies highlighted that this varies. *Radio Sindhu* explained that one programme would ideally take anywhere between 1 and 15 days to be produced in totality depending on the kind of information required and resources available (Shrestha, in-depth interview, April 25, 2018; Srerestha, in-depth interview, April 26, 2018; Syngtan, in-depth interview, April 25, 2018).

With information about thematic areas and production genres in mind, the following sub-section addresses how content are selected and produced for broadcast.

9.1.3 Content Selection and Production

Whether these stations broadcast for 12 or more hours daily, via radio or virtual platforms, content selection and production are key to the successful operation of the CRS. As a result, the case studies highlighted a variety of methods used in this endeavour; Fig. 9.1 visually represents these.

Figure 9.1 highlights the various methods used by the three case studies to select content for production. While the figure represents a consolidated list of methods, the station schedule is unique to *Radio Sagarmatha,* the seasonal calendar is unique to *Radio Namobuddha*, and the content advisory group is unique to *Radio Sindhu*. Each of these methods is explained further below:

- *Seasonal Calendar*—a document that outlines a plan for programmes and issues for the entire year. It includes ideas from the staff, suggestions gathered from the community during field visits by staff, feedback from listeners, issues addressed via other media, and current or trending topics. It is a guideline for the year and

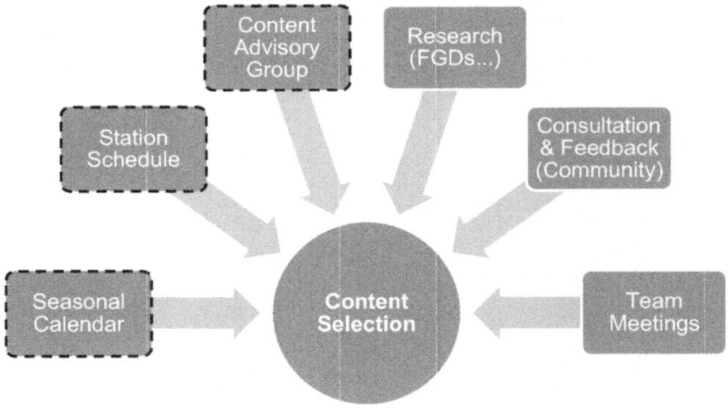

Fig. 9.1 Elements that impact content selection and production in the case studies in Nepal (Source: Author's own illustration)

is updated as information becomes available, and the need arises (Syngtan, in-depth interview, April 25, 2018).

- *Station Schedule*—a document that the station follows and has been created from the knowledge gained from years of research, operation, and adjustments. It highlights the themes for the various time slots and the programmes produced are done with this in mind. However, this schedule is updated whenever the need arises (Srerestha, in-depth interview, April 26, 2018).
- *Content Advisory Group*—this includes individuals associated with various programmes and thematic areas. The group researches topics for production and conducts community discussion sessions, and then relates their findings to the radio team. These types of data are enough to inform content creation for 2 to 3 months[5] (Shrestha, in-depth interview, April 25, 2018).

With regard to the final selection of content for production, *Radio Sagarmatha* highlighted that this is done during the monthly meetings when all team members are present. *Radio Namobuddha* outlined that the CRS team takes part in discussions, but the station manager makes the final decisions taking into consideration the costs associated with production. He stated he has a gate-keeper role with regard to the production and broadcast of programmes as he questions, makes comments, and criticises concepts from the staff before making final decisions. In *Radio Sindhu* the programme producers create concepts and present these to the programme coordinator (programme chief) who will then make the final decisions (Shrestha, in-depth interview, April 25, 2018; Srerestha, in-depth interview, April 26, 2018; Syngtan, in-depth interview, April 25, 2018).

Regarding the need for increased production, all three case studies responded that there is always the need for this. *Radio Sagarmatha* cited the need since it is believed that more content will appeal to larger audiences. *Radio Namobuddha* stated that whenever the CR team goes out to the community for programme production, they are always finding new and emerging issues or topics that need to be addressed. *Radio Sindhu* explained that there is never enough new content being produced to fill all the hours of daily broadcast. However, there are challenges affecting increased production. *Radio Sagarmatha* highlighted that human resource is the largest challenge—there are not enough people to facilitate this. Also, the station manager stated that lack of finances prevents the implementation of all ideas—a sentiment shared by the other two case studies. *Radio Namobuddha* highlighted that the entire process takes time; thus, there are delays between selection and production. In addition to this, the station manager cited the need for well-trained production staff to facilitate an increase in production as well as knowledge about the emerging issues. He further highlighted the need for better audience research to be

[5] One example outlined by the station manager of *Radio Sindhu* was that the content advisory group approached workers in an area where they were constructing houses. There, four men and four women were asked what they would like to hear via the programmes, and they mentioned information about building materials, maps, etc. This information was then shared with the radio team who discussed the order in which to produce these programmes.

conducted for the CRS to understand the community's changing needs. Finally, *Radio Sindhu* highlighted transportation as a challenge in that the CR team is not always able to travel to where they need to be (Shrestha, in-depth interview, April 25, 2018; Srerestha, in-depth interview, April 26, 2018; Syngtan, in-depth interview, April 25, 2018).

9.2 India

According to the four case studies (*Sangham Radio, Tilonia Radio, Radio Luit,* and *Waqt ki Awaaz*), between 95% and 100% of the content broadcast is self-produced. In instances where there is broadcast of external content, these comprise mostly government advertisements or information from non-governmental organisations (NGOs) and international non-governmental organisations (INGOs); however, due to language diversity of the different communities, these are not regular occurrences. Also, while all four case studies highlighted radio broadcast as the primary channel for communication, *Radio Luit* also highlighted the use of social networking platforms for sharing information, which includes Facebook, YouTube, Sound Cloud, and Edaa.in. Furthermore, *Sangham Radio, Tilonia Radio,* and *Radio Luit* highlighted that there could be improvements in how information is shared with their communities. *Sangham Radio* made specific reference to social media platforms in general and *Radio Luit* highlighted that live streaming via a website would be a good addition. However, these three stations highlighted that there are challenges to improve how programmes are shared, which include lack of personnel to undertake such tasks, a policy block on increased transmitter power to reach wider audiences, and lack of a dedicated server to host a website for the station (Aarti Devi,[6] in-depth interview, March 07, 2018; Acharjya,[7] in-depth interview, February 05, 2018; General Narsamma,[8] in-depth interview, April 06, 2018; Shukla,[9] in-depth interview, March 08, 2018).

9.2.1 Thematic Areas

Each of the case studies highlighted multiple thematic areas used in programming, ranging from agriculture and culture to education, entertainment, and gender; Table 9.3 visually presents these categories.

As can be seen in Table 9.3, each station produces content relating to agriculture, culture, education, entertainment, edutainment, environmental, and gender. Also, three CRS produce health-specific content, two cater to the youth and children

[6] Aarti Devi is the station manager for *Tilonia Radio*.

[7] Bhaskar Jyoti Acharjya is the programme executive of *Radio Luit*.

[8] General Narsamma is the station manager for *Sangham Radio* and a key figure in the CR movement in India.

[9] Radha Shukla is the coordinator (instead of the title station manager) for *Waqt ki Awaaz*.

Table 9.3 Thematic areas for programme production in each of the case study in India (Source: Table based on author's own compilation)

Thematic Areas	*Sangham Radio*	*Tilonia Radio*	*Radio Luit*	*Waqt ki Awaaz*
Agriculture	✓	✓	✓	✓
Culture	✓	✓	✓	✓
Disaster		✓		
Education	✓	✓	✓	✓
Entertainment	✓	✓	✓	✓
Edutainment	✓	✓	✓	✓
Environmental	✓	✓	✓	✓
Gender	✓	✓	✓	✓
Health	✓	✓		✓
LGBTQ				
PWD				
Youth and children		✓		✓
Other(s)		✓		

communities, one produces disaster-related programmes, and one identified other thematic areas. Regarding the latter, *Tilonia Radio* highlighted that there are programmes produced relating to government policies and *panchayat* (meaning: village council) activities such as meetings (Aarti Devi, in-depth interview, March 07, 2018; Acharjya, in-depth interview, February 05, 2018; General Narsamma, in-depth interview, April 06, 2018; Shukla, in-depth interview, March 08, 2018).

Even with so many areas currently being addressed, all four case studies highlighted that there is a need for improvements. *Sangham Radio* highlighted that there needs to be an even stronger development focus in the current thematic areas; *Tilonia Radio* highlighted that there is a need for more programmes on government policies and social issues; and *Radio Luit* specifically addressed cultural programmes in that there is a need to ensure their programmes capture the nuances of the different groups in the community since a lot of these folk cultures are becoming lost to the youth population. Regarding additional thematic areas for production, there is a need for LGBTQ content, community-based news, traffic programmes, and content for the elderly (Aarti Devi, in-depth interview, March 07, 2018; Acharjya, in-depth interview, February 05, 2018; General Narsamma, in-depth interview, April 06, 2018; Shukla, in-depth interview, March 08, 2018).

9.2.2 Production Genres

The thematic areas identified by the case studies are produced using a variety of genres (formats) ranging from more serious approaches such as documentaries and

Table 9.4 Production genres for content production in the case studies in India (Source: Table based on author's own compilation)

Production Genres	*Sangham Radio*	*Tilonia Radio*	*Radio Luit*	*Waqt ki Awaaz*
Documentary	✓	✓	✓	✓
Drama	✓	✓	✓	✓
Feature	✓	✓	✓	✓
Interview	✓	✓	✓	✓
Magazine	✓		✓	
Music	✓	✓	✓	✓
News	✓	✓		
PSA (public service ad.)	✓	✓	✓	✓
Report	✓	✓	✓	
Talk-show	✓	✓	✓	✓
Other			✓	✓

reports to more fun approaches such as drama and music. Table 9.4 visually presents the formats identified by the four case studies.

As can be seen in Table 9.4, each station uses a minimum of seven formats with all producing content using documentary, drama, feature, interview, music, PSA, and talk-show formats. Regarding *other* formats, *Radio Luit* highlighted an autobiography format and *Waqt ki Awaaz* mentioned that the diary and puppetry formats learned in workshops have been adapted for radio broadcasting. In light of the restriction on news, it is important to note that the news format identified by two CRS do not refer to news bulletins—programmes produced under this format address current community events and activities as well as the reading of headlines from daily newspapers (Aarti Devi, in-depth interview, March 07, 2018; Acharjya, in-depth interview, February 05, 2018; General Narsamma, in-depth interview, April 06, 2018; Shukla, in-depth interview, March 08, 2018).

Regarding time needed to produce the various formats identified above, this can range anywhere from 30 mins to days or months depending on the amount of work and available resources. Specifically, simpler programmes that do not require much planning, such as features, interviews, and talk-shows, can be done between 30 mins and a day. More complex programmes which need in-depth research and multiple interviews, such as documentaries, can take approximately 2 days[10] to 3 months. However, production time is decreased significantly when staff are able to pre-plan their programme schedules (discussed in the next sub-section) (Aarti Devi, in-depth interview, March 07, 2018; Acharjya, in-depth interview, February 05, 2018; General Narsamma, in-depth interview, April 06, 2018; Shukla, in-depth interview, March 08, 2018).

[10] One day was equated to approximately 6 h of dedicated work.

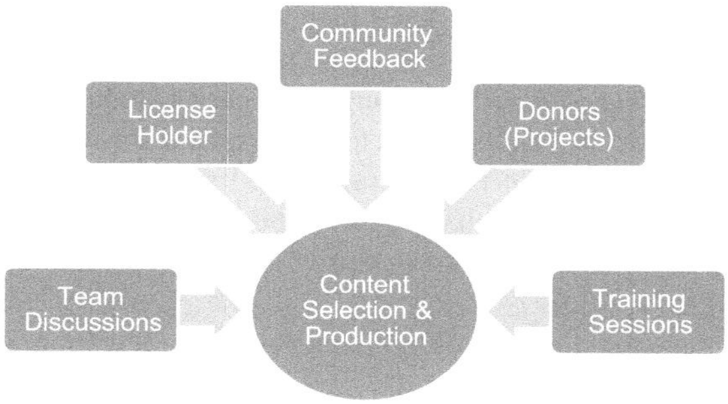

Fig. 9.2 Elements that impact the selection and production of content in the case studies in India (Source: Author's own illustration)

9.2.3 Content Selection and Production

Based on the information from the case studies, there are a variety of methods used to inform content selection and production; Fig. 9.2 visually represents this based on the author's analysis.

Figure 9.2 illustrates five unique elements identified by the case studies that impact the selection and production of content. Each of these is explained in detail below:

- *Team discussions*—these comprise the weekly and monthly staff meetings for each CRS. At these gatherings, all information, such as ideas and feedback from listeners, are discussed and a programme schedule is prepared once responsibilities are assigned.
- *Licence holder*—though not a common occurrence, it was highlighted that the licence holder does have input in the content being produced from time to time, especially where there are smaller stations with small numbers of staff and volunteers who are not very experienced. For example, the staff of Barefoot College assist *Tilonia Radio's* team whenever the need arises.
- *Community feedback*—any information from the community concerning current and prospective programmes are taken into consideration; that is the communities' needs are addressed since the stations are for their benefit.
- *Donors*—sometimes, those providing funds want to focus on specific areas within the communities. As a result, they impact this process since their funds support the production of dedicated content with a specific focus.
- *Training sessions*—ideas generated during various training sessions inform content creation. For example, an information-sharing session on domestic violence might result in a programme about this topic.

Even though there are a variety of elements that influence what programmes are produced, the final decision-making process varies in the CRS. *Sangham Radio* highlighted that the two full-time staff finalise the programme schedule; similarly,

Tilonia Radio and *Waqt ki Awaaz* have their staff make the final decisions; and *Radio Luit's* programme executive makes the final programme schedule. However, as highlighted by *Tilonia Radio*, even though there is a schedule, if a visit to the field results in a more important matter being found out, then this is given precedence in the interest of ensuring current issues are covered promptly (Aarti Devi, in-depth interview, March 07, 2018; Acharjya, in-depth interview, February 05, 2018; General Narsamma, in-depth interview, April 06, 2018; Shukla, in-depth interview, March 08, 2018).

Even though the case studies highlighted a need for a few more thematic areas to be covered, the current formats used for production are sufficient, taking the challenges to increased production into consideration. Specifically, there is a need for more human resources to facilitate higher levels of production as well as increased broadcast hours to share all the content produced—both of which are hampered by the lack of sufficient funds. Overall, the current programmes highlighted by the case studies, are enough to sustain the stations' operations (Aarti Devi, in-depth interview, March 07, 2018; Acharjya, in-depth interview, February 05, 2018; General Narsamma, in-depth interview, April 06, 2018; Shukla, in-depth interview, March 08, 2018).

9.3 Bangladesh

The four case studies (*Radio Padma, Borendro Radio, Radio Bikrampur,* and *Radio Sarabela*) highlighted that they produce between 90% and 100% of their programmes. While there is some content produced by secondary sources, this is not a regular occurrence. In addition to sharing information via radio broadcasting, all four case studies also highlighted doing so via the stations' Facebook pages and websites while *Radio Padma* also identified sharing audio programmes using a mobile phone application created for the station. However, even though they can reach large amounts of communities, three of the four case studies (all except *Radio Padma*) highlighted that there can be improvements in the form of larger transmitters to reach larger audiences, especially since this is a standing demand from communities (Parveen, in-depth interview, December 10, 2017; Salahin & Pallobi, in-depth interview, December 09, 2017; Sarkar, in-depth interview, December 09, 2017; Sutradar, in-depth interview, December 09, 2017).

Apart from these aspects, each case highlighted thematic areas and production genres/formats used in content production, as well as various techniques used to select topics for production.

9.3.1 Thematic Areas

Each of the four case studies identified multiple thematic areas in their programming as represented in Table 9.5.

Table 9.5 Thematic areas for programme production in the case studies in Bangladesh (Source: Table based on author's own compilation)

Thematic Areas	*Radio Padma*	*Radio Borendro*	*Radio Bikrampur*	*Radio Sarabela*
Agriculture	✓	✓	✓	✓
Culture	✓	✓	✓	✓
Disaster	✓	✓	✓	✓
Education	✓	✓	✓	✓
Entertainment	✓	✓	✓	✓
Edutainment	✓			✓
Environmental	✓	✓	✓	✓
Gender	✓	✓	✓	✓
Health	✓	✓	✓	✓
LGBTQ	✓		✓	✓
PWD	✓		✓	✓
Youth and children	✓	✓	✓	✓
Other(s)	✓	✓	✓	✓

As can be seen in Table 9.5, all case studies produce content relating to agriculture, culture, disaster, education, entertainment, environmental, gender, health, and youth and children. Regarding the *other* category, all stations broadcast general development information and news (whether they are full bulletins or just news updates). Also, *Radio Padma* produces beauty, law and human rights, and national content, and *Radio Borendro* produces economics, tourism, and information and communication technologies (ICTs) content. An additional and interesting thematic area highlighted by *Radio Borendro* is called "success stories," where they share the positive achievements of members from their communities. *Radio Bikrampur* also creates ICT-related programmes along with religion and sports, as does *Radio Sarabela*. Additionally, *Radio Sarabela* includes content on travel, weather, career, and local government topics (Parveen,[11] in-depth interview, December 10, 2017; Salahin & Pallobi,[12] in-depth interview, December 09, 2017; Sarkar,[13] in-depth interview, December 09, 2017; Sutradar,[14] in-depth interview, December 09, 2017).

However, even with such a large repertoire of programme ideas, there were noted areas for improvements. *Radio Padma* highlighted the need for more specific social issue content that focus on matters such as dowry, violence, women's empowerment, and eve-teasing. *Radio Bikrampur* mentioned the need to produce more

[11] Shahana Parveen is the Station Manager for *Radio* Padma.

[12] M.D. Musfiqur Salahin, Senior Producer, and Israt Pallobi is a Producer at *Radio Bikrampur*.

[13] Shubrata Sarkar is the Station Manager for Radio Borendro.

[14] Santa Rani Sutradar is the Station Manager of *Radio Sarabela*.

content for specific communities such as seniors, children, and the island communities. *Radio Borendro* and *Radio Sarabela* did not highlight any new thematic areas; however, the latter did emphasise a need to increase the quality of programmes through innovations such as having children produce their own weekly programmes with minimum guidance from the radio teams (Parveen, in-depth interview, December 10, 2017; Salahin & Pallobi, in-depth interview, December 09, 2017; Sarkar, in-depth interview, December 09, 2017; Sutradar, in-depth interview, December 09, 2017).

9.3.2 Production Genres

The case studies highlighted a variety of production genres for programme creation; Table 9.6 visually presents this.

As can be seen in Table 9.6, while all case studies utilise a variety of formats, there appears to be a preference for features, interviews, magazines, news, and talk-shows. The average total production time for these formats range from one hour to six hours, which can be accomplished from 1 day to 1 week, and with one or several staff and volunteers collaborating. In contrast, documentaries and drama formats take significantly longer to produce—approximately 3 days (72 h)—and require more production time, larger production teams, and talent; thus, they are only done when necessary (Parveen, in-depth interview, December 10, 2017; Salahin & Pallobi, in-depth interview, December 09, 2017; Sarkar, in-depth interview, December 09, 2017; Sutradar, in-depth interview, December 09, 2017).

In addition to the above, as highlighted by *Radio Padma* and *Radio Sarabela*, one format that these stations want to be able to utilise in the future is "live

Table 9.6 Production genres for content production in the case studies in Bangladesh (Source: Table based on author's own compilation)

Production Genres	*Radio Padma*	*Radio Borendro*	*Radio Bikrampur*	*Radio Sarabela*
Documentary	✓	✓		✓
Drama	✓	✓	✓	✓
Feature				✓
Interview	✓	✓	✓	✓
Magazine	✓	✓	✓	
Music				✓
News			✓	
PSA	✓	✓	✓	✓
Report	✓	✓		
Talk-show	✓	✓	✓	✓
Other		✓		

broadcasts from the field" and not only from the studio. The reason this has not been implemented yet is due to the costs associated with sourcing fully functional and independent mobile units which will enable stations to reach those communities that cannot physically reach the stations to tell their stories. However, stations have used creative means of involving the community, such as sending representatives equipped with cell phones, so that live interviews from the field can be included in programmes (Parveen, in-depth interview, December 10, 2017; Sutradar, in-depth interview, December 09, 2017).

Further to this, *Radio Borendro* highlighted the need for more investigative forms of reporting to be done. While having pieces that create awareness and share information with the community is important, there is also the need to have individuals who can examine topics from a more critical standpoint and be equipped to ask the more serious questions (Sarkar, in-depth interview, December 09, 2017).

9.3.3 Content Selection and Production

Regardless of the daily hours of broadcasting, CRS uses various techniques to ensure proper content selection and production; Fig. 9.3 highlights these.

As can be seen in Fig. 9.3, the four case studies highlighted six techniques in total that are used to select content for production. It must be noted that no one station used all six methods, and the information provided represents a consolidated list of methods. These are explained below.

- *Original Survey*—when a CRS is being set up in Bangladesh, the individuals involved in that process survey the community to ascertain what the community's needs are. This highlights the type of content that would benefit the community—the thematic areas. As the station becomes operational, this document

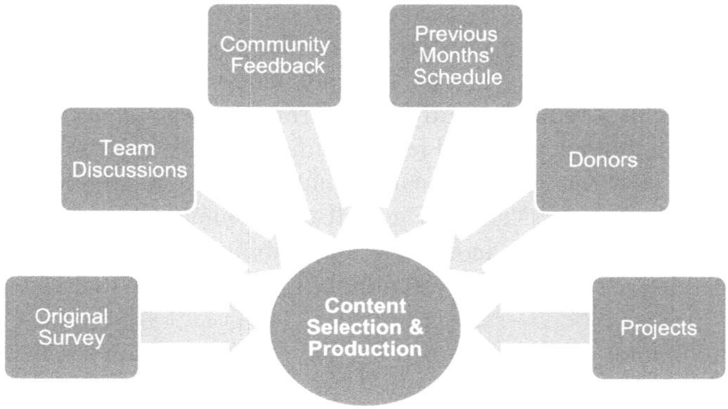

Fig. 9.3 Elements that impact content selection and production of content within the case studies in Bangladesh (Source: Author's own illustration)

guides the staff and volunteers in ensuring that they respond to the external community's needs.

- *Team Discussions*—even though there is an original survey, the staff and volunteers will use their knowledge (guided by feedback and current events) to ensure appropriate thematic areas are focused on. The monthly meetings take into consideration the feedback from the communities.
- *Feedback*—the audiences' responses help to guide the programming decisions. Sometimes listeners hear a programme about something that affects them and would like more detailed information; therefore, they communicate this to the station team. If there is a follow-up programme then this new request is incorporated if possible; however, if there was no planned follow-up programme, such information helps with future scheduling.
- *Previous months' schedules*—due to the habits of listening, stations tend to broadcast the same types of shows at the same time—like clockwork. Therefore, scheduling does affect the selection and production of programmes. Furthermore, the previous months' schedule will guide the programmes for the following month since there might be a need for follow-on programmes.
- *Donors*—sometimes, people who donate money to CRS do so because of areas of interests. If they like a programme, they donate money to the station with a specific request that the money goes to that programme. If they see a need for a new or different programme, they donate money for that specifically—this is called targeted donations.
- *Projects*—NGOs and INGOs, among other entities, normally have specific projects which they are focusing on. Thus, their collaborations with CRS are informed by these project-related goals. Sometimes, if such programming did not exist before, the targeted funding will see the introduction of a new programme (as with donors).

Radio Padma's main reference is the original survey conducted, which highlighted the needs of the community as being programmes on social issues such as gender discrimination, sexual harassment, and early marriages. Keeping this initial survey in mind, the team addresses the more time-sensitive issues (relating to these topics) in their programmes (Parveen, in-depth interview, December 10, 2017).

Radio Borendro is guided mostly by informal surveys of the listeners by the producers—both through mediated feedback mechanisms, such as phone calls and text messages, and via interpersonal communication, in addition to feedback received from the listeners' clubs. The staff and volunteers arrange programming according to their importance and assign responsibilities at monthly meetings based on the availability and interests of volunteers (Sarkar, in-depth interview, December 09, 2017).

Radio Bikrampur is guided mostly by the previous month's schedule. At the monthly meetings, the feedback received from the listeners and critiques by staff and volunteers is taken into consideration when planning the next month's schedule. Additionally, listeners make demands which the team addresses as they see fit.

While guided by the original research, the focus is determined by current events (Salahin & Pallobi, in-depth interview, December 09, 2017).

Radio Sarabela is still guided by the initial survey conducted as this CRS has only been operational for a little over 2 years. However, they tweak the schedule based on feedback received from the listeners, specifically the listeners' clubs. Also, decisions are made by the staff and volunteers, guided by informal inputs from the listeners, at the monthly meetings where ideas are discussed and assigned for programme production (Sutradar, in-depth interview, December 09, 2017).

While the case studies did identify a need for improvements regarding programming, they did highlight that the stations have sufficient content regarding the important areas identified (Parveen, in-depth interview, December 10, 2017; Salahin & Pallobi, in-depth interview, December 09, 2017; Sarkar, in-depth interview, December 09, 2017; Sutradar, in-depth interview, December 09, 2017).

9.4 Summary

On average, stations self-produce at least 80% of the content they broadcast with the remainder being content produced by other sources such as government advertisements and PSAs from development organisations. In addition to radio broadcasts, these initiatives have also been using complimentary social networking platforms such as Facebook, YouTube, and SoundCloud to share their programmes.

9.4.1 Thematic Areas

Regarding the thematic areas used in content production, of the 12 categories provided by the author, 6 were identified by all the case studies: agriculture (farming, crops, seasons), culture (folklore, customs), education, entertainment (songs, drama), environmental (climate change), and gender (women's issues and empowerment in particular). In addition to this, health (HIV/Aids, maternal health), edutainment, youth and children (bullying, child marriages, child labour), and disaster (updates about current disaster, disaster risk reduction strategies, disaster preparedness) were also very popular thematic areas across the region. Regarding PWD and LGBTQ content, while there were some productions around these themes, they were not very popular.

Apart from these generic categories, other thematic areas were identified—while some of these can fit under headings identified by the author based on international groupings, they were identified separately due to the level of importance afforded to them. In Nepal, these included social issues, sustainable energy, and public hearings from the villages. In India, the government content such as information about important policies and *panchayat* activities (as is the case with the public hearings in Nepal). Finally, Bangladesh identified several other thematic areas for production which included development content, development news, beauty, law and human

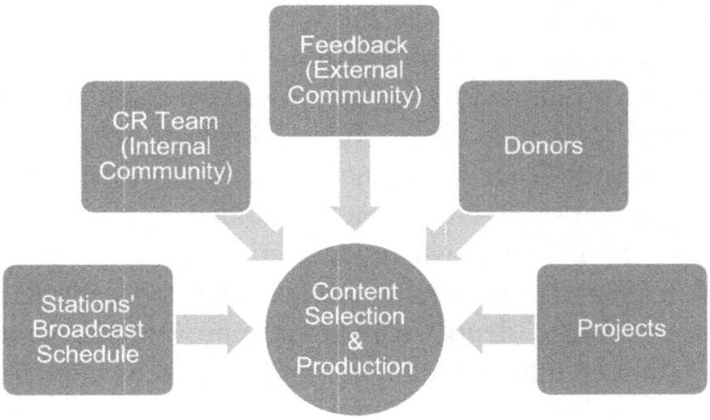

Fig. 9.4 Elements that impact content selection and production in South Asia based on the case studies (Source: Author's own illustration)

rights, economics, tourism, ICT, religion, sports, travel, weather, career, and local government.

9.4.2 Production Genres

Overall, of the ten genres identified, interview, PSA, talk-show, and drama format appear to be the most popular genres used in content production. Additionally, documentary, report, feature, magazine, and music are also widely utilised. Due to the differing country-level policies on news being broadcast via CR initiatives, this is not a very popular format but at least a few stations produce development-based news bulletins. Apart from these identified, generic genres, in Nepal, there are also game shows and live discussions; in India, there is an autobiographical and diary format as well as an adaptation of the puppetry format learned in workshops; finally, in Bangladesh, there are live field broadcasts (though not very common).

9.4.3 Content Selection and Production

The methods used in each country regarding content selection and production are unique; however, based on the analysis of the data across Nepal, India, and Bangladesh, there were some similarities to be found; this information is represented in Fig. 9.4.

As can be seen in Fig. 9.4, five key elements impact content selection and production: station's broadcast schedule, internal community's concepts, external community's feedback, donors, and projects. Apart from these key elements, each country has additional elements that impact this process: Nepal has a seasonal calendar, content advisory group, and research; India has licensing individual or organisation's inputs, and the outputs from capacity building and sharing exercises; and Bangladesh has the original survey before station establishment.

Overall, these various elements ensure that the content selected for production are in keeping with the needs of the communities based on expressions by the individuals or activities and current events. However, in some case studies, content production is guided by donors and projects as they will provide the funds for these special programmes. It must be noted that in such instances, these programmes are given the go-ahead only once they are proven to fit the stations' operational policies.

10 Tracing Regional Multiplicity of the Alternative Mediascape in South Asia

10.1 Nepal

As we look at the CR sector in Nepal, although there is no dedicated CR policy, there is a somewhat enabling policy environment guaranteed by the Constitution for independent media, even though there are some notable restrictions. In addition to the freedom and right to expression and communication, there are several key national-level media legislatures which govern the set-up and operation of media entities—both mainstream and alternative. Through the years, each subsequent policy was revised and amended based on the criticisms of the previous one and has resulted in the *National Mass Communications Policy 2016,* which now takes precedence. This policy formally acknowledges community media as a third media sector and has put forward less government control mechanisms as this sector supports more self-regulation. Additionally, the suggested codes of conduct by Mainali et al. (2004), based on the operations of *Radio Sagarmatha,* ensure a more sector-specific approach regarding operation of community radio stations (CRS). Even though Nepal has no specific community media/radio policy, by combining the formal policies and suggested codes, CRS are aptly guided as they serve their communities.

With regard to the management and ownership of CRS in Nepal, through the three case studies'[1] analyses, it was found that these are rather sophisticated and business-like in nature; however, the enactment of the ideals associated with participatory communication ensures that stations function as CR initiatives are envisioned, to some extent. Each case study identified departments, roles, and responsibilities that encompass both administrative and production functions. However, regardless of this hierarchical structure, the case studies utilise a mixed-method strategy that combines horizontal, bottom-up, and top-bottom approaches

[1] The three case studies in Nepal were: *Radio Sagarmatha, Radio Namobuddha*, and *Radio Sindhu*; see *Chap. 4: Profile of Case Studies* for in-depth information of each initiative.

T. Rampersaud-Skorka, *Community Radio in South Asia*, Diversity and Inclusion Research, https://doi.org/10.1007/978-3-031-85201-5_10

to management and communication, in both formal and informal settings, utilising verbal and writing methods to share information regarding daily operations. These approaches have ensured that there is true participation from all involved. Furthermore, these CRS have internal policies and norms which are initiative specific—while some are unique to each station, others have been created based on the suggested codes at the national level. Apart from these key aspects, the CRS also have mechanisms in place that ensure economic sustainability and editorial independence. By exploring a variety of funding opportunities, stations tend to operate on a break-even basis every month, that is their income is equal to their expenditure. Finally, in the interest of ensuring CRS focus on their communities as a priority, they have put in place strict measures to ensure that they maintain their independence, especially from funders.

The case studies in Nepal focus on key ownership and management functions to ensure they operate as effectively and efficiently as possible. Even though the set-up and operation of the initiatives are not always in keeping with the ideals of CR, the stations do identify as CR entities and have proven this through various methods, such as ensuring participation in decision-making and placing the communities' needs first.

Regarding participants, all three case studies highlighted the need for increased community engagement and identified various techniques employed to address this, including capacity building and sharing. Regardless of the small number of direct participants and the desire to increase this, those associated with the CRS have multiple opportunities to contribute towards the development of their communities via the programmes they produce and broadcast.

All three case studies highlighted the sharing of their mostly self-produced content via radio while one identified 24 h broadcast via its website. While there are standard thematic foci for programmes such as agriculture, education, and gender, there are some unique thematic areas such as sustainable energy—all of which are produced using a variety of formats. In general, the case studies highlighted that they want to expand the number of programmes produced but limited resources post a challenge. As a result, their programme selection and production techniques are implemented taking into consideration their access to resources. In general, all three case studies are satisfied with their programmes, especially since each can broadcast for over 10 h daily.

In Nepal, CR forms a bridge between policymakers and the community while they also foster the formation of relationships among all groups in society through knowledge sharing. As Mainali[2] (in-depth interview, April 26, 2018) summarises, it is important for information and knowledge sharing among the various groups, the

---

[2] Raghu Mainali is a community media activist who has been an advocate for and a key stakeholder of the community media sector in Nepal and South Asia for approximately 26 years, since the early 1990s. He has been involved in the development communication field for approximately 31 years. Mainali was involved in the set-up of *Radio Sagarmatha* and, today, continues his activism with CRSC and NEFEJ (Mainali, in-depth interview, April 26, 2018).

motivation of the various communities to take an active role in their development, and general entertainment of the masses. CR is a necessity.

10.2 India

With over two decades of activism and approximately 15 years of having CR initiatives in India, the policy environment can be described as being somewhat enabling since there are active CRS around the country being used by marginalised groups for various purposes. While there is a policy that acknowledges the importance of CR broadcasting in the country, there are still some aspects of this policy that restrict complete freedom of these initiatives. However, the policy environment does support CR initiatives and the ideals associated with people's participation in their processes of development as well as representation of marginalised groups. Also, the internal policies for these initiatives ensure that gaps in the national-level legislature are addressed. Overall, the policy environment can be described as somewhat fertile for the establishment and operation of CR initiatives.

Guided in part by the national-level policies and mostly by the ideals for CR, the ownership and management of the case studies[3] in India reflect a participatory approach. Even though there is the top-down approach, there is a general preference for the horizontal approach regarding decision-making and communication within these initiatives as the latter is more inclusive in nature. However, one key challenge, which is magnified by the policy guidelines, is funding. While the CRS are able to cover their operational expenses every month, they cannot expand to accommodate more staff or even paid volunteers due to scarcity of this resource. However, each case study was clear about putting measures in place to ensure that they maintain their editorial independence from any funding agency as they focus on their communities' needs—even if it means losing out on a possible opportunity to earn funds.

Regarding the categories of community, the internal community for these CRS are small and not representative of their external community. However, even though individuals are not able to directly contribute, there is a feeling of ownership of these initiatives by the internal participants which ensures their continued participation. To compensate for the small number of internal participants (though the numbers are effective for stations' operations), the case studies ensure the implementation of community engagement activities that motivate and mobilise a variety of participants. They use a variety of formats to deliver content on a variety of thematic areas that are relevant to their respective communities.

In India, CRS now need to start operating in a manner that ensures their sustainability to continue serving their communities. However, to do this, there needs to be an update to the existing policy to create a more enabling policy environment—only when this changes will CR initiatives start to flourish.

---

[3]The four case studies in India were: *Sangham Radio, Tilonia Radio, Radio Luit,* and *Waqt ki Awaaz*; see *Chap. 4: Profile of Case Studies* for in-depth information of each initiative.

10.3 Bangladesh

With a Constitution guaranteeing fundamental human rights and freedom, community practitioners need not fear self-expression once they are responsible and operate within the existing policy framework comprising national media policies and a CR Policy as the legal environment ensures that the rights of citizens are not infringed upon. Ideally, this media sector should have self-monitored practitioners, especially since the focus is on the process of creating content for broadcast. However, while it does impose some restrictions, the presence of a CR policy acknowledges the importance of CR in Bangladesh's development. Since the official policies do not include direction in several key areas, codes of conduct, while not enforceable by law, have been created to address the gap. Freedom of the press and freedom of expression, though with some restrictions, have resulted in a fertile media environment which encompasses broadcast, print, and online media across government, commercial, and community ownership.

Furthermore, as evident in the case studies,[4] there are internal policies, either adopted from the mother organisations or specially created for a community radio station, to further guide the staff and volunteers regarding the stations' operations. Furthermore, these internal policies have been effective in ensuring that stations are operated in a participatory manner by having inclusive management and decision-making processes, thus making sure staff and volunteers do feel some amount of ownership over the stations because of their involvement. Also, policies on funding and maintaining editorial independence ensure that these initiatives cater to the needs of their communities first.

Regarding community, these are categorised based on the level of association individuals have with the initiatives. Internal participants are the staff and volunteers who ensure the stations are operational while external participants are mostly individuals who are not involved in the actual operational aspects—they are resource persons or members of the target audiences. While it is easy to understand the dynamics of the internal communities, only general information about the external communities is known. Even though there is always the need for more direct participation (internal community), the overall engagement of the various communities is seen as satisfactory; however, stations do have measures in place to motivate and mobilise participants regularly.

Finally, the case studies produce all their content for broadcast regularly, with a small amount sourced from external parties from time to time. Even though there are multiple thematic areas—ranging from agriculture and culture to education and entertainment, health and gender to youth and children focused programmes—each station has additional thematic areas specific to their communities such as ICTs and development news. Overall, features, interviews, magazines, and talk-shows are used to create programmes on assorted topics. However, more time-intensive formats such as documentaries and drama are also produced from time to time. With

[4]The four case studies in India were: *Radio Padma, Borendro Radio, Radio Bikrampur,* and *Radio Sarabela*; see *Chap. 4: Profile of Case Studies* for in-depth information of each initiative.

such a wide variety of genres, programming is a very enriched area within these initiatives since the possibilities are almost endless.

CR initiatives in Bangladesh are particularly important since they provide a forum for the community to voice their stories as they share their knowledge and gain knowledge in return. They fill a gap by addressing specific communities of interest which are not targeted in mainstream media. It is important to note that not only are challenges faced by marginalised communities highlighted, the solutions by these same communities are also shared. As a result, there is a need for the financial challenges to be addressed to ensure the sustainability of the stations since finances do affect all other aspects. However, even with limited resources, stations do create a truly participatory environment.

10.4 Guiding Principles for CR in South Asia

Throughout the extensive and comprehensive mapping of the CR sectors in Nepal, India, and Bangladesh, there were some guiding principles for CR operation in the region noticed by the author. Overall, these guidelines represent and support media democratisation and empowerment of traditionally marginalised groups of people and community participation.

Specifically, they were identified from the various discourses around the key elements relating to CR around the world drawn from an understanding of the five areas highlighted in this book's conceptual framework that was discussed at length in *Chap. 3: Contextualising Community Radio*. These are: paradigmatic shifts in understanding communication; participatory communication and development; public sphere, counter public sphere, civil society; notions of community; and alternative media, community media, citizens' media. Additionally, the discussions around concepts such as "voice poverty" and "NGO-ization" also bore some influence. In addition to these conceptual entry points, the author also followed *Our Media, Our Principles* by Malik (2015), which highlighted 13 codes[5] that guide CR operation in India. Malik (2015) presented these codes following an in-depth analysis of the theoretical underpinnings as well as the core, non-negotiable, and globally acceptable norms for democratic and alternative media. Based on Malik's (2015) framework and regarding the theoretical entry points utilised by the author, the following are a list of the guiding principles (codes of conduct) CR practitioners appear to follow in Nepal, India, and Bangladesh. Furthermore, these guiding principles highlight the key thematic areas addressed in this book, which are *policy*

[5] The codes identified by Malik (2015, pp. 5): (1) ensure community ownership and management; (2) serve a recognisable community and be not-for-profit; (3) reflect diversity and sensitivity in programming content; (4) reinforce content development leading to social change; (5) enhance community participation; (6) strengthen capacity building and training opportunities; (7) protect and augment cultural and linguistic diversity; (8) provide voice to the voiceless and encourage inclusivity; (9) promote right to communicate and contribute to democratic communication; (10) espouse self-sustainability mechanisms; (11) exercise editorial independence; (12) advocate for an enabling policy environment; and (13) facilitate adherence to codes of practice.

environment, ownership and management, community, and programming. It is also important to note that while some of these codes are derived from Malik's (2015) framework due to the similarities in Nepal, India, and Bangladesh, not all were found applicable within the larger regional context, due to their particularities of India as a nation.

The researcher observed three principles at the national levels across all three countries. Firstly, CRS are used to *promote community and national unity* since they focus largely on participation and inclusion as societies undergo social and cultural transformations due to social change. Overall, there is support for liberty of thought, expression, and belief, which promote unity and non-discrimination; as such, "they do not broadcast content that would instigate conflict as they uphold the values and principles of freedom and sovereignty of the country" (Code of Conduct for Community Radio (CR) Operation, 2009). Secondly, through official acknowledgement by all three countries, CR is the third tier of broadcasting; therefore, there is support for *democratic access to media initiatives*. By ensuring there is a platform for alternative voices (to the mainstream private stations and government-owned stations), equality of status and opportunity are reflected. As highlighted by Nagarajan[6] (in-depth interview, June 18 & 19, 2018) and Dutta[7] (in-depth interview, March 23, 2018) previously, these initiatives provide access to marginalised groups which in turn empowers them to participate since CRS, in addition to being *for* and *about* these communities, are *by* the communities. Finally, these initiatives are supported with the knowledge that there will be a *responsible use of media* which ensures that these entities operate keeping in mind the need for accuracy, balance, clarity, and objectivity in programmes which focus on the community first and everything else second. In doing so, the CR movements are assured continuity.

Concerning each of the thematic areas used for mapping, the author identified specific principles followed for CR operation in Nepal, India, and Bangladesh based on analyses of the data in the preceding chapters and borrowing from the frameworks and readings mentioned earlier in this section. These guiding principles are presented in Table 10.1.

As can be seen in Table 10.1, there are five principles regarding policy environment, eight for ownership and management, and four each for community and programming. The 22 points provide an exhaustive list of principles that CR sectors within Nepal, India, and Bangladesh, and the South Asian region in general, may follow with regard to the mentioned thematic areas. They highlight core operational

---

[6] Mr. Ramakrishnan Nagarajan, Executive Director, Ideosync Media Combine, India, and member of the Community Radio Forum (India), has been working in the development communication field for approximately 24 years and specifically with CR for 19 years. He assists CRS in setting up and becoming operational, training activities for CRS, lobbying for CRS in India, and networking with other stakeholders for the betterment of CR in India and South Asia (Nagarajan, in-depth interview, June 18 & 19, 2018).

[7] Dr. Ankurran Dutta has been working in the development communication field for approximately 13 years. As a media teacher and work various experiences with organisations such as CEMCA (India), he is focused on promoting the use of community media in India since they allow the common people to be producers of their own stories (Dutta, in-depth interview, March 23, 2018).

Table 10.1 Guiding principles for CR operation in South Asia observed in the CR sectors of Nepal, India, and Bangladesh (Source: Table based on author's own compilation)

Thematic Area	Principles
Policy environment	1. Strengthen the democratic process of society by promoting the rights to communicate and information. 2. Operate within the existing policy environment. 3. Advocate for an enabling policy environment. 4. Facilitate adherence to codes of practice. 5. Reinforce ethical practices.
Ownership and management	6. Ensure community ownership, management, and operation. 7. Support participatory management techniques and practices. 8. Be not-for-profit. 9. Espouse self-sustainable mechanisms. 10. Exercise editorial independence. 11. Ensure transparency in operation. 12. Guarantee diversity in licensing of initiatives. 13. Ensure non-allegiance with any (political) organisations that might impact independence and objectivity.
Community	14. Provide a voice to the voiceless and encourage inclusivity. 15. Protect and augment cultural diversity. 16. Serve a recognisable community. 17. Encourage and enhance representative community participation.
Programming	18. Reflect diversity in programming. 19. Reflect sensitivity in programming. 20. Produce content leading to positive social change. 21. Ensure representative programming.

principles associated with this phenomenon that optimise people's participation with regard to media over traditional broadcasting techniques. By highlighting ideals associated with the representation of the diversity of societies, these codes observed within the community radio mediascape of Nepal, India, and Bangladesh reinforce the core values of CR: participation, inclusion, and equality in ownership, management, and operation.

10.5 CR in South Asia: Challenges and Opportunities

Community radio stations in Nepal, India, and Bangladesh have been established as a necessary source of information and platform for expression for various communities that are traditionally marginalised by the mainstream media. Furthermore, these initiatives are being used by people to communicate with each other, using their unique languages, as they present and represent the variety of cultural norms and practices in the South Asian region. From facilitating and engaging communities in processes of development to creating awareness about the various issues in society, these initiatives have been key to positive social change of various groups of people as they provide a voice to the stakeholders and enable people the opportunity to take an active role in their own growth and progress. Therefore, community radio is a tool that can be used towards the building of more resilient communities as they encourage people's active participation (Basnet, in-depth interview, April 23, 2018; Pavarala, in-depth interview, July 11, 2018).

Taking the analysis of the detailed mapping of the CR sectors in Nepal, India, and Bangladesh further, by addressing the policy environment, ownership and management philosophies, community, and programming across the 11 case studies in all 3 countries, a regional picture about the CR sector in South Asia from a macro-level view is now formed.

Overall, as can be seen, CR in South Asia has evolved over the years to be a key player within the larger media environment. While they do tend to reflect some similarities found in mainstream media, they are different in that they focus on marginalised groups in society—in providing a voice to these groups. However, they do not exist without challenges. As Basnet[8] (in-depth interview, April 23, 2018) highlighted, the biggest challenge is people's participation; once this is perfected then everything else will flow. Manali (in-depth interview, April 26, 2018) added to this by highlighting that new technologies present a challenge since many have technophobia, and the lack of finances to establish and invest in such initiatives is also a deterrent. Nagarajan (in-depth interview, June 18 and 19, 2018) highlighted that complicated and long licensing processes are also constraining for the establishment of CRS. Finally, Pavarala[9] (in-depth interview, July 11, 2018) highlighted that there needs to be a more enabling policy environment which would snowball into more initiatives being established that cater to the core principles of community media.

Overall, these challenges emphasise issues surrounding sustainability—financial, social, and institutional (Ramakrishnan et al., 2017). This is a position that is strongly supported by Pavarala (in-depth interview, July 11, 2018), who mentioned that sustainability is the biggest challenge: initiatives need to ensure they have multiple sources of funding so that if one leaves then there are others available; and they need to ensure there is enough people to have continued operation. Overall, it is difficult for these initiatives to sustain themselves as they are all competing for limited resources. However, due to some creative methods (such as bartering), they can ensure operation on a monthly basis.

In closing, a quote from the AMARC Asia-Pacific the author encountered at the beginning of the research journey seems apt: "Everyone has a right to life, with dignity. All people have the undeniable right to be informed about decisions affecting the quality of their lives such as the right to health, right to education, right to work, the right to free expression, and the right to information" (AMARC

[8] Suman Basnet is the Regional Coordinator of AMARC Asia-Pacific—the World Association of Community Radio Broadcasters. For more than 15 yrs, he has been working in the community media field as an advocate and activist for CR with a focus on (1) disaster risk reduction and CR, (2) women's empowerment, and (3) empowerment of the marginalised societies (Basnet, in-depth interview, April 23, 2018).

[9] Prof. Vinod Pavarala is a Professor and Chairholder, UNESCO Chair on Community Media, University of Hyderabad, India. He has over 20 years of teaching, research, and advocacy experience in the development communication and community media fields (Pavarala, in-depth interview, July 11, 2018).

Asia-Pacific, 2010, p. 1). CR in South Asia ensures that these rights are upheld by providing a voice to the voiceless and democratic access to media fora—places where diversity, equity, and inclusion are key tenants in an ever-evolving world.

References

AMARC Asia-Pacific. (2010, February 20-23). *Bangalore community radio declaration–consolidated points*. 2nd AMARC Asia-Pacific regional conference: Voices for a sustainable and sound future.

Code of Conduct for Community Radio (CR) Operation. (2009). *SANCOM*. Retrieved March 30, 2017, from http://www.sancomonline.net/wp-content/uploads/2015/02/Code-of-Conduct-CR-Operation-in-Bangladesh-English.pdf.

Mainali, R., Chapagain, Y., & Subba, B. (2004). *Community radio organisation development guidebook*. CRSC/NEFEJ with support of Free Voice.

Malik, K. K. (2015). Our media, our principles: Building codes of practice for community radio in India. *Journalism Studies, 16*(5), 750. https://doi.org/10.1080/1461670X.2015.1054195

Ramakrishnan, N., Arora, V., & Dutta, A. (2017, April 11–12). *Strengthening Community Radio in India*. Presented at A National Consultation.

Appendices

Appendix 5.1: Lists of Active CRS in Nepal, India, and Bangladesh as of December 2017

NEPAL	
#	Name of CRS
1	3 Angels Community Radio 94.6 MHz
2	Afno FMHzM 90.4 MHz
3	Appan FM 104.6 MHz
4	Baglung FM 96.4 MHz
5	Bheri Aawaj 95.6 MHz
6	Bheri FM 105.4 MHz
7	Bulbule FM 103.4 MHz
8	Community Radio Parasi 90.2 MHz
9	ECR FM 104.2 MHz
10	Gorkhali Radio 106 MHz
11	Grace FM 107.6 MHz
12	HajurKo Radio 102.1 MHz
13	Himchuli FM 92.2 MHz
14	Ilam FM 93 MHz
15	Jagaran FM 90.8 MHz
16	Jaleshwor Nath FM 90.4 MHz
17	Janaki FM 106 MHz
18	Krishi FM 101.5 MHz
19	Krishi Radio 105 MHz
20	Madi Seti FM 105.8 MHz
21	Manakamana FM 98.7 MHz
22	Mero FM 93.6
23	Mero Sathi FM 107.2 MHz
24	Metro FM 94.6 MHz
25	Myagdi Kali FM 88.2 MHz
26	Nagarik FM 107.5 MHz
27	Narayani FM 103.8 MHz
28	Nepalgunj Samudayik Radio 104.8 MHz

T. Rampersaud-Skorka, *Community Radio in South Asia*, Diversity and Inclusion Research, https://doi.org/10.1007/978-3-031-85201-5

NEPAL	
#	Name of CRS
29	Nuwakot FM 106.8 MHz
30	Phoolwari Samudayik Radio 105.4 MHz
31	Prime FM 104.5 MHz
32	Radio Aakasbani 94.4 MHz
33	Radio Aakashganga 107.6 MHz
34	Radio Aandhikhola 105.4 MHz
35	Radio Aawaz 88.8 MHz
36	Radio ABC 89.8 MHz
37	Radio Abhiyan 107.4 MHz
38	Radio Achham FM 94.8 MHz
39	Radio Afno FM 104.8 MHz
40	Radio Afno FM 104.8 MHz
41	Radio Amargadhi FM 97.4 MHz
42	Radio Appan Mithila 94.4 MHz
43	Radio Arghakhanchi 105.8 MHz
44	Radio Arpan 104.5 MHz
45	Radio Baarasinga FM 102.2 MHz
46	Radio Babai 106.0 MHz
47	Radio Bajhang FM 91.0 MHz
48	Radio Bajura 104 MHz
49	Radio Bandganga 90.6 MHz
50	Radio Bardibas 94 MHz
51	Radio Barpak 106.4 MHz
52	Radio Betana 97.1 MHz
53	Radio Bhanubhakta 104.2 MHz
54	Radio Bheri FM 98.6 MHz
55	Radio Bheriganga 91.4 MHz
56	Radio Bhimeshwor 90.8 MHz
57	Radio Bhojpur 93.8 MHz
58	Radio Bhorukawa FM 92.8 MHz
59	Radio Bhotewodar 90.8 MHz
60	Radio Bihani 89 MHz
61	Radio Bihani 97.6 MHz
62	Radio Bijayabasti 90.1 MHz
63	Radio Buddha Aawaj 89.6 MHz
64	Radio Budinanda 96.5 MHz
65	Radio Chankheli 98.8 MHz
66	Radio Chapakot 91.6 MHz
67	Radio Chautari FM 91.4 MHz
68	Radio Chhimeki 107.2 MHz
69	Radio Chhinnamasta FM 101.4 MHz
70	Radio Chitwan 94.6 MHz
71	Radio Chomolonma 95.2 MHz
72	Radio Chomolungma 98.6 MHz
73	Radio Chulimalika 101.8 MHz
74	Radio Dadadara 104 MHz

NEPAL	
#	Name of CRS
75	Radio Damauli FM 94.2 MHz
76	Radio Darchula 90 MHz
77	Radio Darpan 88.4 MHz
78	Radio Daunne 103.4 MHz
79	Radio Deukhuri 105.8 MHz
80	Radio Deurali 101 MHz
81	Radio Devdaha 106.6 MHz
82	Radio Devghat 102.6 MHz
83	Radio Dhading 106 MHz
84	Radio Dhankuta 106.2 MHz
85	Radio Dhorpatan 104.1 MHz
86	Radio Dhrubatara 89.8 MHz
87	Radio Dhrubatara 89.9 MHz
88	Radio Didi Bahini 95.2 MHz
89	Radio Dolpa 101.4 MHz
90	Radio Ekata 92.4 MHz
91	Radio Friends FM 90.9 MHz
92	Radio Galkot 102.4 MHz
93	Radio Ganatantra FM 95.1 MHz
94	Radio Gandaki 90.2 MHz
95	Radio Gantatara Rapti FM 95.1 MHz
96	Radio Gaumukhi 106.7 MHz
97	Radio Gaushala 93.6 MHz
98	Radio Gemitribeni 94.3 MHz
99	Radio Ghodaghodi FM 88.3 MHz
100	Radio Gorkha 92.8 MHz
101	Radio Goshaikunda 96.5 MHz
102	Radio Gujramai FM 93.8 MHz
103	Radio Gunjan FM 105.3 MHz
104	Radio Hamro 103.4 MHz
105	Radio Hapure 89.4 MHz
106	Radio Hemja 88.5
107	Radio Highway 103.5
108	Radio Himal 92.8
109	Radio Jagaran 93.6
110	Radio Jagriti 87.9
111	Radio Jajarkot 105.6
112	Radio Jalapa 104.5
113	Radio Jaljala 96.4
114	Radio Janakpur 97.0
115	Radio Janasanchar 107.9 MHz
116	Radio Janasandesh FM 103.6 MHz
117	Radio Janpariya 102.4 MHz
118	Radio Jharana 88 MHz
119	Radio Jhilimila 107.8 MHz
120	Radio Jiwan Jyoti 90 MHz

NEPAL	
#	Name of CRS
121	Radio Jwala Samudiyik FM 100.4 MHz
122	Radio Kailash 103.4 MHz
123	Radio Kairan 96.4 MHz
124	Radio Kalapani 102.2 MHz
125	Radio Kalinchowk FM 106.4 MHz
126	Radio Kanchanpur 90.2 MHz
127	Radio Kapilvastu 104.2 MHz
128	Radio Kapurkot FM 106.1 MHz
129	Radio Karnali 105.2 MHz
130	Radio Karnali Aawaz 94.2 MHz
131	Radio Khalanga FM 107.6 MHz
132	Radio Khandabari 105.8 MHz
133	Radio Kohalpur 101.2 MHz
134	Radio Kripalu 99 MHz
135	Radio Krishnasar FM 94.00 MHz
136	Radio Kushum 90.0 MHz
137	Radio Laligurash 105.2 MHz
138	Radio Lalitpur 100.9 MHz
139	Radio Lamjung 88.4 MHz
140	Radio Langtang 90.3 MHz
141	Radio Lekhnath 106.6 MHz
142	Radio Likhu 91.3 MHz
143	Radio Lisne Aawaj 103.6 MHz
144	Radio Loktantra 89.4 MHz
145	Radio Lumbini FM 96.8 MHz
146	Radio Madanpokhara 106.9 MHz
147	Radio Madhesh 106.6 MHz
148	Radio Madhesh 89.3 MHz
149	Radio Madhesh Jana Aawaj 98.6 MHz
150	Radio Madhyabindu FM 101 MHz
151	Radio Madhyapaschim 91.4 MHz
152	Radio Madhyapurba FM 104 MHz
153	Radio Madi FM 107.6 MHz
154	Radio Mahakali 96.2 MHz
155	Radio Mahila Aawaz 90 MHz
156	Radio Makalu Dhankuta 92.2 MHz
157	Radio Makwanpur 101.3 MHz
158	Radio Malashree 100.5 MHz
159	Radio Malika 97.4 MHz
160	Radio Malikarjun 107.2 MHz
161	Radio Manakamana 102.4 MHz
162	Radio Manaslu 103.9 MHz
163	Radio Mandabi 97.0 MHz
164	Radio Marsyangdi 95.0 MHz
165	Radio Mayadevi 106.1 MHz
166	Radio Meeta F. M 106 MHz

NEPAL	
#	Name of CRS
167	Radio Melamchi 107.2 MHz
168	Radio Menchhayayem 103.4 MHz
169	Radio Mirchi 89.6 MHz
170	Radio Mountain 94.6 MHz
171	Radio Mugu 107.4 MHz
172	Radio Mukteswor 100.4 MHz
173	Radio Mukti 95.5 MHz
174	Radio Muktinath 90.8 MHz
175	Radio Mustang 89.0 MHz
176	Radio My FM 107.4 MHz
177	Radio Myagdi 104.4 MHz
178	Radio Nagarik 90.8 MHz
179	Radio Namobuddha 106.7 MHz
180	Radio Narayani 105.2 MHz
181	Radio Nari Aawaj 100.6 MHz
182	Radio Naya Abhiyan 99 MHz
183	Radio Naya Karnali 102.8 MHz
184	Radio Naya Nepal FM 104.5 MHz
185	Radio Naya Yug 107.3
186	Radio Nepal Bani FM 94.9 MHz
187	Radio Newa FM 106.6 MHz
188	Radio Nikash 93.4 MHz
189	Radio Nunthar FM 102.6 MHz
190	Radio Pahichan 105.3 MHz
191	Radio Palung 107.2 MHz
192	Radio Panchadewal 100.5 MHz
193	Radio Parbat 103.6 MHz
194	Radio Paribartan 92 MHz
195	Radio Pariwartan FM 89 MHz
196	Radio Pariwartan FM 89.4 MHz
197	Radio Paschim Aawaz 104.3 MHz
198	Radio Pashchim Today FM 88.8 MHz
199	Radio Pathshala 104 MHz
200	Radio Paurakhi FM 90.4 MHz
201	Radio Prakriti FM 93.4 MHz
202	Radio Pratibodh FM 102.4 MHz
203	Radio Purbanchal 104.4 MHz
204	Radio Pushpaanjali 97.4 MHz
205	Radio Pyuthan 92.0 MHz
206	Radio Rajdevi FM 93.2 MHz
207	Radio Rajmarga 92.1 MHz
208	Radio Ramaroshan 92.0 MHz
209	Radio Ramechhap 95.8 MHz
210	Radio Ramjyanu 89 MHz
211	Radio Rampur 103.6 MHz
212	Radio Rapti FM 104.8 MHz

NEPAL	
#	Name of CRS
213	Radio Rara 106 MHz
214	Radio Rasuwa 102.1 MHz
215	Radio Rautahat 90.8 MHz
216	Radio Rolpa 93.8 MHz
217	Radio Rubaru FM 104.6 MHz
218	Radio Rudraksha 98.8 MHz
219	Radio Sadvab 91.2 FM
220	Radio Sagarmatha 102.4 MHz
221	Radio Sailung FM 92.7 MHz
222	Radio Sajha Aawaz 88.3 MHz
223	Radio Sakhi 95.8 MHz
224	Radio Sakhi FM 106.4 MHz
225	Radio Salhes 88.8 MHz
226	Radio Salyan FM 101 MHz
227	Radio Samabesi 105 MHz
228	Radio Samad 102.6 MHz
229	Radio Samanata 105.4 MHz
230	Radio Sandesh 103.9 MHz
231	Radio Sani Bheri FM 89.2 MHz
232	Radio Sanjibani 91.0 MHz
233	Radio Sano Bheri 100.8 MHz
234	Radio Sansher 106.6 MHz
235	Radio Sanskriti 98.2 MHz
236	Radio Sarangkot 104.6 MHz
237	Radio Sarathi FM 92.6 MHz
238	Radio Sargam 88.8 MHz
239	Radio Sarlahi 105.6 MHz
240	Radio Sarthak 89.1 MHz
241	Radio Saugat 88.1 MHz
242	Radio Saurydaya 92.4 MHz
243	Radio Shaileswori 105.9 MHz
244	Radio Shaligram 100.6 MHz
245	Radio Sharada FM 99.2 MHz
246	Radio Shivasakti 98.3 MHz
247	Radio Siddhababa 98.4
248	Radio Simara 106 MHz
249	Radio Sindhu 105 MHz
250	Radio Sindhuligadhi 92 MHz
251	Radio Sisne FM 92.8 MHz
252	Radio Sky FM 88.4 MHz
253	Radio Society FM 89 MHz
254	Radio Sonamai 103.7 MHz
255	Radio Sudoor Sandesh 104 MHz
256	Radio Sudur Awaz 95 MHz
257	Radio Sumhatlung FM 104.2 MHz

NEPAL	
#	Name of CRS
258	Radio Sunawal 90.7 MHz
259	Radio Sunchhahari FM 101.5 MHz
260	Radio Sungava 104.6 MHz
261	Radio Sunkoshi 105.6 MHz
262	Radio Sunsari 104.6 MHz
263	Radio Surkhet 90.2 MHz
264	Radio Suryodaya 94 MHz
265	Radio Swagatam 89 MHz
266	Radio Swargadwari 102.8 MHz
267	Radio Swarnim 96.3 MHz
268	Radio Syangja FM 89.6 MHz
269	Radio TU FM 107 MHz
270	Radio Tahalka 91.1 MHz
271	Radio Tamor 102 MHz
272	Radio Tanahun 97.2 MHz
273	Radio Taplejung FM 94.0 MHz
274	Radio Terai 107 MHz
275	Radio Terhathum 92.4 MHz
276	Radio Tifadi 99.1 MHz
277	Radio Tikapur FM 101.0 MHz
278	Radio Tinjure 103.8 MHz
279	Radio Today 91 MHz
280	Radio Tripura 89.6 MHz
281	Radio Trishuli 88.4 MHz
282	Radio Triyuga 104 MHz
283	Radio Tulsipur FM 100.2 MHz
284	Radio Udaypur FM 102.4 MHz
285	Radio Unik FM 97.6 MHz
286	Radio Unity 92.2 MHz
287	Radio Unnati FM 92.9 MHz
288	Radio Upathyaka 87.6 MHz
289	Radio Uttar Ganga 102 MHz
290	Radio Voice 102.4 MHz
291	Ramailo Samudayek Radio 100.6 MHz
292	Rupakot Radio 105.0 MHz
293	Rupandehi FM 102 MHz
294	Sahayatri Samudayik Radio 94.2 MHz
295	Saipal FM 100.6 MHz
296	Samagra FM 107 MHz
297	Samudayik Radio Waling 89.2 MHz
298	Sarathi FM 90.7 MHz
299	Saugat FM 103.6 MHz
300	Seti Samudayik FM 93.6 MHz
301	Shakti FM 103.4 MHz
302	Shreenagar FM 93.2 MHz

NEPAL	
#	Name of CRS
303	Shuklaphanta FM 94.4 MHz
304	Sindhu FM 102.8 MHz
305	Solu FM 102.2 MHz
306	Sunaulo FM 107.2 MHz
307	Tribeni FM 94.4 MHz
308	Vijaya FM 101.6 MHz
309	Vision FM 90.5 MHz
INDIA	
#	Name of CRS
1	Aap Ki Awaz 90.8
2	AGN School CR 91.2
3	Agra Ki Aawaz 90.4
4	Ahalia Voice 90.4
5	Alfaz-e-Mewat 107.8
6	Aligarh Alive 90.8
7	Alwar Ki Awaz 90.8
8	Anna Community Radio 90.4
9	Antarvani CRS 90.8
10	Apna Radio 96.9
11	Apno Radio
12	Avtar Radio 90.4
13	Bannari Amman 90.4
14	BBD 90.8
15	Bol Hyderabad 90.4
16	Brahmaputra Community Radio Station 90.4
17	CCS Agricultural University Radio 91.2
18	Chanderi Ki Awaaz 94.4
19	CMS DC CR 90.4
20	CMS Radio 90.4
21	CRS Kuthar 90.8
22	Deccan Radio 107.8
23	Desh Bhagat Community Radio 107.8
24	Divya Vani Neladhani 90.8
25	Dnyanvani 90.4
26	DU CR 90.4
27	Ghazipur CR
28	GMR Radio 90.4
29	GNGC CR 90.4
30	Green CR 90.4
31	Gurgaon Ki Awaaz Samudayik Radio 107.8
32	Guruvani 90.8
33	Hamara MSPICM 90.4
34	Hello Haldwani 91.2
35	Himgiri Ki Awaaz 107.8
36	HINT CR 90.4

INDIA	
#	Name of CRS
37	Holy Cross College 90.4
38	Honey CR 90.8
39	IITK CR 90.4 FM
40	Ilanthalir CR 107.2
41	J G Radio 90.8
42	Jamia Radio 90.4
43	Janadhwani 90.8
44	Janvani CR 90.8
45	Jayoti Vani CR 91.2
46	JIMS CR 96.9
47	Jnan Taranga 90.4
48	Junagadh Janvani 91.2
49	Jyotirgamaya CR 91.2
50	Kalanjiam Samuga Vanoli 90.8
51	Kalpakkam CRS 90.8
52	Kamalvani 90.4
53	Karshaka Vani CR 90.4
54	Kisan Radio Basti 90.4
55	Kisan Vani Sironj 90.4
56	KLE Dhwani 90.4
57	KLR Community Radio 90.4
58	KMIT Tarang 90.4
59	Kongu CRS 90.4
60	KRIMS CR 90.8
61	Krishi CR 90.4
62	Krishi Vigyan Kendra Barh
63	KSR CR 90.4
64	Kumaon Vani 90.4
65	KVK Pravara CR 90.8
66	KVK Sharada Krishi Vahini 90.8
67	Lalit Lokvani CR 90.4
68	Lokvani Radio 90.4
69	Loyola CR 107.4
70	Mandakini Ki Awaaz 90.8
71	Manndeshi Tarang Vahini 90.4
72	Micavaani CR 90.4
73	Mindtree CR 91.2
74	MKC CR 91.2
75	MOP CR 107.8
76	Mugil CR 90.4
77	MUST Radio 107.8
78	Namma Dhwani 90.4
79	Neladani CR 90.8
80	Neotech CR 90.4
81	Nila CR 90.4

INDIA	
#	Name of CRS
82	NIVH Hello Doon 91.2
83	NSHM CR 91.2
84	Pantnagar Janvani 90.8
85	PARD Vaanoli CR 91.2
86	Pasumai CR 90.4
87	Periyar CR 90.4
88	PGP CR 90.8
89	Pragnya CR 90.4
90	PSG CRS 107.8
91	PudiyaUdayam 91.2
92	Puduvai Vaani CRS 107.8
93	Radio 7 90.4
94	Radio Active 90.4
95	Radio Active 90.4—Karnataka
96	Radio Adan 90.4
97	Radio Ala 90.8
98	Radio Amity 107.8
99	Radio Awaaz 91.2
100	Radio Azad Hind 90.8
101	Radio Banasthali 90.4
102	Radio Benziger 107.8
103	Radio Bundelkhand 90.4
104	Radio Chandra Shekhar Azaad Nagar (Bhabra) 90.4
105	Radio Chitkara 107.8
106	Radio DC 90.4
107	Radio Dhadkan 107.8
108	Radio Eminent 90.4
109	Radio FTII 90.4
110	Radio IIMT 90.4
111	Radio JIMS 90.4
112	Radio JU 90.8
113	Radio Khushi 90.4
114	Radio Kissan 90.8
115	Radio Kotagiri 90.4
116	Radio Luit 90.8
117	Radio MACFAST 90.4
118	Radio Madhuban 90.4
119	Radio Manav Rachna 107.8
120	Radio Manipal 90.4
121	Radio Mantra 91.9
122	Radio Mast 90.4
123	Radio Mattoli 90.4
124	Radio Media Village 90.8
125	Radio Mewat 90.4
126	Radio MGIRI 90.4

INDIA	
#	Name of CRS
127	Radio Muskan 90.4
128	Radio Nagar 90.4
129	Radio Namaskar 90.4
130	Radio NGF Palwal 90.4
131	Radio Noida 107.4
132	Radio Noida Lok Manch 91.2
133	Radio Popcorn 90.4
134	Radio Raman 90.4
135	Radio Rimjhim 90.4
136	Radio Sanskar 90.4
137	Radio Sarang 107.8
138	Radio SD 90.8
139	Radio Sharda 90.4
140	Radio Siddhartha 90.8
141	Radio Sirsa 90.4
142	Radio Snehi 90.4
143	Radio SRFTI 90.4
144	Radio Surabhi 90.4
145	Radio Swayamshakti 90.4
146	Radio Tilonia 90.4
147	Radio Universal 106.8
148	Radio VatsaGulm 90.8
149	Radio Vikalp 90.4
150	Radio Vishnu 90.4
151	Radio Vishwas 90.8
152	Radio Zindagee 90.8
153	Raipur CRS 90.4
154	Ramana Dhwani 90.4
155	Rathinavani CR 90.8
156	Ravenshaw Radio 90.4
157	Rudi No Radio 90.4
158	Saiyere Jo Radio 90.4
159	Salaam Namaste 90.4
160	Samudayik Henval Vani 90.4
161	Sangham Radio 90.4
162	Sanjha Radio 90.8
163	Sarathi Jhalak 90.4
164	Shyamalavani CRS 90.4
165	Sivanthi CR 90.4
166	SRM Muthucharam CR 90.4
167	SSM CR 90.8
168	Suno Sharda FM 90.8
169	SVFM CRS Tirupati 90.4
170	Swaranant CRS 90.4
171	Tashi Delek CR 90.4

INDIA	
#	Name of CRS
172	Thendral CR 91.2
173	TNAU CRS 107.4
174	Uttam Radio 90.4
175	Vallabh Krishak Radio 90.4
176	Vallabh Vidyanagar Campus Radio 90.4
177	Vanya Radio Bijori 90.4
178	Vanya Radio Chanda 90.4
179	Vanya Radio Chandrashekhar Azad Nagar (Bhabra)
180	Vanya Radio Chicholi 90.4
181	Vanya Radio Khalwa 90.4
182	Vanya Radio Nalchha 90.8
183	Vanya Radio Sesaipura 90.8
184	Vasundhara Krishi Vahini 90.4
185	Vayalaga Vanoli 90.4 FM
186	Venudhwani CR 90.4
187	Vidyavani CR 107.4
188	VIT CR 90.8
189	Vivek CR 90.4
190	Voice of Azamgarh 90.8
191	Voice of SOA Community 90.4
192	Waqt Ki Awaaz 91.2
193	Yeralavani CR 91.2

BANGLADESH	
#	Name of CRS
1	Krishi Radio 98.8
2	Radio Bikrampur 99.2
3	Radio Borendro 99.2
4	Radio Chilmari 99.2
5	Radio Jhenuk 99.2
6	Radio Lokobetar 99.2
7	Radio Mahananda 98.8
8	Radio Meghna 99.0
9	Radio Mukti 99.2
10	Radio NAF 99.2
11	Radio Nalta 99.2
12	Radio Padma 99.2
13	Radio Pollikontho 99.2
14	Radio Sagar Giri 99.2
15	Radio Sagor Dwip 99.2
16	Radio Sarabela 98.8
17	Radio Sundarban 98.8

Appendix 5.2: Screenshot of CRS Basic Profile Form in the CMD (created using Microsoft Access)

ID
1

Name of initiative
Krishi Radio 98.8

Type of media
Community Radio

Country
Bangladesh

Location
Rural

Date established
Thursday, December 12, 2013

Established by
Agricultural Information Service, Ministry of Agriculture (Government)

Description of initiative
Krishi Radio, located in Borguna's Amtoli, has started is test transmission on January 01, 2013. It is the only government community radio among the community radios, established by Agricultural Information Service assisted by the United Nation's Food and Agricultural Organization. The station has begun its journey with the slogan that "Amar Radio, Amar Kotha Bole".

Partners
Agricultural Information Service, Bangladesh NGO's Network for Radio and Communication, United Nation's Food and Agricultural Organization.

Street address
Amtoli Upazilla Complex, Barguna, Barisal

Phone number
01913029381

E-mail address
krishiradioais@gmail.com

Website
https://bnnrc.net/krishi-radio/

Other

Audience profile
Men, Women

Thematic Area
Culture, Environmental, Gender, Health, Other

Content Genre
Music, News, Other

Miscellaneous
2 listening groups; broadcast time: 9am to 11am, 3pm to 5pm; challenges: financial, irregular volunteers, need training

Appendix 5.3 Screenshot of CRS In-Depth Profile Form in the CMD (created using Microsoft Access)

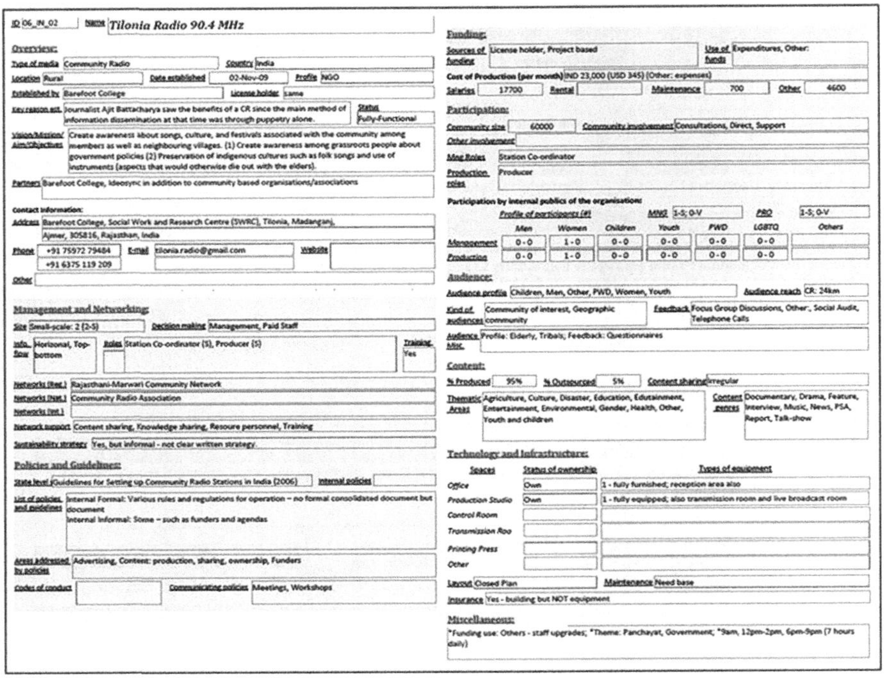

ID 06_IN_02 Name Tilonia Radio 90.4 MHz

Overview:
Type of media: Community Radio | Country: India
Location: Rural | Date established: 02-Nov-09 | Profile: NGO
Established by: Barefoot College | License holder: same
Key reason est.: Journalist Ajit Battacharya saw the benefits of a CR since the main method of information dissemination at that time was through puppetry alone. | Status: Fully-Functional
Vision/Mission/Aim/Objectives: Create awareness about songs, culture, and festivals associated with the community among members as well as neighbouring villages. (1) Create awareness among grassroots people about government policies (2) Preservation of indigenous cultures such as folk songs and use of instruments (aspects that would otherwise die out with the elders).
Partners: Barefoot College, Ideosync in addition to community based organisations/associations

Contact information:
Address: Barefoot College, Social Work and Research Centre (SWRC), Tilonia, Madanganj, Ajmer, 305816, Rajasthan, India
Phone: +91 75972 79484; +91 6375 119 209 | E-mail: tilonia.radio@gmail.com | Website:
Other:

Management and Networking:
Size: Small-scale: 2 (2-5) | Decision making: Management, Paid Staff
Info. flow: Horizonal, Top-bottom | Roles: Station Co-ordinator (S), Producer (S) | Training: Yes
Networks (Reg.): Rajasthani-Marwari Community Network
Networks (Nat.): Community Radio Association
Networks (Int.):
Network support: Content sharing, Knowledge sharing, Resoure personnel, Training
Sustainability strategy: Yes, but informal - not clear written strategy.

Policies and Guidelines:
State level: Guidelines for Setting up Community Radio Stations in India (2006) | Internal policies:
List of policies and guidelines: Internal Formal: Various rules and regulations for operation – no formal consolidated document but document
Internal Informal: Some – such as funders and agendas
Areas addressed by policies: Advertising, Content: production, sharing, ownership, Funders
Codes of conduct: | Communicating policies: Meetings, Workshops

Funding:
Sources of funding: License holder, Project based | Use of funds: Expenditures, Other:
Cost of Production (per month): IND 23,000 (USD 345) (Other: expenses)
Salaries: 17700 | Rental: | Maintenance: 700 | Other: 4600

Participation:
Community size: 60000 | Community involvement: Consultations, Direct, Support
Other involvement:
Mng Roles: Station Co-ordinator
Production roles: Producer

Participation by internal publics of the organisation:
Profile of participants (#) | MNG: 1-5; 0-V | PRO: 1-5; 0-V

	Men	Women	Children	Youth	PWD	LGBTQ	Others
Management	0-0	1-0	0-0	0-0	0-0	0-0	
Production	0-0	1-0	0-0	0-0	0-0	0-0	

Audience:
Audience profile: Children, Men, Other, PWD, Women, Youth | Audience reach: CR: 24km
Kind of audiences: Community of interest, Geographic community | Feedback: Focus Group Discussions, Other:, Social Audit, Telephone Calls
Audience Misc.: Profile: Elderly, Tribals; Feedback: Questionnaires

Content:
% Produced: 95% | % Outsourced: 5% | Content sharing: Irregular
Thematic Areas: Agriculture, Culture, Disaster, Education, Edutainment, Entertainment, Environmental, Gender, Health, Other, Youth and children | Content genres: Documentary, Drama, Feature, Interview, Music, News, PSA, Report, Talk-show

Technology and Infrastructure:

Spaces	Status of ownership	Types of equipment
Office	Own	1 - fully furnished; reception area also
Production Studio	Own	1 - fully equipped; also transmission room and live broadcast room
Control Room		
Transmission Roo		
Printing Press		
Other		

Layout: Closed Plan | Maintenance: Need base
Insurance: Yes - building but NOT equipment

Miscellaneous:
*Funding use: Others - staff upgrades; *Theme: Panchayat, Government; *9am, 12pm-2pm, 6pm-9pm (7 hours daily)

Appendix 5.4: List of Active CRS Websites Accessed as of December 2017

#	Name	Website:
Nepal		
1	3 Angels Community Radio 94.6 MHz	http://3angelsradio.org.np
2	Afno FM 90.4 MHz	http://radioafnofmrukum.com
3	Baglung FM 96.4 MHz	http://baglungfm.com.np/
4	Bheri FM 105.4 MHz	https://radiobheri.com.np/about-us/
5	Bulbule FM 103.4 MHz	http://www.bulbulefm.com.np/
6	Community Radio Parasi 90.2 MHz	http://radiomukti.org
7	ECR FM 104.2 MHz	http://www.radioparyabaran.org.np
8	Gorkhali Radio 106 MHz	http://www.radiogurkhali.com

#	Name	Website:
9	Grace FM 107.6 MHz	http://www.gracefm.com.np
10	HajurKo Radio 102.1 MHz	http://hajurkoradio.org.np
11	Ilam FM 93 MHz	http://www.ilamfm.org
12	Jagaran FM 90.8 MHz	http://jagaran.com.np
13	Janaki FM 106 MHz	http://www.janakifm.com.np
14	Manakamana FM 98.7 MHz	http://manakamanafm.org.np
15	Mero FM 93.6	http://merofm.com.np
16	Myagdi Kali FM 88.2 MHz	http://myagdikali.com.np
17	Nagarik FM 107.5 MHz	http://www.nagarikfm.com.np
18	Narayani FM 103.8 MHz	http://radionarayani.org.np
19	Nuwakot FM 106.8 MHz	http://www.nuwakotfm.org
20	Prime FM 104.5 MHz	http://www.primefm.com.np
21	Radio Aandhikhola 105.4 MHz	http://www.radioandhikhola.org
22	Radio Aawaz 88.8 MHz	http://www.radioaawaj.org.np
23	Radio ABC 89.8 MHz	http://radioabc.com.np/
24	Radio Abhiyan 107.4 MHz	http://www.radiolisnefm.org
25	Radio Achham FM 94.8 MHz	http://www.radioachham.com.np
26	Radio Afno FM 104.8 MHz	http://afnofm.org/dadeldhura
27	Radio Afno FM 104.8 MHz	http://okhaldhunga.afnofm.org
28	Radio Amargadhi FM 97.4 MHz	http://radioamargadhi.org/contact-us.php
29	Radio Appan Mithila 94.4 MHz	https://www.facebook.com/pg/radioappanmithila/about/?ref=page_internal
30	Radio Arghakhanchi 105.8 MHz	http://www.arghakhanchi.com/index.php?action=video
31	Radio Arpan 104.5 MHz	http://www.radioarpan.com
32	Radio Babai 106.0 MHz	http://www.radiobabai.org.np
33	Radio Bajura 104 MHz	http://www.radiobajura.org.np/
34	Radio Betana 97.1 MHz	http://radiobetana.com
35	Radio Bheri FM 98.6 MHz	http://radiobheri.com.np
36	Radio Bheriganga 91.4 MHz	http://www.radiobheriganga.com.np
37	Radio Bhimeshwor 90.8 MHz	https://www.facebook.com/pg/Radio-Bhimeshwor-908-MHZ-Dolakha-192021384316960/posts/?ref=page_internal
38	Radio Bhojpur 93.8 MHz	http://www.radiobhojpur.org.np
39	Radio Bhotewodar 90.8 MHz	http://www.radiobhotewodar.org.np
40	Radio Bihani 89 MHz	http://www.radiobihani.org.np/
41	Radio Bihani 97.6 MHz	http://www.radiobihani.org.np
42	Radio Buddha Aawaj 89.6 MHz	http://www.buddhaawaaz.com
43	Radio Chautari FM 91.4 MHz	http://www.radiochautari.org

#	Name	Website:
44	Radio Chhinnamasta FM 101.4 MHz	https://www.facebook.com/pg/Radio-Chhinnamasta-FM-1014-MHz-655639437809241/about/?ref=page_internal
45	Radio Chitwan 94.6 MHz	http://radiochitwan.com.np/
46	Radio Chomolungma 98.6 MHz	http://www.cfm.org.np
47	Radio Dadadara 104 MHz	https://dadadara.com.np/
48	Radio Damauli FM 94.2 MHz	http://www.damaulifm.org
49	Radio Darpan 88.4 MHz	www.facebook.com/radiodarpan88.4mhzbardibas/
50	Radio Daunne 103.4 MHz	http://radiodaunne.org.np
51	Radio Devdaha 106.6 MHz	http://www.radiodevdaha.org/about.php
52	Radio Devghat 102.6 MHz	http://www.radiodevghat.org.np/
53	Radio Dhading 106 MHz	http://www.radiodhading.org
54	Radio Dhankuta 106.2 MHz	http://www.radiodhankuta.org.np
55	Radio Dhrubatara 89.8 MHz	http://www.dtfm.org
56	Radio Didi Bahini 95.2 MHz	http://www.radiodidibahini.org
57	Radio Dolpa 101.4 MHz	http://www.radiodolpa.org.np
58	Radio Ekata 92.4 MHz	http://www.radioekata.com.np/
59	Radio Friends FM 90.9 MHz	http://www.friendsfm.com.np
60	Radio Ganatantra FM 95.1 MHz	http://www.gfm.com.np
61	Radio Gandaki 90.2 MHz	https://gandakimedia.com/
62	Radio Gemitribeni 94.3 MHz	http://gemitribenifm.org.np
63	Radio Ghodaghodi FM 88.3 MHz	http://radioghodaghodi.org.np/contact.php
64	Radio Gorkha 92.8 MHz	http://www.hamrogorkha.com/
65	Radio Gunjan FM 105.3 MHz	http://www.gunjanfm.com/about.php
66	Radio Hamro 103.4 MHz	http://www.hamroradiofm.org.np
67	Radio Highway 103.5	http://www.radiohighway.com.np
68	Radio Himal 92.8	http://himalfm.org
69	Radio Jagaran 93.6	http://jagaran.radio.net
70	Radio Jajarkot 105.6	http://www.radiojajarkot.org.np
71	Radio Jalapa 104.5	http://www.radiojalapa.com/
72	Radio Jaljala 96.4	http://www.radiojalapa.com/
73	Radio Janakpur 97.0	http://radiojanakpur.org.np/about-us/
74	Radio Janasanchar 107.9 MHz	http://www.jfm.com.np
75	Radio Janpariya 102.4 MHz	http://www.radiojanapriya.org.np
76	Radio Kailash 103.4 MHz	http://radiokailash.org.np
77	Radio Kairan 96.4 MHz	http://www.radiokairan.com
78	Radio Kalapani 102.2 MHz	http://kalapanifm.com.np

#	Name	Website:
79	Radio Kalinchowk FM 106.4 MHz	https://kalinchokfm.com
80	Radio Kanchanpur 90.2 MHz	http://www.radiokanchanpur.org.np
81	Radio Kapurkot FM 106.1 MHz	http://radiokapurkot.org.np
82	Radio Karnali 105.2 MHz	http://www.kirdarc.org
83	Radio Karnali Aawaz 94.2 MHz	http://radiokarnaliaawaj.com
84	Radio Khalanga FM 107.6 MHz	http://radiokhalanga.org.np
85	Radio Khandabari 105.8 MHz	http://www.kfm.com.np
86	Radio Kohalpur 101.2 MHz	http://www.kohalpurfm.org.np
87	Radio Kripalu 99 MHz	http://radiokripalu.com.np/
88	Radio Krishnasar FM 94.00 MHz	http://krishnasarfm.org.np
89	Radio Kushum 90.0 MHz	http://radiokushum.org.np
90	Radio Laligurash 105.2 MHz	http://www.radiolaligurans.com.np
91	Radio Lalitpur 100.9 MHz	http://www.radiolalitpur.com.np
92	Radio Lamjung 88.4 MHz	http://www.radiolamjung.org
93	Radio Langtang 90.3 MHz	http://www.mirchifm.com.np
94	Radio Lisne Aawaj 103.6 MHz	http://www.radiosanobheri.com
95	Radio Lumbini FM 96.8 MHz	http://www.radiolumbini.org
96	Radio Madanpokhara 106.9 MHz	http://www.community-radio-madanpokha
97	Radio Madhesh 106.6 MHz	http://www.radiomadhesh.com
98	Radio Madhesh Jana Aawaj 98.6 MHz	http://www.madheshjanawajfm.org.np
99	Radio Madhyapaschim 91.4 MHz	https://www.radiomp.org
100	Radio Madi FM 107.6 MHz	http://radiomadi.org.np
101	Radio Mahakali 96.2 MHz	http://www.radiomahakali.org
102	Radio Mahila Aawaz 90 MHz	http://mahilaawaj.org.np
103	Radio Makalu Dhankuta 92.2 MHz	http://www.radiomakalu.org.np
104	Radio Makwanpur 101.3 MHz	http://www.radiomakawanpur.com
105	Radio Malika 97.4 MHz	http://www.malikafm.org.np
106	Radio Manakamana 102.4 MHz	http://radiomanakamana.org
107	Radio Mandabi 97.0 MHz	http://www.mandavifm.com/
108	Radio Melamchi 107.2 MHz	http://www.radiomelamchi.com
109	Radio Menchhayayem 103.4 MHz	http://mfm.com.np/
110	Radio Mirchi 89.6 MHz	http://www.mirchifm.com.np
111	Radio Mugu 107.4 MHz	http://www.radiomugu.com.np

#	Name	Website:
112	Radio Mukti 95.5 MHz	http://radiomukti.org
113	Radio Muktinath 90.8 MHz	http://www.radiomuktinath.org.np/
114	Radio Namobuddha 106.7 MHz	http://www.radionamobuddha.org
115	Radio Narayani 105.2 MHz	http://narayanifm.org.np
116	Radio Nari Aawaj 100.6 MHz	http://www.radionariaawaj.com.np
117	Radio Naya Karnali 102.8 MHz	http://www.rnkfm.com.np
118	Radio Naya Nepal FM 104.5 MHz	http://www.nayanepalfm.com.np
119	Radio Naya Yug 107.3	http://www.radionayayug.org.np
120	Radio Nepal Bani FM 94.9 MHz	http://www.nepalbani.org.np
121	Radio Nikash 93.4 MHz	http://www.radionikas.com
122	Radio Nunthar FM 102.6 MHz	http://nuntharfm.com
123	Radio Pahichan 105.3 MHz	http://www.radiopahichan.org.np
124	Radio Palung 107.2 MHz	http://www.radiopalung.org
125	Radio Panchadewal 100.5 MHz	http://www.radiopanchadewal.org.np
126	Radio Paribartan 92 MHz	http://radioparibartan.com.np
127	Radio Pariwartan FM 89.4 MHz	http://radiopariwartan.org.np
128	Radio Paschim Aawaz 104.3 MHz	http://www.radiopaschimaawaj.org.np
129	Radio Pashchim Today FM 88.8 MHz	http://www.epaschimtoday.com
130	Radio Pathshala 104 MHz	http://www.radiopathshala.com
131	Radio Paurakhi FM 90.4 MHz	http://www.radiopaurakhi.org.np
132	Radio Prakriti FM 93.4 MHz	http://www.radioprakriti.com
133	Radio Purbanchal 104.4 MHz	http://www.radiopurbanchal.org.np
134	Radio Pushpaanjali 97.4 MHz	http://www.radiopuspanjali.com.np
135	Radio Rajmarga 92.1 MHz	http://rajmargasanchar.org.np
136	Radio Ramaroshan 92.0 MHz	http://rfm.org.np
137	Radio Ramechhap 95.8 MHz	http://www.radioramechhap.org.np
138	Radio Rapti FM 104.8 MHz	http://www.radiorapti.org.np
139	Radio Rasuwa 102.1 MHz	http://radiorasuwa.com.np
140	Radio Rautahat 90.8 MHz	http://rautahatfm.org/
141	Radio Rolpa 93.8 MHz	http://www.radiorolpa.org
142	Radio Rubaru FM 104.6 MHz	http://rubarufm.org.np
143	Radio Rudraksha 98.8 MHz	http://radiorudraksha.com
144	Radio Sadvab 91.2 FM	http://www.radiosadvab.com/about/about-us

#	Name	Website:
145	Radio Sagarmatha 102.4 MHz	http://www.radiosagarmatha.org.np
146	Radio Sailung FM 92.7 MHz	http://radiosailung.org/
147	Radio Sakhi 95.8 MHz	http://www.radiosakhi.com.np
148	Radio Salhes 88.8 MHz	http://www.radiosalheshfm.com.np
149	Radio Samabesi 105 MHz	http://www.radiosamabeshi.com.np
150	Radio Samad 102.6 MHz	http://samadfm.org
151	Radio Sano Bheri 100.8 MHz	http://www.radiosanobheri.com
152	Radio Sanskriti 98.2 MHz	https://www.facebook.com/pg/RadioSanskriti98.2MHz
153	Radio Sarangkot 104.6 MHz	http://radiosarangkot.com.np
154	Radio Sargam 88.8 MHz	http://www.radiosargam.org.np
155	Radio Sarlahi 105.6 MHz	http://www.radiosarlahi.org
156	Radio Saugat 88.1 MHz	http://radiosaugat.onlinesiraha.com
157	Radio Shaileswori 105.9 MHz	http://www.sfm.org.np
158	Radio Shaligram 100.6 MHz	http://www.radiosaligram.com.np
159	Radio Sharada FM 99.2 MHz	http://www.radiosarada.org
160	Radio Shivasakti 98.3 MHz	http://radioshivshakti.org.np
161	Radio Siddhababa 98.4	http://www.radiosiddhababa.org.np
162	Radio Sindhu 105 MHz	http://radiosindhu.org
163	Radio Sindhuligadhi 92 MHz	http://www.radioaandhikhola.org
164	Radio Sisne FM 92.8 MHz	http://www.radiosisne.com.np
165	Radio Sky FM 88.4 MHz	http://ww.skyfm.org.np
166	Radio Society FM 89 MHz	http://www.societyfm.com.np
167	Radio Sonamai 103.7 MHz	http://www.radiosonamai.org.np
168	Radio Sudoor Sandesh 104 MHz	http://www.sudoorsandesh.com.np
169	Radio Sudur Awaz 95 MHz	http://www.radiosudoorawaz.com.np
170	Radio Sumhatlung FM 104.2 MHz	http://sumhatlungfm.com.np
171	Radio Sunawal 90.7 MHz	http://www.radiosunwal.com.np
172	Radio Sunkoshi 105.6 MHz	http://www.radiosunkoshi.org.np/
173	Radio Syangja FM 89.6 MHz	http://radiosyangja.org
174	Radio Tamor 102 MHz	http://www.radiotamor.com
175	Radio Tanahun 97.2 MHz	http://www.radiotanahun.com
176	Radio Taplejung FM 94.0 MHz	http://www.radiotaplejung.com
177	Radio Terai 107 MHz	http://radioterai.com.np
178	Radio Terhathum 92.4 MHz	http://www.radioterhathum.com.np

#	Name	Website:
179	Radio Tikapur FM 101.0 MHz	http://www.tikapurfm.org/
180	Radio Tinjure 103.8 MHz	http://www.radiotinjure.com
181	Radio Trishuli 88.4 MHz	http://radiotrishuli.com.np
182	Radio Tulsipur FM 100.2 MHz	http://www.radiotulsipur.com.np/
183	Radio Udaypur FM 102.4 MHz	http://www.radioudayapur.org.np/
184	Radio Unik FM 97.6 MHz	http://uniquefm.com.np
185	Radio Unity 92.2 MHz	http://www.radiounity.com.np
186	Radio Upathyaka 87.6 MHz	http://radioupatyaka.com.np
187	Radio Uttar Ganga 102 MHz	http://www.radiouttarganga.org.np
188	Rupandehi FM 102 MHz	http://www.rupandehifm.org
189	Sahayatri Samudayik Radio 94.2 MHz	https://www.facebook.com/pg/Radio-Sahayatri-FM-942-MHz-okhaldhunga-264874806997922/posts/?ref=page_internal
190	Saipal FM 100.6 MHz	http://saipal.listenfm.org/
191	Samagra FM 107 MHz	http://www.radiosamagra.org
192	Sarathi FM 90.7 MHz	http://www.radiosarathi.org.np/
193	Saugat FM 103.6 MHz	http://www.saugaatfmbaitadi.org
194	Seti Samudayik FM 93.6 MHz	http://radiosetifm.simplesite.com
195	Shakti FM 103.4 MHz	http://www.radioshakti.com.np
196	Solu FM 102.2 MHz	http://www.solufm.org.np
197	Tribeni FM 94.4 MHz	http://www.tribenifm.com
198	Vijaya FM 101.6 MHz	http://www.vijayafm.org.np
199	Vision FM 90.5 MHz	http://visionfm.org/
India		
200	Aap Ki Awaz 90.8	http://www.aapkiawazfm.com
201	Alfaz-e-Mewat 107.8	http://www.smsfoundation.org
202	Alwar Ki Awaz 90.8	http://www.radioalwar.com
203	Antarvani CRS 90.8	http://www.mahadasoha.com
204	Avtar Radio 90.4	http://www.avtarradio.com
205	Bannari Amman 90.4	http://www.bitsathy.com
206	BBD 90.8	http://www.bbdu.ac.in
207	Bol Hyderabad 90.4	http://bolhyd.commuoh.in/
208	Brahmaputra Community Radio Station 90.4	http://www.radiobrahmaputraa.webs.com/, www.facebook.com/radiobrahmaputra90.4fm
209	Chanderi Ki Awaaz 94.4	http://www.chanderikiawaaz.in
210	CMS DC CR 90.4	http://www.cmseducation.org/crs
211	CMS Radio 90.4	http://www.cmseducation.org/crs
212	Deccan Radio 107.8	http://www.siasat.com
213	Desh Bhagat Community Radio 107.8	http://www.deshbhagatradio.com/
214	DU CR 90.4	http://ducr.du.ac.in/

#	Name	Website:
215	Ghazipur CR	http://www.pgcghazipur.ac.in
216	GMR Radio 90.4	http://www.gmrit.org
217	Green CR 90.4	http://www.greenfm.techmindinfo.com
218	Gurgaon Ki Awaaz Samudayik Radio 107.8	http://www.trfindia.org
219	Hamara MSPICM 90.4	http://www.panwarinstitutes.org
220	Hello Haldwani 91.2	http://radio.uou.ac.in
221	Himgiri Ki Awaaz 107.8	http://www.hzu.edu.in
222	Ilanthalir CR 107.2	http://www.rgniyd.gov.in
223	J G Radio 90.8	http://www.jgsirsa.com
224	Janadhwani 90.8	http://www.svym.org
225	JIMS CR 96.9	http://www.jims.in
226	Jnan Taranga 90.4	http://www.kkhsou.in/jnantaranga
227	Junagadh Janvani 91.2	http://www.jau.in
228	Kalanjiam Samuga Vanoli 90.8	http://www.dhan.org
229	Kamalvani 90.4	http://www.kamalvani.org
230	Kisan Radio Basti 90.4	http://kssbasti.org/radio
231	Kongu CRS 90.4	http://www.kongu.ac.in
232	Krishi CR 90.4	http://www.uasd.edu.in
233	Krishi Vigyan Kendra Barh	http://www.bausabour.ac.in
234	KSR CR 90.4	http://www.ksrfm.com
235	KVK Pravara CR 90.8	http://www.kvk.pravara.com
236	KVK Sharada Krishi Vahini 90.8	http://www.kvkbaramati.com
237	Lokvani Radio 90.4	http://www.ambujacementfoundation.org
238	Loyola CR 107.4	http://www.loyolacollege.edu
239	Manndeshi Tarang Vahini 90.4	http://www.manndeshi.org
240	MKC CR 91.2	http://www.mkce.ac.in
241	MOP CR 107.8	http://www.mop-vaishnav.ac.in
242	MUST Radio 107.8	http://www.mustradio.in
243	Namma Dhwani 90.4	http://www.myrada.org
244	Neladani CR 90.8	http://www.djvk.org
245	Neotech CR 90.4	http://Neotechgroup.com
246	Pasumai CR 90.4	http://www.pasumairadio.com
247	Periyar CR 90.4	http://www.periyarcommunityradio.weebly.com
248	PGP CR 90.8	http://www.pgpcet.ac.in
249	Pragnya CR 90.4	http://www.griet.ac.in
250	PSG CRS 107.8	http://www.psgtech.edu/psgcrs
251	PudiyaUdayam 91.2	http://www.sarvam.aurosociety.org
252	Puduvai Vaani CRS 107.8	http://www.pondiuni.edu.in

#	Name	Website:
253	Radio 7 90.4	http://www.icfia.org
254	Radio Active 90.4—Karnataka	http://www.radioactive.edu.in
255	Radio Ala 90.8	www.facebook.com/radioala90.8fm
256	Radio Amity 107.8	http://www.amity.edu
257	Radio Awaaz 91.2	http://www.fmradioawaaz.org
258	Radio Banasthali 90.4	http://www.banasthali.org
259	Radio Benziger 107.8	http://www.Communityradiobenziger.org
260	Radio DC 90.4	http://www.radiodcfm.com
261	Radio FTII 90.4	http://www.ftiindia.com
262	Radio JIMS 90.4	http://www.jimsd.org
263	Radio JU 90.8	http://www.jaduniv.edu.in/radioju
264	Radio Kissan 90.8	http://www.radiokissan.org
265	Radio Luit 90.8	http://www.idolgu.in/student_support/radio_luit_FM_90.8
266	Radio MACFAST 90.4	http://www.radiomacfast.org
267	Radio Madhuban 90.4	http://www.radiomadhuban.in
268	Radio Manav Rachna 107.8	http://www.radiomanavrachna.org
269	Radio Manipal 90.4	http://www.manipal.edu
270	Radio Mattoli 90.4	http://www.radiomattoli.com
271	Radio Media Village 90.8	http://www.mediavillage.com
272	Radio Mewat 90.4	http://www.radiomewat.org
273	Radio MGIRI 90.4	http://www.mgiri.org
274	Radio Muskan 90.4	http://www.radiomuskan.org
275	Radio Nagar 90.4	http://www.snehalaya.org
276	Radio Namaskar 90.4	http://www.radionamaskar.in
277	Radio Noida 107.4	http://www.radionoida.fm
278	Radio Popcorn 90.4	http://www.visionbharat.com/radiopopcorn
279	Radio Rimjhim 90.4	http://radiorimjhim.wordpress.com
280	Radio Sarang 107.8	http://staloysiuscollege.co.in
281	Radio SD 90.8	http://www.radiosdfm.com
282	Radio Sharda 90.4	http://www.radiosharda.com
283	Radio Siddhartha 90.8	http://www.radiosiddhartha.com
284	Radio Surabhi 90.4	http://www.iiec-odisha.org
285	Radio Tilonia 90.4	http://www.barefootcollege.org
286	Radio Universal 106.8	http://www.universalcollege.org
287	Radio Vishwas 90.8	http://www.kvkbaramati.com
288	Ramana Dhwani 90.4	http://www.srmab.org
289	Rathinavani CR 90.8	http://www.rathinavani.com
290	Rudi No Radio 90.4	http://www.sewaacademy.org/
291	Saiyere Jo Radio 90.4	http://www.kmvs.org.in

#	Name	Website:
292	Salaam Namaste 90.4	http://www.salaamnamaste.in
293	Sangham Radio 90.4	http://www.ddsindia.com
294	Sanjha Radio 90.8	http://www.radiosanjha.com
295	Shyamalavani CRS 90.4	http://shyamalavani.in
296	Sivanthi CR 90.4	http://www.aditanarcollege.in
297	SRM Muthucharam CR 90.4	http://www.srmuniv.ac.in/muthucharam
298	SSM CR 90.8	http://www.ssmce.ac.in
299	Suno Sharda FM 90.8	http://Sharda.ac.in
300	Swaranant CRS 90.4	http://www.kvkwashim.com
301	Thendral CR 91.2	http://www.nalamdana.in
302	Uttam Radio 90.4	http://www.uttamradio.com
303	Vasundhara Krishi Vahini 90.4	http://www.radiovasundhara.com
304	Vayalaga Vanoli 90.4 FM	http://www.vayalagafm.in
305	Venudhwani CR 90.4	http://www.klevenudhwanifm.org
306	Vidyavani CR 107.4	http://vidyavani.unipune.ac.in
307	VIT CR 90.8	http://www.vit.ac.in/about/community/radio
308	Vivek CR 90.4	http://www.vivekhighschool.in
309	Waqt Ki Awaaz 91.2	http://www.shramikbharti.org.in
310	Yeralavani CR 91.2	http://www.yerala.org
Bangladesh		
1	Krishi Radio 98.8	https://bnnrc.net/krishi-radio/
2	Radio Bikrampur 99.2	https://bnnrc.net/radio-bikrampur/
3	Radio Borendro 99.2	https://bnnrc.net/borendro-radio/
4	Radio Chilmari 99.2	http://chilmari.communityradio.com.bd/
5	Radio Lokobetar 99.2	https://www.facebook.com/Lokobetar99.2fm/
6	Radio Mahananda 98.8	https://www.radiomahananda.fm/startofrm/
7	Radio Meghna 99.0	http://radiomeghna.net/
8	Radio Mukti 99.2	http://mukti.communityradio.com.bd/
9	Radio NAF 99.2	http://naf.communityradio.com.bd/en
10	Radio Nalta 99.2	https://www.facebook.com/pg/radionalta99.2fm/posts/?ref=page_internal
11	Radio Padma 99.2	http://www.radiopadma.fm/
12	Radio Pollikontho 99.2	https://bnnrc.net/radio-pollikontho/
13	Radio Sagar Giri 99.2	https://bnnrc.net/radio-sagorgiri/
14	Radio Sagor Dwip 99.2	https://bnnrc.net/radio-sagor-dwip/

#	Name	Website:
15	Radio Sarabela 98.8	http://radiosarabela.fm/
16	Radio Sundarban 98.8	https://bnnrc.net/ radio-sundarban/

Appendix 6.1. Guidelines for CRS Operation in Nepal

Source:

Mainali, R., Chapagain, Y., and Subba, B. (2004). Community Radio Organisation Development Guidebook. CRSC/NEFEJ with support from Free Voice, The Netherlands: Kathmandu, Nepal.

Organisational Guidelines:

i. *Human Resource Plan of Community Radio*—this takes into consideration the vision and long-term plan of the station, the hours of broadcasts, and the programming specifics of CRS. A human resource plan helps the CRS to better understand its personnel needs and how to place individuals based on their core skills and interests.

ii. *Human Resource Management Policy and Procedures*—this outlines the core values and management principles of the station, the human resource categories, and terms of services for staff, volunteers, and trainees/interns. This plan specifically outlines recruitment and selection criteria in addition to staff mobilisation, performance management, staff compensation and benefits, working environment, and termination.

iii. *Public Consultation and Maintenance of Transparency Policy and Procedures*—this focuses on the importance of the station to be supported by the community being served. It outlines the types of public consultation activities, their ideal frequency of occurrence, and suggested locations.

iv. *Dealing with Competition Plan*—this plan highlights approaches regarding competition from all other types of media (print and broadcast) and focuses on outlining strategies where the CRS can be unique to receive public support.

v. *Resource Mobilisation Policy and Procedures*—this focuses on the financial, physical, technical, and human resources as they relate to the station's needs in order for the CRS to remain beneficial to its community. It addresses aspects dealing with advertisements, conducting fundraising activities, and remaining independent from funding sources.

vi. *Collaboration Policy*—this addresses the need of the station to develop symbiotic relationships with appropriate organisations in order to increase efficiency, effectiveness, and sustainability. It focuses on creating and maintaining key partnerships.

vii. *Documentation and Knowledge Management Policy*—in order to ensure that stations are effective and have a better impact on their communities, this highlights how information can be collected, stored, and retrieved for better operations. It addresses the systems and mechanisms in place for management and operation of the library (print and audio).

viii. *Operational Plan*—this covers all information relating to the smooth running of the station with regard to ensuring each minute of broadcast is meaningful. It covers administrative protocols such as opening and closing of the station, security, logs for various activities, and a code of conduct; on-air protocols such as airing of signature tunes, station ID and promotions, how to broadcast advertisements, and handing and taking over from different staff; and programming protocols such as maintaining a programme log-sheet, the lengths for different formats of programmes, and respect of copyright.

ix. *Station Management Systems and Protocols*—this is the clearly defined items that help to orient personnel to the station and help with better organisation which results in more orderly operation including the planning system such as the participatory manner of administration; the communication system which highlights the importance of openness and transparency; the decision-making system which addresses items such as centralisation of information and authority of different personnel; and the monitoring and evaluation system.

Apart from the above, the CRS can choose to have specific policies for non-staff personnel which address how these types of human resources are managed in relation to their mobilisation and what roles they can fulfil in the station. These include:

x. *Volunteer Mobilisation Policy* and

xi. *Policy about Trainees/Interns*

Financial Guidelines:

With regard to the station's finances, there are specific guidelines that can be implemented to ensure good financial management practises that ensure the stations are sustainable while they remain independent from their sources of funding. Further, such policies ensure accountability and transparency with regard to funds and highlight what aspects of the station's operations receive funds and for what purposes. The following plans were suggested:

(i) *General Accounting Principles and Guidelines*, and

(ii) *Accounting Policies.*

Technical Guidelines:

It is also important for stations to ensure that all their technologies are properly maintained in order to ensure longer life and better quality of outputs. The following plans ensure this:

(iii) *Maintenance Plan and Procedure*, and

(iv) *Technology Upgrading Plan.*

Broadcasting Guidelines:

Finally, even though the Constitution and national legislature identify specifics in relation to broadcasting, internal guidelines would ensure initiative specific focus on key legal issues as well as ethical operations. This type of plan can also help initiatives to standardise the language, style, and content of programmes for each CRS to create a station identity while ensuring that programmes keep within agreed upon procedures as listeners' interests, human rights, democratic norms, and constructive approaches are taken into consideration. The following policy is suggested to meet these needs:

(v) *Policy governing informative and educative program.*

Appendix 6.2. Committees Associated with Regulation of CR in Bangladesh

Source:

Community Radio Installation, Broadcast and Operation Policy 2017. (2018). Ministry of Information, People's Republic of Bangladesh.

The mandates of the committees identified above are explained below based on the information in the 2017 Policy (pp. 3–4, 12):

(i) *National Regulatory Committee* observes the implementation of the community media policy, reviews regulations and makes suggestions for timely amendments, and generally ensures the policy is operational.

(ii) *Technical Sub-committee* (of the National Regulatory Committee) finalises a list, and submits the same to the National Regulatory Committee, of eligible applicants.

(iii) *Central Monitoring Committee* ensures the adherence to the terms and conditions, regulations with regard to advertisements, and general implementation and operation criteria of the policy, in addition to overseeing the technical aspects of the station are followed, and overall monitoring of the operation of the stations.

(iv) *Local Advisory Committee* comprises key stakeholders from the community; this committee monitors the station at the local level and aids whenever necessary, such as making recommendations based on the strengths and weaknesses of the station and encouraging participation of the community and resource persons.

(v) *Management Committee* ensures the participation of community members and oversees the general operation of the station with regard to the overall aim of the station. This committee is governed by previously drafted by-laws and comprises members who have an enormous understanding of the targeted community—their culture, values, and day-to-day lives (Fig. 1).

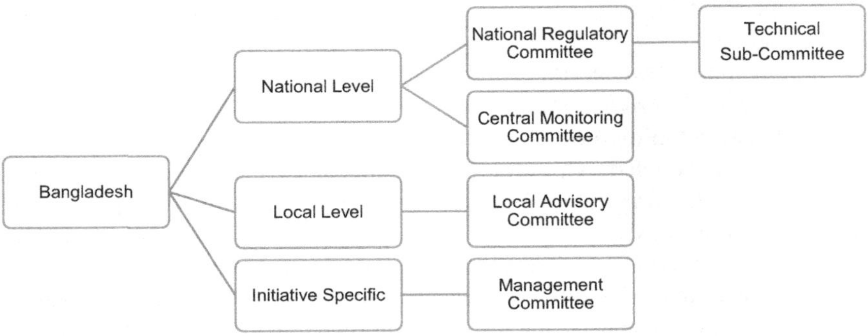

Fig. 1 Committees associated with regulation of CR in Bangladesh based on the Community Radio Installation, Broadcast and Operation Policy 2017

The manufacturer's authorised representative in the EU is Springer Nature Customer Service Centre GmbH, Europaplatz 3, 69115 Heidelberg, Germany. If you have any concerns regarding our products, please contact ProductSafety@springernature.com

Printed and bound by CPI Group (UK) Ltd, Croydon, CR0 4YY
30/09/2026
02225599-0003